Media Convergence

Media Convergence

Networked Digital Media in Everyday Life

Graham Meikle
*Senior Lecturer, Communications, Media and Culture,
University of Stirling*

Sherman Young
*Associate Professor, Department of Media, Music,
Communication and Cultural Studies, Macquarie University*

First published 2012 by
PALGRAVE MACMILLAN

Palgrave Macmillan in the UK is an imprint of Macmillan Publishers Limited, registered in England, company number 785998, of Houndmills, Basingstoke, Hampshire RG21 6XS.

Palgrave Macmillan in the US is a division of St Martin's Press LLC, 175 Fifth Avenue, New York, NY 10010.

Palgrave Macmillan is the global academic imprint of the above companies and has companies and representatives throughout the world.

Palgrave® and Macmillan® are registered trademarks in the United States, the United Kingdom, Europe and other countries.

ISBN 978–0–230–22893–1   hardback
ISBN 978–0–230–22894–8   paperback

This book is printed on paper suitable for recycling and made from fully managed and sustained forest sources. Logging, pulping and manufacturing processes are expected to conform to the environmental regulations of the country of origin.

A catalogue record for this book is available from the British Library.

A catalog record for this book is available from the Library of Congress.

10   9   8   7   6   5   4   3   2   1
21   20   19   18   17   16   15   14   13   12

Transferred to Digital Printing in 2012

Contents

Acknowledgements

Graham thanks Fin, Rosie and Lola and would like them to know that he's now free to come to the park.

Sherman thanks Amanda, Harper and Truman. You can use the computer now.

Introduction

In January 2010, US Secretary of State Hillary Clinton delivered a speech on Internet freedom in Washington DC. She spoke of 'the right of people to freely access information', and said that 'access to information helps citizens to hold their governments accountable'. Her government, she said, stood 'for a single internet where all of humanity has equal access to knowledge and ideas' (Clinton 2010). The limits of this position were to be both tested and revealed throughout 2010, as the US administration and the world responded to a series of revelations facilitated by the activist whistleblower site WikiLeaks.

In April 2010, WikiLeaks released a video they titled 'Collateral Murder', which they claimed showed civilians, including two Reuters journalists, being shot dead by US forces. In July, they provided more than 90,000 classified documents from the Afghan war to *The Guardian*, *The New York Times* and *Der Spiegel*. This was dwarfed on 23 October, when those same three publications, along with Al Jazeera, *Le Monde* and UK broadcaster Channel 4 published simultaneous stories about the occupation of Iraq. These reports all drew upon a cache of 391,832 classified US military documents obtained by WikiLeaks. And on 29 November, the Cablegate events began, with the publication in five major western newspapers of stories based on 251,287 secret cables sent from more than 250 US embassies.

This time, the WikiLeaks website came under extraordinary political pressure – it lost its access to the domain name Wikileaks.org. Amazon (which provided its web space), PayPal, Visa and MasterCard all withdrew their services from the organization. A loose coalition of supporters using the collective label 'Anonymous' engaged in a string of electronic civil disobedience actions against the websites of these companies, coordinating through spaces such as 4chan, Facebook and Internet Relay Chat channels. The attempts to block access to the WikiLeaks website provided an important demonstration of John Gilmore's famous observation that 'the Net interprets censorship as damage and routes around it' (quoted in *Time*, 6 December 1993). By 10 December 2010, the entire contents of the site were mirrored on more than 1500 other websites.

WikiLeaks shows the contours of the convergent media environment that is the subject of this book. The events WikiLeaks initiated in 2010 played out through networked digital media, as its 'Collateral Murder'

1

video circulated through blogs, YouTube, Facebook, Twitter and Wikipedia. But these events also played out through longer-established industries such as newspapers and magazines, through broadcast television and radio, as WikiLeaks built collaborations with leading newspapers and broadcasters to analyse, distribute and publicize its caches of classified data. This illustrates the complex media environment that we now inhabit, an environment built on both broadcast and broadband. To say we *inhabit* this media environment is not to overstate the case – at least for those of us in the UK, Australia and North America, which are the parts of the world we focus on in this book. In the UK, for example, the average person spends almost nine hours a day using media – watching TV, reading newspapers, listening to the radio, texting, gaming and using the Internet. More time than we spend asleep, more time than we spend at work. On average, 45 per cent of our waking hours are spent with media (an average of 7 hours and 5 minutes), and by using more than one kind of media at the same time, we cram in an average of 8 hours and 48 minutes media time every day (Ofcom 2010a: 1–2). The media are no longer just what we watch, listen to or read – the media are now what we do.

Convergence

This book is about convergence – the coming together of things that were previously separate. More than that, this book is about media convergence in everyday life. Other books about convergence variously focus on the political economy of contemporary media industries (Dwyer 2010), on establishing a research agenda for digital media scholars (Jensen 2010), or on the activities of specialized groups of media fans (Jenkins 2008). But in this book we emphasize more everyday uses of networked digital media – Facebook and iTunes, Google and Wikipedia, and the BBC iPlayer among them. We use the term *convergent media* throughout the book to refer to media content, industries, technologies and practices that are both digital and networked. We avoid the term *new media* (cf. Manovich 2001; Lievrouw and Livingstone 2006; Flew 2008; Lister *et al.* 2009; Giddings and Lister 2011). All media were new once, and to place an emphasis on the 'new' can be misleading. If we emphasize technological novelty, then this can obscure the crucial processes of transition, of both adoption and adaptation, through which a medium comes to seem part of the furniture (Gitelman and Pingree 2003). More than this, there are also some very real problems in deciding what is to count as 'new'. The World Wide Web is already twenty years old – Tim Berners-Lee activated the first website in December 1990 (Berners-Lee 2010). The Internet which underpins the web is more than forty years old – the first message on the ARPANET was sent in October 1969 (Abbate 1999). The history of the mobile phone might be traced back as far as Marconi or even Morse, or through long trajectories of development in CB radio and pagers (Goggin 2006; Ling and Donner 2009), until the first-generation commercial cellular phones at the end of the 1970s (Green and Haddon 2009). Some of the earliest videogames date to 1958 (*Tennis For Two*) and 1962 (*Spacewar!*) (Newman 2004). The image-manipulation application Photoshop has been with us for twenty years; word processors, desktop publishing and email for longer; and even the iPod for ten. Are any of these media still *new*? DVDs and MP3s once seemed new, but then so did the telegraph, the telephone and electric light (Marvin 1988; Fischer 1992; Standage 1998). At the time of writing, various kinds of cutting-edge technologies might be represented by location-based social media tools (Foursquare), augmented-reality phone apps (Layar) or legal streaming-music services (Spotify), but readers in the not-too-distant future are likely to find all of those unexceptional.

We also avoid the term *digital media* in this book, except where we are focusing on specific properties of specific digital forms or in conjunction with the term *networked*. We do not use the term 'digital media' as a general label for the convergent media environment. This is because the digitization of media content is now so pervasive and so firmly established that the term is unhelpful as a general label. All media now involve digital technologies in at least some stages of their production, distribution or reception. Even a centuries-old form like the newspaper at its most modest level – the local free-sheet – is written on word processors, laid out on desktop publishing packages, and sent to its printers electronically. Moreover, the significant characteristic of contemporary media is not just that they are digital but that they are also networked, enabling complex relationships of two-way communication. Convergent media for us, then, are *networked digital media*.

And we avoid the term *revolution*, which can be used by even the most incisive analysts of the convergent media environment (such as Castells 2000 or McChesney 2007). 'The rhetoric of the digital revolution', as Mark Andrejevic points out, 'assumes a fundamental discontinuity between the old media and the new' (2004: 24). Instead, in this book we ground our discussion of convergent media in longer historical trajectories, linking news blogs to established news organizations, creative audiences to decades of audience theory and research, and the increased degree of personal visibility afforded by social network media to older issues.

Convergence, Roger Silverstone once suggested, is 'a dangerous word' (1995: 11). Silverstone was concerned that the word had come to mean so many different things to so many people, applied to technological developments, industry structures, changing forms of media texts, and shifts in the relationships between audiences and media. For Silverstone, this was a problem, although we would suggest that being able to explain many different kinds of media phenomena with a single concept is a useful thing. But Silverstone was right that the term 'convergence' means different things to different people, and perhaps as a result the term also attracts a certain scepticism – 'the promise of further wonders', as Hesmondhalgh assesses convergence (2007: 261). Murdock (2000) made a significant contribution by distinguishing between, first, the convergence of cultural forms (which we discuss in Chapter 4 as textual convergence); second, industrial convergence (to which we turn in Chapter 2); and third, technological convergence, which he termed 'the convergence of communications systems' (2000: 37–8). This third form is our focus in Chapter 1.

For Klaus Bruhn Jensen convergence describes 'a historically open-ended migration of communicative practices across diverse material technologies and social institutions' (2010: 15). Jensen identifies three broad modes of communication that are affected by this, which he labels 'the three degrees'. The first involves bodies and tools of inter-personal communication, including both face-to-face conversation and writing. The second degree he identifies as 'technologies', a label for the few-to-many media forms of the broadcast paradigm (although it is not clear how writing, as applied to letters, books or email, is free from technological mediation). And Jensen's third degree is 'meta-technologies', or digital media which remediate and recombine the other degrees. Jensen's analysis is incisive and original, but conflates too many important distinctions into its 'first degree' – face-to-face communication is different in crucial ways from mediated one-to-one communication through phones, letters, email or chat, most obviously in that those latter kinds of communication usually occur between people who are not present in the same place at the same time (Thompson 1995).

Where Jensen is concerned with modes of interaction, others take a political economy perspective on convergence. For Tim Dwyer, convergence describes 'the process whereby new technologies are accommodated by existing media and communication industries and cultures'

(Dwyer 2010: 2). In this analysis, networked digital media appear just as a kind of superstructural phenomenon on top of the established media industries. The limitations of this approach are clear in Dwyer's case study of Myspace, which sees this network entirely as a broadcast platform (2010: 57–9). Myspace has certain things in common with certain platforms in the broadcast paradigm, but it is better understood as a social media tool which creates a complex environment, mixing one-to-one personal communication with the broadcast model of messages sent to nobody in particular. We will discuss social media in more detail in Chapter 3, which will extend the points raised here about the analyses of both Jensen and Dwyer.

Other authors have also stressed the convergence of computing, communications and content (Pool 1983; Rice 1999; Barr 2000; Flew 2008; Küng, Picard and Towse 2008), generating powerful insights. Bolter and Grusin describe convergence as *remediation* – 'the representation of one medium in another' (1999: 45). For these authors 'Convergence is the mutual remediation of at least three important technologies – telephone, television, and computer' (1999: 224). The importance of their argument is in its insistence that networked digital media do not replace older media but join them in a complex convergent environment: 'the remediation is mutual: the Internet refashions television even as television refashions the Internet' (1999: 224). But, in contrast, other scholars miss the point of convergence entirely: 'That people can listen to their radio over their digital television – so what? That they can make telephone calls on their computers – so what?' (Winston 2005: 377). However, in recent years, convergence has become firmly identified – even over-identified – with the work of Henry Jenkins (2001, 2004), in particular his 2006 book *Convergence Culture* (references in this book are to the updated paperback edition of 2008).

'In the world of media convergence', writes Jenkins, 'every important story gets told, every brand gets sold, and every consumer gets courted across multiple media platforms' (2008: 3). For Jenkins, convergence can be defined as

> the flow of content across multiple media platforms, the cooperation between multiple media industries, and the migratory behavior of media audiences who will go almost anywhere in search of the kinds of entertainment experiences they want. (2008: 2)

The title of his book identifies not only convergence but a convergence *culture* – something different and something bigger than just a set of specialized media practices (see also Jenkins and Deuze 2008; Perryman 2008; Deuze 2010). For some critics, this relies rather too much on generalizing from the practices of very small groups (Couldry 2010a). Jenkins's case studies largely focus around dedicated fans who have the economic and cultural resources to engage with their favourite media in unusual depth. *Convergence Culture* is best seen as a contribution to the literature on fan studies, with which Jenkins has been associated since the early 1990s (Jenkins 1992, 2006b). Key chapters explore online discussion forums surrounding the reality TV show *Survivor,* amateur contributions to the *Star Wars* canon, and coordinated fan fiction around the Harry Potter universe. This is both the biggest strength of the book – its detailed and revealing case studies of fan behaviour – and its biggest limitation, because Jenkins generalizes and extrapolates throughout the book from the behaviour of particular groups who may not after all turn out to be harbingers of wider trends that will diffuse throughout society. To devote an enormous amount of time to remaking a *Star Wars* film, or to fully exploring every last nuance of the world of *The Matrix* (across games, virtual worlds and graphic novels as well as the trilogy of films), or to establishing oneself as a leading voice in an online forum for *Survivor* fans – each of these demands resources of money, cultural capital and above all time, which marginalize the potential for many people to join in (Couldry 2011; Gregg and Driscoll 2011). As is true of all literature in fan studies, Jenkins's examples may not, in fact, apply to other, less dedicated groups. We will address the changing roles of media audiences in more detail in Chapter 5.

Both Jenkins (2008: 10–11) and Castells (2009: 58) credit Ithiel de Sola Pool's 1983 book *Technologies of Freedom* as the first to draw attention to convergence, although from this early vantage point he did not have a great deal to say about computers:

A process called the 'convergence of modes' is blurring the lines between media, even between point-to-point communications, such as the post, telephone, and telegraph, and mass communications, such as the press, radio, and television. A single physical means – be it wires, cables, or airwaves – may carry services that in the past were provided in separate ways. Conversely, a service that was provided in the past by any one medium – be it broadcasting, the press, or telephony – can now be provided in several different physical ways. So the one-to-one relationship that used to exist between a medium and its use is eroding. That is what is meant by the convergence of modes. (Pool 1983: 23)

And in *The Media Lab*, Stewart Brand described MIT Media Laboratory Director Nicholas Negroponte's 'vision' of convergence: 'all communication technologies are suffering a joint metamorphosis, which can only be understood properly if treated as a single subject, and only advanced properly if treated as a single craft' (1988: 11).

But such technological convergence would have ramifications, which were identifiable some time ago. Pool noted, for example, that legal and regulatory approaches towards print, telephony and broadcasting systems had all evolved separately and distinctly, so their practical convergence would create regulatory dilemmas (a point explored in the greatest depth by Benkler 2006). The possibilities of technological convergence, when combined with increasingly convergent ownership patterns, would effect a blurring of earlier distinctions – print publishing, for example, which was subject to one specific set of legal conventions, would be increasingly drawn into the regulatory domains affecting broadcasting and telecommunications.

Contestation and continuity

The emergence of WikiLeaks on the political stage was a vivid example of the *transformation* of the media from the broadcast paradigm of the twentieth century into a more complex, twenty-first-century convergent environment. And yet the WikiLeaks events also point to some crucial *continuities*. Viewed from a certain angle, the WikiLeaks story seems to be all about the new – it was a YouTube sensation, a Facebook sensation, a Twitter sensation. But viewed from a different angle, the story is one of long-established media industries and practices. For one thing, WikiLeaks was also a newspaper phenomenon. All the online sharing and argument, all the social networking and collaborative chatter, were catalysed by the publication of material provided by WikiLeaks to *The Guardian*, *The New York Times* and other long-established news organizations. The convergent media environment, then, is characterized by both contestation and continuity.

With the Cablegate developments, WikiLeaks' figurehead Julian Assange became the focus of an international manhunt. Before his arrest in London in December 2010 on charges relating to alleged sexual offences in Sweden, a string of US political figures had issued threats: Sarah Palin called for him to be 'hunted down like Osama Bin Laden'; one senior Canadian political aide called publicly for his assassination. The US government warned university students that discussing WikiLeaks on

Facebook could damage their job prospects. Providing information to news media was shown to be a new kind of thought crime, whereas storytelling based on that information appeared to remain a protected activity – there were no public calls from elected officials or political aides for the editor of *The Guardian* to be assassinated.

With each of the four key WikiLeaks events in 2010, much attention went to the nature of the publication rather than to the content of the documents, with WikiLeaks itself and Julian Assange in particular the focus of considerable attention (see for example Assange 2010a, 2010b; Greenberg 2010; Khatchadourian 2010). Many details lent these events an air of radical media transformation – the online distribution of such huge quantities of secret data; the exotic name of the site itself; and the intriguing figure of Assange, who until his arrest was said to be in constant transit, hauling encrypted computers in his luggage (some observed that he resembled a hacker protagonist from one of William Gibson's cyberpunk novels). The medium and the messenger were in this case as fascinating as the message, leading to a certain amount of hyperbole. Journalism scholar Jay Rosen, for instance, described WikiLeaks as 'the world's first stateless news organization' (2010).

But WikiLeaks is not a news organization, stateless or otherwise. Placing a quarter of a million raw documents on a website is not the same thing as producing news, which is an industrial process of creating and distributing non-fiction drama, of giving shape and structure to raw information. WikiLeaks does not produce news – rather, it is a source of raw material for news organizations which simultaneously makes that raw material available to anyone through its website. Its role in channelling information to news media has more in common with the communication strategies of powerful sources like the Pentagon or the Metropolitan Police than with journalism (Fishman 1980; Ericson, Baranek and Chan 1989). Where WikiLeaks differs from such established sources is in exemplifying what McNair calls the 'cultural chaos' of a global networked media environment: 'the possibilities allowed [...] for dissent, openness and diversity rather than closure, exclusivity and ideological homogeneity' (2006: vii).

Assange himself wrote that the project illustrated a new form of 'scientific journalism':

Scientific journalism allows you to read a news story, then to click online to see the original document it is based on. That way you can judge for yourself: Is the story true? Did the journalist report it accurately? (Assange 2010b)

Benkler has described this as the 'see for yourself' culture of the Internet (2006: 218), enhanced by the link structure of the web, in which trust, reputation and authority do not simply derive from the organization providing the news, but also from the capacity to trace their sources for oneself.

One important conclusion to draw from WikiLeaks and its campaign to enforce radical transparency on powerful institutions is that it highlights how the convergent media environment is characterized by both contestation and continuity – new actors and old industries, contending modes of distribution and visibility, complex assemblages of networked digital media. To see this, ask yourself why WikiLeaks involves established media organizations at all, rather than just posting its caches of data on its own website. Those organizations bring distribution networks that complement rather than replace the WikiLeaks website. They add the credibility and authority of long-established news brands to what could otherwise be dismissed as a niche website with a weird name, and they set the agenda for other news media to follow. As an activist project, WikiLeaks wants to bring attention to the documents it makes available. News organizations can help with this. Most importantly, they bring journalists who – at their best – can analyse and sift the raw material, can test evidence and redact details that may endanger named individuals, can offer context to help the reader interpret the material, and can shape the data into stories, reports and commentaries that make sense of the material for audiences who lack, of course, the time and expertise to process these hundreds of thousands of specialized documents for themselves – although those documents are available online in their raw form for anyone who wishes to try. WikiLeaks, then, illustrates a convergent media environment – networked digital communication – emerging through complex relations of contestation and continuity.

Such tensions and interplay between contestation and continuity are central to the study of media and communication. From one perspective, communication is all about contestation, about transformation, about the exchange of information and meaning. 'Communication', writes Klaus Bruhn Jensen, 'is the human capacity to consider how things might be different' (2010: 6). Much media use can be understood as the sending of messages across space for the management of complex societies (Beniger 1986). Messages, information, communication itself are 'differences that make a difference' (Jensen 2010: 40). But from another perspective, communication is also about maintaining continuity, about maintaining society and culture through time (Carey 1989), as we share in rituals of simultaneity and storytelling, from watching

X Factor along with millions of distant others to sharing video clips on Facebook. In this view, communication is not just about bringing about transformation through the dissemination of new information, but also about maintaining relationships, about maintaining the continuity of cultures through time.

The tensions between contestation and continuity have also animated the 'Media Studies 2.0' debate. This was initiated in polemical online posts by William Merrin (2008, 2009) and David Gauntlett (2007, 2009), which argue that the study and teaching of media have not kept pace with developments in either media technology or in users' experiences of a convergent media environment. In particular, it points to the blurring of the line between production and consumption. This debate, in part perhaps because of the polemical nature of its first statements, has been fiercely contested (see for example Andrejevic 2009; Dovey and Lister 2009; Miller 2009; as well as the 2009 special issues of *Television & New Media* [vol. 10, no. 1] and *Interactions* [vol. 1, no. 1]) and it is true that it may reify an unreal Media Studies 1.0. But it does crystallize the tensions between continuity and contestation – between the broadcast era in which 'some get to speak and some to listen, some to write and some to read, some to film and some to view' Carey (1989: 87), and the emerging participatory culture which, as Lessig observes, 'could be both read and write' (2004: 37).

This book recognizes and explores the ways in which 'the people formerly known as the audience' (Rosen 2006) are developing new ways of interacting with media – creating, editing, organizing, collaborating, sharing – at the same time as the average UK viewer's hours spent watching broadcast television have increased to almost four per day (Ofcom 2011: 131). The convergent media environment is making possible an enormous redistribution of a certain kind of power – the power to speak, to write, to argue, to define, to persuade – symbolic power (Bourdieu 1991; Thompson 1995; Meikle 2009; Couldry 2010a). For many people, the media are no longer just what they watch, listen to or read – the media are now what people *do*.

Social media platforms such as Facebook, Myspace and Twitter bring together different forms of communication and interaction, blurring the lines between one-to-one, one-to-many and many-to-many communication. They make possible an unprecedented convergence between messages exchanged directly between specific individuals and messages sent randomly to nobody in particular. It is a communication environment that Castells (2009) characterizes as 'mass self-communication', although we would distance ourselves from the word 'mass' here, which has had a problematic status for many media scholars for some time – the problem with the word 'mass' is that it always seems to refer to other people, never ourselves. We all know ourselves to be more complicated, more discriminating, more distinctive than simply a part of an amorphous mass. As Raymond Williams once argued, there are in fact no masses – 'there are only ways of seeing people as masses' (1961: 300). Seeing people as masses was very convenient for twentieth-century media industries – but in the twenty-first century, it is proving much harder, as audiences discover their increased capacity to exercise symbolic power.

This book explores that media environment, addressing Facebook and iTunes, Wikipedia and blogging, lolcats and Hitler remixes, *Guitar Hero* and political videogames. But it is also grounded in the research, insights and concerns of earlier approaches to media. The convergent media environment is being shaped not only by such emerging transformations but also by contested continuities. Established media industries struggle to deal with the shock of the new – a proliferation of competing platforms, a reconfiguration of audiences, and a convergent context in which media products can be shared, copied and remixed by millions, on a global scale and in real time. But at the same time, assumptions and precedents from the twentieth century persist in the shaping of policy and regulation, in debates about censorship and subsidy, in struggles over intellectual property, copyright and access. So this book also examines examples that speak to continuities – the BBC and Rupert Murdoch, discourses of news and of media policy, understandings of media audiences, ownership and texts that are grounded in decades of research and debate.

About this book

In this book we first examine four key dimensions of convergence, giving each a chapter in turn – technological, industrial, social and textual. In the second half of the book, we then go on to explore the implications of these forms of convergence for audiences and for governments and regulators. In Chapter 1 we focus on the convergence of content, computers and communications – the technological convergence of digital networked media that enables the computer company Apple to become a dominant force in selling music or to team up with Rupert Murdoch to develop a new kind of 'newspaper' for its tablet device the iPad. In Chapter 2 we turn to those organizations that are driving and being driven by this, examining some of the most important and emblematic media institutions of the convergent environment – the BBC, Google and News Corporation. Chapter 3 explores the rise of social network media, concentrating on Facebook, a complex space which enables the convergence of one-to-one communication with the broadcast model of messages sent to nobody in particular. In Chapter 4 we discuss three key ways in which media texts converge – the mash-up model in which texts are sampled, remixed and reimagined; the multimedia model in which different textual systems – words, images, sounds – come together in the same space on the same device; and what Jenkins (2008) has labelled the transmedia model, in which stories and texts are dispersed across multiple platforms.

With these four major kinds of convergence mapped, the second half of the book explores some of their most important implications. Chapter 5, 'Creative Audiences', identifies the key ways in which audiences can now interact with media – accessing, organizing, creating, manipulating, collaborating upon and sharing media content in the networked digital environment. Chapter 6 turns to the ways in which convergent media make the invisible visible, enabling new power relationships as users monitor, display and connect. Chapter 7 looks at some key implications of convergent media for our experiences of mediated time and space. Chapter 8 identifies some of the main consequences of convergent media for policy makers and regulators.

To some extent these chapter divisions are artificial, as is true of many books. Certain key themes occur and recur within more than one chapter, unable to be contained within a single discussion, and the book is to be read horizontally across chapters rather than vertically as a series of separate, unconnected topics. For example, questions of visibility are not confined to Chapter 6, which explicitly focuses on these, but also appear in our discussion of social network media in Chapter 3 and in Chapter 7 on convergent media, time and space. Questions of remix, similarly, are addressed in both Chapter 4 on convergent texts and Chapter 5 on creative audiences. This is not a bug but a feature, and the reader is encouraged to see the book not as a collection of connected discussions but as a continuous exploration of networked digital media. And of course, the reader will make their own connections between ideas as they read.

Content, Computing, Communications 1

As this is being written, an Apple software application called iTunes is running in the background. It's a taken-for-granted application, used by tens of millions every day. But stop for a moment and ask yourself what iTunes is for. First, of course, you can use it to listen to music – the clue is rather in the name. But you can also import music, either by ripping CDs, buying from the iTunes Store, or by importing files acquired by other means. You can then use iTunes to organize those files, tag them, rate them, combine them into playlists and share those playlists either online on local networks or by burning them to CD or DVD. You can organize your listening through smart playlists that will automatically select music to your specifications – recent additions, five-star songs, particular genres, tunes by a certain artist or containing a certain key-word, or through its 'iTunes DJ' shuffle option. And you can also use its 'Genius' function to create playlists including recommendations based on your existing music library.

But iTunes, now in Version 10 at the time of writing, has long since ceased to be just about music. All forms of media content now converge in this space. Films and TV programmes can also be down-loaded, stored, organized and watched directly within iTunes. Podcasts can be automatically updated and synced to other devices. So can books and audiobooks, games and, of course, ringtones. Software apps, includ-ing those of major newspapers and magazines and of major social net-work services, can be downloaded. iTunes can connect to live streams from radio stations broadcasting online around the world. iTunes U can download lectures and presentations, and in some cases textbooks, from scores of universities. And its Ping social network service offers some limited capacity to connect with friends and interact around shared music.

iTunes also connects and manages other devices – phones, portable music players, tablet computers – updating their software, backing up their key files, syncing address book contacts and to-do lists, and both enabling and restricting access to their contents. And the application is the gateway to the iTunes Store, accessible globally from fixed and portable computing devices and open 24 hours a day, 7 days a week. As of September 2011, Apple's website claims an inventory for its iTunes stores of more than 10,000 movies, 350,000 apps and 12 million songs, and claims that more than 15 billion apps and more than 10 billion songs have been sold.

In short, iTunes has become a media hub, a place where a large part of our media use occurs, and one which bypasses longer-established modes of media distribution such as the packaging of CDs and DVDs or the broadcasting of TV and radio content. It was originally introduced by Apple in 2001 as a means for users of their Macintosh computers to 'rip, mix and burn' their music collections. With the introduction of the iPod in October of the same year, it became the means to transfer music to that device. But it was only with the introduction of the iTunes music store in April 2003 that the full potential of the package became apparent, as it was now both digital and networked. iTunes is representative of a digital, networked media environment, built upon the possibilities of technological convergence.

iTunes illustrates the processes of convergence that are the subject of this chapter. The application is built around the coming together of three things that were previously separate (Rice 1999, Barr 2000, Flew 2008). First, media content – music, images, films, TV, radio, newspapers, magazines, books and games. Second, computer hardware and software. And third, communications, specifically networked telecommunications enabling connectivity, downloads and sharing, as well as conversational interaction (Bordewijk and Kaam 1986). This dimension of convergence – content, computing, communications – is our focus in this chapter. The next section expands upon the significance of the words 'digital' and 'network' for convergent media. It then goes on to examine the importance of technology in thinking about convergent media and communication, taking the development of the Internet as an extended example.

The digital bit

If Pool was right in 1983 to identify a 'convergence of modes', then how was this convergence happening? The first important cause of this convergence is the shift to digital media. 'Media may be converging', observed James Carey in 1997, 'but only in the *minor* sense that computer power permits the conversion of words and images into numbers' (1997: 324, emphasis added). But there is nothing minor about the transition to digital media. As discussed by Lev Manovich, the first key aspect of this shift is that all media forms can now be represented numerically: 'Numerical representation turns media into computer data, thus making it programmable' (2001: 52). So once you have media expressed as numbers, then you can do maths with them – enlarging a photo, compressing an audio recording, editing a written text. The second key aspect is that digital media objects are 'modular', that is, they are made up of discrete objects that retain their independent identities. At any given moment, for example, your Facebook page may display within a single window an OK Go music video from YouTube, an album of photos from your friend's housewarming party, and a triumphant announcement that someone has acquired a somersaulting pig for their Farmville empire. The page you see is made up of these separate items, each of which exists independently elsewhere, combined into the single document of your Facebook news feed (this recombination of different texts is itself another form of convergence, which we pursue in Chapter 4). At a larger level, the web itself, Manovich points out, is also modular, made up of billions of web pages, each of which is in turn made up of separate media items, each of which can be accessed independently.

Other key dimensions of digital media that follow from the above are automation, variability and transcoding (Manovich 2001: 32–48). Automation is a feature of many digital applications – RSS and podcast feeds that update whenever new content is available, word processing documents that automatically configure documents to templates and save changes without prompting, videogame engines that respond to the player's input to generate the environment through which the user navigates, or web pages that pull elements together at the user's request. Those same automatically generated web pages also illustrate the principle of variability – what you see when you visit the home page of Amazon may be different from what other users will see, depending on your location, your browsing and purchase histories (and if variability sounds like an unqualified good thing, note that at some online retailers you may be offered the same item as another user at a different price). Finally, by transcoding, Manovich describes the mutual influence of culture and computer logic, as the previous four principles are applied to cultural expression and established cultural practices are extended into digital media. So the modernist artistic strategy of collage, for instance, is transcoded as the basic cut-and-paste operation in computer pro-grammes (2003: 22). A key example of transcoding is his discussion of the database as a cultural form, making possible cultural expressions which privilege the logic of a database – to be searched and navigated by the user – to complement the cause-and-effect logic of narrative. We will return to this point in Chapter 7.

A beautiful and astonishing illustration of all these characteristics of digital media is Chris Milk's 2010 music video/software application 'The Wilderness Downtown', made to accompany Arcade Fire's song 'We Used to Wait'. To begin, the visitor enters the street address of the house where they grew up, which the site uses to retrieve Google Maps and Street View images of the actual street, which are then incorporated into the music video. As the song plays, multiple overlapping browser windows open automatically, overlaying film of a kid running through suburban streets, animation of a flock of birds, and rotating images of the user's actual childhood home, which is engulfed by a forest of computer-generated trees at the climax. 'The Wilderness Downtown' demonstrates all of the principles of digital media identified by Manovich – it achieves its considerable emotional impact by drawing upon digitized images from the user's own life, which are turned into programmable elements, added automatically as discrete modules to the overall film, an experi-ence which is not only variable but customized to the past personal experience of each unique visitor. Song and image, memory and expe-rience, are transcoded with the execution of a software programme, drawing on and contributing to a database of discrete elements – a transcoding process about which 'The Wilderness Downtown' is explicit. At one point a window opens and invites the user to write a postcard to their younger self – physical copies of some of these were distributed during Arcade Fire's 2010 tour. As the site explains this:

> A postcard is created by an analog signal: you. This site takes that postcard and converts it to digital. The Wilderness Machine brings it back to analog. Look for it on tour with the band in North America. If you're lucky enough to get someone's postcard from it, plant it. A tree will grow out of it.

The Net works

So the first key level of the convergence illustrated by iTunes is that media content is now *digital*. The second key level is the *networking* of digital media content and of its users. What kind of network do we mean? After all, at the technical level, devices can be connected in different kinds of network topologies, giving each individual node greater or lesser control over the others (Gane and Beer 2008). Drew points out that to talk of media networks today connotes something intrinsically positive. Networks are viewed as something democratic, something equally distributed, something that contrasts with the hierarchies of the twentieth century – but many networks are not, in fact, like that, with one-way, few-to-many, TV broadcast networks providing one example (Drew 2005: 222). Networks can be centralized, as in the Panopticon prison model discussed below in Chapter 6, in which the prison guard is at the centre and the prisoners at the peripheries. Or they can be decentralized, as in the airline network in which long flights involve stopovers or transfers at major hubs. Or they can be distributed, as in the road system, in which there are multiple combinations of routes to destinations and no central hubs (Galloway 2004: 29–37).

But in terms of *computer* networks, the key principle for thinking about convergent media is the end-to-end architecture of the Internet as we know it at present (Lessig 2001; Zittrain 2008). The Internet was built on an end-to-end principle of network design, which allowed its builders to keep the network infrastructure itself as simple as possible, and which allowed more complicated applications and uses to be made by end users. In an end-to-end network, the infrastructure just carries data. What happens to that data at either end is up to the end users. If someone has a new idea for a computer application, they don't have to change the entire Internet. They can just write a programme, and other users can use it. Lessig (2001) points out that the electricity system works on end-to-end principles – you plug in your new appliance, and it works without your needing to reconfigure the national grid. So does the roads system – if you have a car and a licence, you just get on the roads and go without further permission.

This approach decentralized the development of the Internet. In Tim Berners-Lee's words, 'as long as we accept the rules of sending packets around, we can send packets containing anything to anywhere' (quoted in Lessig 2001: 40). The end-to-end architecture made possible the rapid global connection of disparate networks into the Internet, and the rapid global connection of non-specialist users of the web. It's a very formidable technical accomplishment. But future developments in convergent media may follow different directions. There is no technical or legal or other reason why end-to-end design should continue to be the key principle: 'The principles of end-to-end are protected (if at all) through norms' (Lessig 2001: 58). To return to the example of iTunes again, Apple's store is online but in a closed proprietary space, from which users cannot link directly to any other online space they might choose; we will return to this point at the end of this chapter.

'Why is the network', ask Lovink and Rossiter, 'this empty signifier, the emerging-becoming-dominant paradigm of our age?' (2011: 280). They are certainly right that the image of the network is now central to much writing on contemporary media. This is in large part due to the work of Manuel Castells. The network, according to Castells, is the message (2001: 1). In particular, the network of networks known as the Internet provides the infrastructure for new forms of social organization, which Castells analyses as 'the network society' (2000). Convergent communications make it possible for networks to function and to be sustainable at larger scales and sizes than was previously possible. This, writes Castells, offers flexibility and adaptability, enabling networks to capitalize on the disadvantages of centralized bureaucracies or vertically structured corporations. The new emphasis on networks has been driven by the globalization of finance and industry; by decades of identity-based political and social movements (sexual, ethnic, nationalist, religious, as well as ecological); and by the rapid development of telecommunication and computing technologies (1998: 335–60). These three processes provided the context and impetus for the rise of the Internet (2001: 2), which in turn underpins what Castells terms the network society. As Latour points out (2005: 129), Castells combines two distinct senses of 'network', addressing both connected computers and wider forms of social organization under the same single term. Castells privileges the particular network of the Internet as that which is pivotal to his concept of the network society.

This network society, organized by and through networks rather than hierarchies, makes possible a reconfiguration of social, political and economic power, although this is not necessarily a democratization of those resources, and may well result in an unequal concentration of power resources in certain kinds of node within certain kinds of network – for example, the global bond markets that stalk national currencies or the handful of media corporations that dominate the global communications system (News Corporation or Google, for example, discussed in more detail in the following chapter). Finance and capital flow through networks. So too do ideas and images, technologies and innovations, and so too do people – businesspeople, tourists, students, refugees and migrants (Appadurai 1996; Urry 2007). In the network society, the space of places meets the space of flows, which Castells defines as 'the technological

and organizational possibility of practicing simultaneity without con-
tiguity' (Castells 2009: 34). And in the network society the linear clock
time of the modern era gives way to 'timeless time':

> the desequencing of social action, either by the compression of time
> or by the random ordering of the moments of the sequence; for
> instance, in the blurring of the lifecycle under the conditions of flex-
> ible working patterns and increased reproductive choice. (Castells
> *et al.* 2007: 171)

We will return to this concept in Chapter 7.

Layer upon layer

One of Jenkins's most useful contributions to concepts of convergence is
his identification of what he calls the 'Black Box Fallacy' (2008: 13–16).
This is a response to the common objection to the concept of technological convergence that it can imply an unrealistic teleology, a smooth
trajectory towards a single point of media contact – a single black box in
our homes into which all our media use converges, replacing the multiple boxes (TV, PC, DVD player, games console, music system) that clutter
many living rooms at present. Jenkins dismisses this, pointing out that
many households are seeing more and more black boxes, rather than
whittling these down to one. Why does this matter? It points towards
the crucial understanding that processes of technological convergence –
indeed, as discussed below, of *all* technological development – are contested. Rather than an inexorable movement towards a single dominant
system, processes of convergence are contested and unpredictable.

Benkler (2006: 383–459) argues that all mediated communication
involves three layers, which he calls the physical, logical and content layers. The physical layer refers both to the devices we use to
communicate – phones, computers, televisions, games consoles – and
to the physical infrastructure and channels that connect those devices
and their users – the phone system, broadcast networks, broadband,
cable, wireless links. The logical layer describes the software protocols,
algorithms and communications standards that enable connectivity
between devices and users – these would include the TCP/IP protocols
that enable computers to connect across different networks, 3G phone
standards, 802.11 wireless communication standards, and the HTTP
and HTML protocols that underpin the web. The content layer refers to

the messages and ideas, the information and entertainment, the stories, songs and images that we share.

In the convergent era, each of these layers has seen developments that could facilitate greater openness and creative opportunities for users. At the physical layer, examples would include open wireless networks and greater broadband capacity. At the logical layer, open-source software and peer-to-peer network tools, building on the principle of openness that has underpinned wave after wave of networking innovation from the earliest developments in the Internet (Castells 2001: 9–35). And at the content layer, open publishing models such as Creative Commons licences and collaborative projects such as Wikipedia (Benkler 2006: 395). But each layer has also seen developments that could lead to greater constraints and restrictions. At the physical layer, network operators seek ways to maximize their commercial advantage, threatening the principle of 'network neutrality' through which all data is given equal priority (Berners-Lee 2010; Wu 2010). Devices such as Apple's iPad and iPhone tightly control what applications the user can install and what they can be used to do, while at the logical layer, their proprietary software operating system imposes further constraints upon the user. At the content layer, established media industries, such as those in film and recorded music, lobby hard for the extension of copyrights, the restriction of sampling and the criminalization of sharing. Processes of convergence, then, are contested. There is no obvious single end-point of development in any arena of convergent communication. Rather, there are ongoing contests and negotiations, legal crackdowns and user subversions, commercial expansion and altruistic innovation. Developments and possibilities are not only adopted but also adapted.

Technology is a contest

'Stories about technology', writes James Carey, 'play a distinctive role in our understanding of ourselves and our common history' (1989: 9). Across popular culture, from *Frankenstein* to the TV news, stories about technology animate our fantasies of escape and liberation (*Avatar*) and our fears of domination and control (*The Matrix*). In many of the stories we tell each other about technology, it appears as a force somehow external to society (Winner 1977; Wajcman 1994). The fictional genre most engaged with technology is science fiction, the narratives of which often suggest, as Constance Penley observes, 'that if technology can go wrong or be abused, it will' (1990: 118; see also Wark 1997, Murphie and Potts 2003). We are too often ready to defer to technology as a panacea or to blame it when things go wrong. As such, it's tempting to treat technology as something separate and external to society. Instead, we should think about technology as an integral part of everything we do. 'We're inside of what we make', argues Donna Haraway, author of 'A Manifesto for Cyborgs', 'and it's inside of us. We're living in a world of connections – and it matters which ones get made and unmade' (quoted in Kunzru 1997).

Technology is about the expression of ideas. Real, individual, social, cultural and very human ideas about how we should live our lives. Things like computer chips, internal combustion engines or mobile telephones don't emerge fully formed from a vacuum. They are produced and developed within complex relationships between people, institutions and technical possibilities. In this section, we canvass some of the key perspectives on technology that are fundamental to understanding convergent media.

Discussions of media and technology usually begin with a ritual invocation of Marshall McLuhan – and this book is no different. 'Societies', wrote McLuhan, 'have always been shaped more by the nature of the media by which men [*sic*] communicate than by the content of the communication' (McLuhan and Fiore 1967: 8). In aphorisms like this, or his provocative slogan 'the medium is the message' (1964: 7), McLuhan tried to steer communications scholars away from their prevailing emphasis on media texts. To say that the medium of television was itself the message would be to argue that the intrinsic properties of the broadcast medium had a greater social and cultural importance than had any of the programmes that had ever appeared on it. That television is a one-way system, that it has been for most of its history predominantly domestic, that it organizes its programmes to an industrial schedule, that it is in many cases funded by commercial advertising – these characteristics have been more influential and significant than the actual content of TV programmes.

McLuhan's emphasis was on the *effects* of technologies; he had less to say about their *causes*, for which he is generally castigated as a technological determinist (Williams 1974; Smith and Marx 1994). One powerful line of response is the Social Construction of Technology approach (MacKenzie and Wajcman 1999), which looks instead to those social actors and groups that are most able to influence the development and implementation of technologies. Lelia Green (2002) offers the mnemonic 'ABC' – A for army (or more broadly, of course, the military), B for bureaucracy (or government) and C for corporations or commercial interests.

To take these in turn, the army first, there are many examples of military investment fuelling the development of communications technologies, some more obvious (the Internet) than others. Wark (1992) offers the example of technologies developed to enable satellites to detect the launching of missiles finding a domestic application within camcorders, so that a technology designed to identify the flare of a rocket from space can also capture an image of a child blowing out the candles on a birthday cake with the room lights off. For the role of the bureaucracy, or of government more broadly defined, consider the development of the standardized form, an innovation designed to manage, organize and process information – specifically by eliminating or ignoring information, in order to process it more easily:

> Imagine how much more processing would be required if each new case were recorded in an unstructured way, including every nuance and in full detail, rather than by checking boxes, filling blanks, or in some other way reducing the burdens of the bureaucratic system to only the limited range of formal, objective, and impersonal information required by standardized forms. (Beniger 1986: 16)

As to the C category of corporate or commercial power, of course, it should come as no surprise that there are important links between communications technologies and commercial power. After all, even writing itself is believed to have begun not for the purposes of poetry or philosophy but for accountancy (Robinson 2003). The example below of the DVD develops further this point about commercial interests and the development of communications media.

The contrasting poles that we have discussed so far mark two key approaches to understanding technology. But as Castells observes: 'the dilemma of technological determinism is probably a false problem, since technology *is* society, and society cannot be understood or represented without its technological tools' (2000: 5, original emphasis). Langdon Winner points out that the Social Construction of Technology approach risks suggesting that the technologies themselves do not really matter (1986: 21). He crafts an alternative perspective that shows how technologies can embody political ideas – in some cases, this may be because a given technological system brings with it a political obligation for regulation; Winner's example is nuclear power, but we could apply his argument that certain systems are too important to be left to the marketplace to more recent innovations such as networked databases containing personal or medical information. Winner also shows how, in other cases, technologies can be political in a different sense: 'instances in which the invention, design, or arrangement of a specific technical device or system becomes a way of settling an issue in the affairs of a particular community' (1986: 22). The example below of attempts to restrict the copying of DVDs is one key illustration of this. The value of Winner's perspective is that it avoids the extremes of either the determinist or social constructionist approaches, maintaining a focus on the ways in which technologies are part of social relations rather than external to them. 'The things we call "technologies"', writes Winner, 'are ways of building order in our world' (1986: 28).

'Technology', as Bruno Latour (1991) puts it, 'is society made durable'. Latour shows how human and non-human actors ('actants') combine into complex networks of social relations (1991, 2005). As an example, we will update Latour's 1991 example of the hotel room key and consider the format of the DVD. The introduction of the DVD was an opportunity for the film industry to expand its revenues. It also turned out to create a new market for TV programmes, allowing broadcasters to extend into a publishing model (Kompare 2006; Brookey 2007). But it posed problems for those industries too. Distributing films in a digital format of course allowed them to be viewed with higher-quality video and audio than did VHS tapes, and the format allowed space for special features such as commentary tracks. But the downside for the industry was that once those films were digital, people could do all the things they always do with digital media – such as copy them and share them.

So consider the steps the film industry took to dissuade users from copying their disks. They added copyright warning messages at the start of each disk, drawing attention to the harsh penalties that would befall anyone copying the film. These messages highlight the legal force that the content industries have mobilized to have unauthorized viewing of a *Lord of the Rings* movie turned into a criminal offence. But it seemed likely that users would fast-forward past those, so they also had to add a tiny piece of code that prevented the player from skipping the warning. The disks also contain other pieces of code to constrain users. For one, DVDs are region-coded: manufacturers divide the world up into zones – six geographical regions, plus four other codes, such as 'all' – and market disks only in a specific region in an attempt to restrict piracy and constrain parallel imports from regions with lower prices. This also requires hardware manufacturers to implement the region-coding system within DVD players, although devices which can handle multiple regions are now very common. Because the films are encoded in a digital format, as noted already, they are open to copying, manipulation and sharing. The encryption standards on DVDs were cracked quickly (Kilker 2003; Huang 2007), and free software applications such as Handbrake are able to extract the files from disks. So, again, the code was changed to subvert this process. The user ripping a disk risks an error message reading that the copy could not be completed because the disk has 'bad sectors' – deliberate insertions of software code that inhibit the copying process.

This example illustrates the complex networks of relationships between human actors (film studios, regulators, hardware manufacturers, hackers, end users) and technological devices (DVDs, players, software applications). Taken together, they constitute a technological system and a set of social relationships, embodying within the object of the DVD itself a complex contest of ideas about intellectual property, commercial value and fair use. Technologies are social and cultural systems. They are combinations of ideas and artefacts, ideologies and techniques with which we can engage. For example, we can understand the technology of television as such a system. Television is not just a box with a screen, a tuning device and a remote control. It is a combination of physical engineering, industrial infrastructure (programme-making and distribution), business model (audience commodification) and end user, together with a host of cultural practices, expectations and norms. Together, these components are assembled into what we know as television – a coherent system expressing the dominant idea of free-to-air broadcasting.

But such ideas are not fixed – they are contested. Free-to-air broadcasting is no longer the only model and is instead both complemented and challenged by a range of subscription, on-demand and online alternatives (see Chapter 7 for more on this). What we see as fixed technologies are really only moments of stability in an ongoing battle of ideas and possibilities – a battle in which institutions with different motivations and desires seek control over the activities that particular techniques enable. Radio is the classic example of that contest – a technological system in which the idea of one-way mass communication replaced an earlier idea of two-way communication (Brecht 1993 [1932]). The ability to broadcast was constrained socially, not technically (McChesney 1996, Hargittai 2001). As Peters has it:

> It is a mistake to equate technologies with their societal applications. For example, 'broadcasting' (one-way dispersion of programming to an audience that cannot itself broadcast) is not inherent in the technology of the radio; it was a complex social accomplishment. (1999: 34)

The one-way radios in our kitchens and cars exemplify the fact that technologies do not exist entirely in some kind of scientific or engineering realm, but are shaped in a wider social reality. We should understand that while technological systems have physical limitations, particular implementations are informed and shaped by human ideas and desires. What we understand as media technologies are no different. For example, the open web and a closed proprietary network such as the iTunes Store share technical approaches to network engineering but allow different uses. These systems are motivated by different ideas of what end users should be allowed to do. So it would be wrong to attribute an inevitable or intrinsic nature to any technology. Instead, if we are concerned about the impact of a technology, we should identify where ideas are contested, and engage in those contests. There are four main realms where technologies are shaped – in design, the marketplace, policy debates and end usage.

The actions of a technology's initial designer are just the first act in a process of negotiations towards a stable system. Designers have particular worldviews and express their political, ethical and economic prejudices through technological implementation. Of course, technologies are rarely created by individuals – a point developed more fully in the next section of this chapter – and so the worldview expressed is the result of a contest between everyone involved in the design process. Often, it is a compromise between concerns of engineering, marketing and accounting. All too rarely do concerns beyond sales potential form any part of the design equation. Such concerns may only be addressed if our education systems produce engineers and scientists who are also exposed to humanities traditions.

The marketplace is where broader technological concerns are commonly addressed. Champions of market solutions argue that consumer choices can determine corporate priorities for technological systems. Such a simplistic approach ignores market power and the biases of the design process. But it does suggest that users can – and should – select those technologies which reflect their chosen human values. And, of course, policy can reshape a technological system. Radio's current form was dictated not by designers but by a combination of market-driven corporate desires and government regulation. The social and economic idea of broadcasting was introduced and enforced by policy decisions. Rather than rely on 'consumer sovereignty', citizens should engage with the broad range of policy debates that impose particular ideas or models on technological usage.

Finally, end users also shape technologies. 'It is a proven lesson from the history of technology', writes Castells, 'that users are key producers of the technology, by adapting it to their uses and values, and ultimately transforming the technology itself' (2001: 28). Users can choose not only to adopt a new medium of communication, but also to adapt it – a truth still best expressed in novelist William Gibson's observation that 'the street finds its own uses for things' (1995: 215). There are many examples of users appropriating technologies and in the process becoming co-producers of their eventual uses (Oudshoorn and Pinch 2003, Eglash, Di Chiro and Fouche 2004; see also Kevin Kelly's blog *Street Use* at <http://www.kk.org/streetuse>). In his history of the first decades of the telephone in America, Claude Fischer shows how the telephone was marketed as a *practical* tool rather than a social one. Business uses were marketed first, then emergency uses, and only then domestic uses. 'Sociability, obviously an important part of the telephone today, was ignored or resisted by the industry for almost the first half of its history' (Fischer 1992: 84). He argues that the 'discovery' of social uses of the telephone shows how users can innovate new uses of a medium for themselves, and in the end decide which uses of that medium will come to be pre-eminent (1992: 85). Howard Rheingold offers a similar way of thinking about the development of the Internet:

> The computer and the Internet were designed, but the ways people used them were not designed into either technology, nor were the most world-shifting uses of these tools anticipated by their designers or vendors. Word processing and virtual communities, eBay and e-commerce, Google and weblogs and reputation systems *emerged*. (Rheingold 2002: 182, original emphasis)

The extraordinary growth of SMS text messaging is one more illustration. SMS was originally viewed as a one-way provision for phone companies to alert subscribers that they had voicemail waiting (Jensen 2010: 63). The phone industries were initially unsure how to make money from text services, although they developed mechanisms for this as SMS began to take off, particularly with younger users, quickly in some countries (Scandinavia, Japan, the Philippines) and more slowly in others (the US, Hong Kong) (Green and Haddon 2009: 43–4). Some estimates put the annual number of texts now sent globally at 2 trillion (Ling and Donner 2009: 39). The point to note is that the phenomenal growth of text messaging was user-led.

Technologies, then, are not unchangeable. Rather, they are contested systems that allow competing possibilities to be realized. Technologies are not inevitable, all-powerful forces that leave no room for alternative values or concerns. These are contests that we can be a part of, where we can shape technologies, but only if we confront those ideas and values with which we do not agree. 'Science and technology multiply around us', wrote the late J. G. Ballard. He went on: 'To an increasing extent they dictate the languages in which we speak and think. Either we use those languages, or we remain mute' (1974: 7).

Who invented the Internet?

This section draws together the preceding discussions of technological convergence and technology as a contest, by addressing a simple question. Who invented the Internet? We could observe first that 'the Internet' is a convenient label for a broad range of diverse phenomena, and should not be reduced to a single thing, or a single date of origin, just as Eisenstein observed that to speak of 'the printing press' is to bind together a range of different developments. Eisenstein defines printing as a set of processes and innovations, rather than a single invention, a single moment in Gutenberg's workshop. To speak of the invention of the printing press is, she argues 'a shorthand way of referring to a cluster of innovations (entailing the use of movable metal type, oil-based ink, wooden handpress, and so forth)' (1993: 13). The same observation can be applied to the Internet – email, BitTorrent, chat, search, and Internet telephony have as many points of difference as they have points of commonality, although all build on the convergence of computing, content and communications.

To begin to answer our question of who invented the Internet, we could trace conceptual roots of convergent media at least to the early parts of the twentieth century, if not even earlier, if we were to focus on non-linear writing strategies of modernist authors such as Joyce, Eliot or Borges as antecedents of hypertext (Tofts and McKeich 1998; Tofts, Jonson and Cavallaro 2002). But a key root was Vannevar Bush's 1945 proposal for a prototypical hypertext device he called the *memex*, which would enable users to follow and create lines of association between texts. The human mind, Bush wrote, 'operates by association', so he saw a need for a mechanized means of storing and retrieving information through making connections. He imagined a personal library/database, in the form of a desk with screens and a keyboard. Using advanced microfilm technology, this memex would enable the user to store her entire library and all her notes on it, to retrieve and edit these easily, and to create networks of connections ('trails') that could be shared. 'Wholly new forms of encyclopedias will appear', Bush wrote, 'ready made with a mesh of associative trails running through them, ready to be dropped into the memex and there amplified'.

Bush's memex, as such, was never built. But his ideas directly influenced a number of others who would be key to the development of the net, such as Douglas Engelbart, Tim Berners-Lee, or Ted Nelson, the latter of whom coined the word 'hypertext' to describe 'non-sequential writing' (Nelson 2001: 170) – 'a network of links between words, ideas and sources that has neither a centre nor an end' (Snyder 1996: 18). While Nelson's attempt to build a network he calls Xanadu has never been fully realized, we can observe that he is a hardcore practitioner of hypertext in other ways. His 1993 book *Literary Machines* features seven Chapter Ones and seven Chapter Threes, as well as a Chapter Zero. Nelson recommends reading the chapters more or less at random, stopping off frequently at Chapter Two, the only one with numbered pages (Tofts and McKeich 1998: 27). Nelson's unrealized hypertext project Xanadu would have been a read-write network, in which any user could insert a reciprocal link into anyone else's document. In essence, any user would be able to edit any document, whether they'd written it or not. This looked unfeasible for many years, but is now a daily reality on Wikipedia, for example.

Links were central to this vision. Tim Berners-Lee, the key creator of the World Wide Web, has suggested that, from one angle, 'the world can be seen as only connections' (1999: 14). After all, he says, we think of a dictionary as a warehouse of meanings – but a dictionary only defines words by linking them to other words. Berners-Lee built on this idea that 'information is really defined only by what it's related to, and how it's related' (1999: 14). So links came to structure his concept for the web. 'Hypertext', he writes, 'would be most powerful if it could conceivably point to absolutely anything' (1999: 19). An earlier visionary of the Internet, J. C. R. Licklider of MIT, had written in 1962 of an envisaged 'Galactic Network', imagining a global network of computers through which anyone could connect with data on any other machine (Leiner *et al.* 2000). For this to happen, though, computers had to be enabled to connect to each other.

So perhaps the invention of the Internet was instead with the theorization of packet-switching telephony in the early 1960s, through which messages could be broken up and sent through multiple routes to be reassembled at their destination. Packet-switching was theorized independently by Paul Baran in the US and by Donald Davies in the UK, and underpinned the eventual implementation of the ARPANET in 1969. Baran was theorizing a communications network that could survive a nuclear war; Davies wanted an improved public network for communication that would be faster, more responsive, more efficient (Hafner and Lyon 1996: 66; Abbate 1999: 7–41).

Building on the concept of packet-switching, the first experimental dial-up network connection was achieved in 1965 (Leiner *et al.* 2000). The first nodes on the Pentagon's ARPANET were connected in 1969. The first message was intended to read 'LOGIN', but the receiving computer crashed on the G, and so it was actually the Biblical-sounding 'LO' (Hafner and Lyon 1996: 153) – an accidental echo of Morse's first telegraph message in 1844, 'What hath God wrought?' (Standage 1998: 49). Was packet-switching then the invention of the Internet? Or was the crucial development instead the introduction of the TCP/IP protocols in 1973 by Vint Cerf and Bob Kahn? This enabled communication between different networks, not just within a network. Any network could now connect to any other (Castells 2000: 47–8).

But a medium is not just a technological structure – it is also a cultural formation. When we talk about the Internet, we are not just talking about infrastructure but also about the messages, habits and cultural norms of its users. And these messages, habits and norms have moved the Internet far from the original intentions of its designers. 'The network was not originally to be a medium for interpersonal communication', Abbate reminds us, 'it was intended to allow scientists to overcome the difficulties of running programs on remote computers' (1999: 2; see also Leiner *et al.* 2000). So was the invention of the Internet actually when ARPANET's users began to appropriate the network for personal use?

Perhaps the real breakthrough was Ray Tomlinson's hack of the network's messaging system to create email at the start of the 1970s, including his decision to adopt the now-iconic @ symbol? (Hafner and Lyon 1996: 190–2; Naughton 1999: 147–50; Milne 2010: 137–62). Or perhaps the real impetus came from email's CC function, which enabled this one-to-one messaging system to open out into group communication (Shirky 2003; Baym 2010: 13–15)? Or the first unofficial discussion groups, using the network to talk about science fiction (Castells 2000: 46) or, it is rumoured, arrange dope deals (Abbate 1999: 107)? Or the creation of Project Gutenberg, which has provided online access to classic texts since 1971 (Abbate 1999: 86)? What about the first games played across the network, such as *Adventure* or *MUD1*, or the invention of the emoticon :-)? (Hafner and Lyon 1996: 206–17, Taylor 2006, Baym 2010: 60). What about the expansion of discussion networks such as the Usenet system from 1979 on, including the creation of the alt.sex, alt. drugs and alt.rock-n-roll groups in 1988 (Naughton 1999: 179–84)?

Each of these innovations was a hack. Hackers built the Internet. These days, the word suggests those who might be trying to subvert the network, but without hackers there would *be* no Internet and, for that matter, no personal computer either. To say this is to draw upon the original sense of the word 'hacker' (Levy 1984). In this original usage, a 'hack' was an elegant solution to a technological problem – Jon Postel, for example, a key figure in the development of the net, recalled that when he saw the details of the first email application in 1972 he thought: 'Now there's a nice hack' (Hafner and Lyon 1996: 192). In its original sense, hacking described improving a system rather than damaging it, sharing information rather than stealing it, making technological breakthroughs rather than break-ins. And within our frame of technology as a contest, the shifting connotations of the word suggest that the term 'hacker' is one forum in which our anxieties with contemporary technology are enacted and contested.

Levy describes an early Hacker Ethic, built on such tenets as 'mistrust authority – promote decentralization' and 'all information should be free' (1984: 26–36). 'The hacker', as Turkle put it, 'is a person outside the system who is never excluded by its rules' (1984: 208). The early hacker ethic, in Paul Taylor's analysis, had at its core three features: 'the ingenious use of any technology; the tendency to reverse engineer technology to do the opposite of its intended design; and the desire to explore systems' (Taylor 2005: 628). 'If *everyone* could interact with computers with the same innocent, productive, creative impulse that hackers did', Levy writes, 'the Hacker Ethic might spread through society like a benevolent ripple, and computers would indeed change the world for the better' (1984: 36). Despite decades of commercialization, this perspective remains fundamental to many key innovations in convergent media (Himanen 2001) – open-source software, the World Wide Web, Wikipedia – and it can be used to offer perspective on some of the most important contests of this area, such as those over control of Benkler's physical, logical and content layers. In his 2004 book *A Hacker Manifesto*, McKenzie Wark extends the concept of 'hacker' beyond computing. Hackers, for Wark, are all those who work with ideas, with the creation of new concepts from raw information. So not just programmers, but poets, mathematicians, musicians and biologists as well. Wark's hackers create concepts. But the means through which those concepts are distributed, their patenting and copyrighting, are increasingly in the name of, and on the terms of, others.

Perhaps, then, the commercialization of the Internet was its real invention, opening it up as a domestic medium on a mass scale? Throughout the 1980s, the Internet grew to incorporate more non-military, non-scientific networks (Abbate 1999: 181) and ARPANET itself was dismantled by the end of 1989 (Hafner and Lyon 1996: 256). The network was privatized from 1991 onwards, and subsequently, access to the net itself became a commodity with the rise of Internet Service Providers (Leiner *et al.* 2000). Or perhaps all of this was simply a prologue to the development of the web by Tim Berners-Lee and his collaborators and its release by CERN in 1991, enabling a hypertext network that could incorporate images as well as text? Or perhaps the crucial thing was the marketing of web browsers from November 1993, with the release of Mosaic and subsequently Netscape? (Abbate 1999: 216–7).

Or as a final suggestion, perhaps the entire history sketched so far is really a pre-history of a phase we are only now entering – one characterized less by an open architecture and more by control over Internet content and Internet-connected devices. 'The Internet', writes Manuel Castells, 'is, above all else, a cultural creation' (2001: 33). He describes how the net was shaped by grassroots traditions of computer networking; by free distribution of modem protocols, of bulletin board systems, of the Usenet newsreader system. He describes the origins of the open-source movement, and of Berners-Lee's development of the web. What all of these have in common is a predisposition towards *openness*. Castells writes that the leading innovators in the development of the net had a desire 'to allow the network to evolve as an open system of computer communication, able to reach out to the whole world' (2001: 19). The Internet was developed, in Castells's phrase, through and towards an 'architecture of openness' (2001: 26).

In the days of ARPANET, there was no distinction between the producers of the network and its end users. Those building it were building it for their own use (Abbate 1999: 5). This led them to consciously design an open, end-to-end system, one that allowed any user to implement new features. Abbate argues that many of the net's most successful features, such as email and the web, were products of this design (1999: 5–6). The network was, in Zittrain's term, generative. 'Generative systems', he writes, 'are built on the notion that they are never fully complete, that they have many uses yet to be conceived of, and that the public can be trusted to invent and share good uses' (2008: 43). Zittrain writes that the end-to-end principle of network design was initially a pragmatic decision by early network designers. It allowed those designers to push complications to the end-points of the network, and freed them from the need to anticipate unforeseen possibilities and design around them. It was an architectural choice which has since been taken up as an ethical norm. Not just 'this is the way the net should be because it's practical', but 'this is the way the net ought to be because it's *just.*' This slippage, in Zittrain's analysis, depends on assuming the end user can choose how their device works, something that is no longer a safe assumption as tethered appliances like the iPhone become more widely used, and as much Internet activity takes place within walled gardens like Facebook or spaces like iTunes which are convergent – networked, digital – but are separated from the wider net and comprise enclosed proprietary environments (Zittrain 2008: 164–5).

Zittrain sees 'sterile tethered appliances' such as the iPad as the most likely threat to the generative potential of convergent media: 'lock down the device, and network censorship and control can be extraordinarily reinforced' (Zittrain 2008: 125). Zittrain's basic distinction between generative and sterile is made in his comparison of the Apple II (1977) and the Apple iPhone (2007). The earlier computer was one that the user could fool around with, one for which anyone could write and freely share applications, and one which could be reconfigured as the user chose. The latter device is one under much tighter lockdown by Apple – 'jailbreak' your device to gain control over it and Apple might remotely 'brick' it the next time you try to update your phone's firmware. True, there are now hundreds of thousands of applications available for the iPhone, but access to these, and control of their means of distribution, as well as the parameters of the software they can be written with, are all under exceptionally tight control from Apple, whose criteria for accepting or rejecting an application proposed for the iTunes Store have been criticized as being, at best, opaque. Apple, in the words of one of the sharpest observers of convergent media, Cory Doctorow, is 'a company that is deploying lots of technology in an attempt to break the Internet by making it worse at copying' (2008: ix–x). Of course, reality is more nuanced than such critics may care to admit. While the Apple II may have been more hackable, the ecosystem within which the iPhone resides includes an app store which enables hackers to more easily distribute their hacks than they could in the Apple II era, as can be seen in the huge number of available apps; 'all innovation and functionality', however, as Wu points out, 'are ultimately subject to Apple's veto' (2010: 292). Another perspective suggests that convergent technologies are entering a different developmental phase where users are not looking for the ability to hack a device, but just want something that works – in the same way that most car drivers care little about modifying the exhaust system on their family sedans, but are passionate about comfort and reliability. This could be illustrated by the similar rise of Internet-connected gaming consoles such as Sony's PS3, Nintendo's Wii and Microsoft's Xbox360 that satisfy the demands of *particular* millions of users – just not all of them. Technology is a contest.

Conclusion

Other timelines and interpretations of Internet history are, of course, possible. Other signature dates and innovations could be piled up – the ignition of the first dot.com boom with the public share offering of Netscape; the ill-fated AOL/Time Warner merger of 2000, which enacted and brought to a close a particular vision of old and new media convergence; the launch of Google or Wikipedia; or the development of the smartphone, which took the Internet away from connecting computers and towards connecting people. But our point is that *the development of media technologies is an ongoing process, not an event.* Paul Baran, whose own contribution to the development of the Internet is far greater than most, made this point to one interviewer:

> The process of technological development is like building a cathedral. Over the course of several hundred years new people come along and each lays down a block on top of the old foundations, each saying "I built a cathedral." Next month another block is placed atop the previous one. Then comes along an historian who asks, "Well, who built the cathedral?" Peter added some stones here, and Paul added a few more. If you are not careful, you can con yourself into believing that you did the most important part. But the reality is that each contribution has to follow onto previous work. Everything is tied to everything else. (quoted in Hafner and Lyon 1996: 79–80)

Seen from this perspective, perhaps the Internet *has not yet been invented.* What we now think of as the net is quite different from ten years ago, before YouTube, Xbox Live Arcade, Google Street View or the iTunes

Store, and it will perhaps not be too long before each of those in turn also comes to seem old, or even discarded. Technology is a contest – and in the media sphere there is continuity in the dimensions of that contest.

For example, Zittrain's tension between 'sterile' and 'generative' approaches is not new, but can be seen in the introduction of media technologies throughout history as established producers defend their turf and those previously excluded get excited about the potential of the new. Moreover, there can be a tendency to romanticize – it would be interesting to imagine current media cultures if early two-way radio technology had remained dominant. Would the wider availability of broadcast capacity have led to significant change, or would the more sophisticated content of those with larger resources have come to dominate the airwaves anyway? Technical possibility may be a pre-requisite, but it does not in itself guarantee particular social outcomes – it is only one dimension of the contest.

Media forms – and not just the Internet, but also television, radio, newspapers, cinema, recorded music, games – are constantly being invented and re-invented as they are taken up by new people in new contexts for new ends. The existing openness of the Internet not only attracts uses privileging that openness, but also attracts uses made possible by its low cost of entry and apparent ubiquity. The Internet activities of corporations, large and small, are driven by profit, not by ideology, and it's possible that particular implementations have apparently contradictory motivations. For example, while Google likes to cast itself as an exemplar of openness, it remains a global public company with fiduciary responsibility to its shareholders and it's likely that its motivation is not openness itself, but rather the drive for maximum exposure to users, and hence maximum advertising revenue for its platforms. Embracing openness is merely a rational means to those ends, and ultimately the ends will be more important than the means. So contests over how convergent media technology is shaped and used will continue to be complex, and can't be cast in stark terms of black and white, or good and evil. But what is promising about the Internet is that it has widened participation in, and commentary surrounding, its own contested development, which in the present authors' view can only be a good thing.

Convergent Media Industries

2

On 2 February 2011, Rupert Murdoch's News Corporation launched *The Daily*, a news application available only on Apple's iPad tablet device. Much of the attention it attracted was focused on whether or not its particular business model was viable – Murdoch said his target was one million subscriptions, at US99¢ a week. This was a daunting aspiration in an environment in which everything covered by *The Daily* – general news, sport, apps and games, arts, gossip, opinion – was available elsewhere for free. It entered a media environment of continuous real-time updates – rolling news, push notifications, the endless conversation that is Twitter – but was to be updated only once a day, an unlikely proposition for a device built around mobility and continuous connection. Moreover, *The Daily* was restricted to a tethered device of the kind discussed in the previous chapter, and so the ability of non-subscribers to follow links to its content was constrained. But the real importance of *The Daily*, whether its initial form succeeds or not, is that it illustrates the central role of convergent media industries in driving the new media environment. This collaboration between News Corporation and Apple, the shared attempt to create a new business model for online content, and their use of a particular convergent product (the iPad), all illustrate a second key dimension of convergence for this book. Both News Corporation and Apple are leading examples of convergent media industries.

There are two main senses in which media firms can be described as convergent. The first of these describes the ongoing processes of consolidation and expansion through which global media firms become larger, more integrated and more networked. The second sense describes the ways in which media firms are adopting and adapting the potential of the technological convergence explored in the previous chapter. This chapter looks at both senses of convergent media industries. It first

introduces the key global firms in the contemporary media environment, outlining the major trends and issues which arise from their operations. After this, the following three sections focus on particular media
organizations which are important in different ways as convergent media
entities. First, the BBC, a non-commercial public service broadcaster with
a particular social and cultural mandate. Second, News Corporation, one
of the largest commercial media organizations in the world, with interests in newspapers, film, TV, social media, book publishing and a range
of other industries. And third, Google, synonymous with online search
but also a convergent media and communications company, which owns
YouTube and Blogger, is a leading player in email and is developing a very
significant presence in the mobile phone market. In the final section of
this chapter, we build on the discussion of the BBC, Google and News
Corporation to explore the importance of convergent media industries,
taking news as our extended example.

Convergence Inc.

The media landscape of the business pages is one in which communications companies and corporations come together through mergers,
acquisitions and alliances. These corporations grow ever larger, more
diverse, more integrated and more global in scope and operations. Rather
than diminishing the importance of media ownership, the convergent
environment has highlighted the complex questions of power, influence and control. Such questions of ownership continue to matter to
three key groups (Doyle 2002: 171–3). They matter to the corporate
owners themselves as they continue to struggle for commercial and regulatory advantage. They matter to politicians who, rightly or wrongly,
feel that their survival depends on the grace of a friendly news outlet:
'Outside the sphere of the media', as Manuel Castells observes, 'there is
only political marginality' (2004: 370). And ownership matters to media
users, whose access to ideas may be constrained if profit is the sole motivation – if the market is all, then only ideas that are *marketable* are likely
to be marketed (Keane 1991: 90).

In the most comprehensive recent analysis of the media ownership
landscape, Castells identifies seven corporations as the top tier in terms
of revenue and global reach – Time Warner, Disney, Bertelsmann, NBC
Universal, Viacom, CBS and News Corporation. These are global media
businesses active across the full spectrum of mediated communication. He adds to this list the four Internet and computer firms with the

largest and most diversified operations – Apple, Microsoft, Yahoo! and Google (2009: 73–4). We outline the diverse range of media activities of each of these eleven firms below. All information is drawn from the most recently available published annual reports and other corporate information from each firm, as of September 2011, and is indicative rather than exhaustive.

Time Warner is active in four key areas. Warner Bros. produces films, television programmes, games, comic and web properties such as the *Harry Potter* movies. HBO is a cable channel turned television production house – think *True Blood* or *The Wire*. Turner Broadcasting includes CNN and the Cartoon Network, while Time Inc.'s focus is on magazines and their associated Internet presence, including iPad versions of *Time*, *People* and *Sports Illustrated*.

Disney's activities include broadcast networks such as ABC TV in the US, ESPN sports networks, the Disney Channel and Radio Disney stations. As well, Disney Studio Entertainment, which includes Walt Disney Pictures, Pixar and Touchstone, has a catalogue of around 2700 films, both produced and acquired. Disney Interactive Media produces games based on Disney and Marvel characters, as well as web properties such as the Club Penguin social media service for kids. Disneyland and Disney World theme parks in the US, France and Asia are owned, part-owned or licensed by Disney Parks and Resorts. Complementing these are the merchandising, books, magazines and comic publishing sold by the Consumer Products division, often through Disney stores globally.

Like Disney, *NBC Universal*'s 42 companies are active across film (Universal Pictures and Universal Studios boast a catalogue of more than 4000 films), television (including the NBC Network, Telemundo and MSNBC with franchises such as *Law and Order* and *E!*) and online media such as iVillage and Hulu. It too has an interest in theme parks and resorts in the US, Asia and the Middle East. Telecommunications company Comcast owns 51 per cent of NBC Universal.

Bertelsmann AG has different emphases, but is similarly global. Its portfolio includes television and radio – its subsidiaries produce the *Idol* and *Got Talent* reality contest franchises – as well as book publishing in the form of Random House, the world's largest trade publisher. It also produces more than 300 magazine titles. Reach is added with a distribution network of book shops, book and music clubs, and catalogue sales, as well as a range of media and communication services including call centres, software distribution and music merchandising.

Viacom has media networks including MTV, Nickelodeon, Comedy Central and Shockwave games online. It owns Paramount Pictures with more than 3300 films and associated licensing agreements including videogames.

CBS includes the CBS TV network (*60 Minutes, CSI, Survivor, Oprah Winfrey Show*), CBS Films, CBS Interactive (including CNET, GameSpot and Last.FM) and cable networks such as Showtime, which produces leading dramas such as *Dexter* and *Nurse Jackie*. CBS also owns book publisher Simon & Schuster, and is a major presence in local US broadcasting with 28 TV and 130 radio stations.

News Corporation has a range of television interests including the Fox Network and Fox News in the US, Star TV in Asia and BSkyB in the UK. It also owns Twentieth Century Fox with its vast catalogue of films; a range of newspapers around the globe (including *The Wall Street Journal, New York Post* and *The Sun* and *The Times* in the UK); and book publisher HarperCollins.

Apple sells both computer and consumer electronics hardware (Macintosh, iPhone, iPod and iPad ranges) and associated operating system and application software. Much of this is sold through a global network of more than 300 Apple Stores. Its iTunes Stores occupy a pivotal position in online media retail and distribute a range of (largely third-party) music, movies, television shows and software apps.

Google's products include its iconic search service google.com, including Google Images, Scholar, Books and News. As well, it provides a range of applications and services such as Gmail, Docs, Maps, Earth, Street View, YouTube, Blogger, Picasa and Orkut (a social network platform with a major presence in emerging territories such as Brazil and India). Of these, Gmail and Docs are offered as licensed installations to companies, schools or universities. The others are monetized by advertising, which Google enables with its AdWords and DoubleClick services. Providing a platform for these activities, Google offers its Chrome browser and OS as well as the Android OS and Mobile products in the mobile space.

Yahoo! also offers a search product as well as the Yahoo! homepage and toolbar; a range of applications and services including mail, messenger, groups and Flickr; and media solutions such as Yahoo! News, Sport and Finance. Again, it provides a range of services that allow third parties to develop platform offerings and enable revenue streams through advertising placements.

Microsoft's Entertainment and Devices division sells consumer electronics hardware (Xbox, Windows Phone, Zune) but software is still central. Its traditional Windows and Office products are now complemented by online services including its Bing search engine, its MSN (Microsoft

Network) suite of websites and services, and its May 2011 acquisition of communications company Skype.

The diversity and scale of this top tier of media firms shows that ownership in the media environment grows ever-more concentrated (Herman and McChesney 1997; Bagdikian 2004), at the same time as these businesses diversify their platforms and products to increasingly segmented and fragmented audiences. All of these enterprises are also increasingly networked, and key board members and senior executives interlock across multiple organizations, in addition to providing crucial connections to financial and political networks (Castells 2009: 93). Castells observes that it is not simply that media ownership is more concentrated than ever, but also that the major players increasingly pursue partnerships, alliances and joint ventures to exploit synergies in production and distribution. Furthermore, there is increased business between established media corporations and computing companies like Apple and Internet firms like Google, as well as with telecommunications firms. And media networks are linked with other kinds of networks – financial, political, technological; advertising industries, global news agency wholesalers. The capacity to network between different kinds of network is often facilitated through board members and executives who are affiliated across multiple businesses, providing access and leverage between media and financial networks, or political access for media firms (Castells 2009).

> Because the media are predominantly a business, the same major trends that have transformed the business world – globalization, digitization, networking, and deregulation – have radically altered media operations [...] Almost no media organizations are truly global and a decreasing number of media outlets are singularly local. What are global are the networks that connect media financing, production, and distribution within countries and between countries. The major organizational transformation of media that we observe is the formation of global networks of interlocked multimedia businesses organized around strategic partnerships (Castells 2009: 71–2)

Castells provides four key examples of these networked media industries: Hulu, the online television streaming service (NBC Universal, News Corporation and Disney); the CW Network, a US broadcast network (CBS and Time Warner); MSNBC (Microsoft, NBC); and ESPN Star Sports Asia (News Corporation, Disney). To his list we could add Yahoo! and

Microsoft's 'Search Alliance' in which Microsoft's Bing engine powers Yahoo! search, while Yahoo! handles the global premium ad sales for both – and of course, the previously mentioned iPad app *The Daily*, where News Corporation provides exclusive media content for Apple's tablet device.

Capitalizing on convergence

The second sense in which we use the term 'convergent media industries' describes the ways in which media firms are adopting and adapting the potential of the technological convergence explored in the previous chapter. Media industries develop by responding to the possibilities offered by the affordances of communications technologies. In some cases, they incorporate these into their existing business; in others, they significantly change the scope and prevailing uses of the technology, and in so doing change the scope and scale of their own business. The digitization and networking of production and distribution means that the overlap between previously distinct sectors is now very substantial. While Amazon, for example, has its roots in retailing, its website is a significant media presence – its book reviews facility, for instance, does a job that was previously the sole domain of newspaper literary supplements. Amazon's ventures into the ebook market have seen it enter the consumer electronics domain, and as it encourages authors to bypass traditional publishers and write solely for its Kindle platform, the gap between being a bookseller and a book publisher has essentially been eliminated. Similarly, Apple, as a dominant player in music sales and a key intermediary in the distribution of movies, TV shows, games and now books, is these days as much a media company as a computer company. As all forms of media content converge in the digital space, media firms are now all in the software business, in that all are engaged in the movement of zeroes and ones between networked digital devices.

This environment, again, is characterized by contestation but also by continuity. Consider the recorded music industry, in which, despite a decade of attrition by file-sharing, the recording companies continue to find ways of exploiting the convergent media environment – some of the most high-profile examples of how convergent media are supposedly revolutionizing the record industry in favour of the artists and fans can instead be seen as successful appropriations of convergent media by the established industry.

The discovery of Arctic Monkeys in the UK, for instance, is often described as a Myspace phenomenon, through which the band were believed to have bypassed the record industry: 'Have the Arctic Monkeys changed the music business?' asked *The Guardian* (25 October 2005). The band's debut album in 2006 was at the time the fastest-selling album in UK pop history. And yet the role of Myspace in their discovery was as a forum for their earliest fans to connect with each other and to share files ripped from home-made demo CDs produced and given away at gigs by Arctic Monkeys before the band had signed a record deal, in effect demonstrating to the labels that the band had a following (David 2010). Arctic Monkeys were the beneficiaries of an environment in which fans can be crowd-sourced as A&R scouts by record companies (Sexton 2009). And even though their label, Domino, is an indie, they have licensed their publishing through EMI in major territories including the US. So their case is not a revolutionary insurrection, but rather a convergence in which the established record industry, battered as it has been in the last decade, is still pivotal.

A similar observation applies to the online pay-what-you-like release of *In Rainbows* by Radiohead in 2007, although the band were at a very different stage of their career than were Arctic Monkeys. Radiohead, having concluded their contract with EMI, initially made the album freely available online in an 'honesty box' format (at a relatively low audio quality of 160kbps), with a reported 1.2 million downloads in the first three weeks, most paying nothing at all (David 2010). But the band then went on to license the album to various labels around the world, including in a lucrative deluxe box-set version. This eventual CD release went to number one in both the UK and the US, among other territories, which means that the entire download project can be seen as an elaborate promotional campaign for the CD (Wikström 2009; Harvey 2011). The Radiohead example differs from that of Arctic Monkeys in that the latter act were unknowns breaking into the business, whereas Radiohead were a very established act between contracts. One crucial consequence of this is that Radiohead were able to retain control of copyright, significantly shifting the revenues for *In Rainbows* in their favour; it remains to be seen, however, how far less-established acts can push such strategies.

This chapter now turns to focus on three organizations which represent different aspects of convergent media industries – the BBC, News Corporation and Google – before drawing together the themes and concerns raised throughout the chapter in an extended discussion of news in the convergent media environment.

The BBC

The UK broadcast sector is a mix of publicly funded and commercial organizations, operating across free-to-air analogue and digital platforms as well as subscription-based satellite and cable services, and increasingly experimenting with convergent systems. By far the most influential institution is the British Broadcasting Corporation (BBC). It runs ten national TV channels, 55 radio stations, a network of websites, the iPlayer and Red Button interactive services, as well as the World Service, which broadcasts in 27 languages other than English, and its commercial arm BBC Worldwide. According to the BBC's annual report for 2009/10, 97 per cent of UK adults make some weekly use of BBC services. The BBC receives the bulk of its funding from the sale of compulsory TV licences. As of September 2011, a licence typically costing £145.50 is required for all UK households that watch or record TV broadcasts, whether on a television, a computer, a phone or other device.

The BBC is the world's most influential public service broadcaster. On one level, public service broadcasting (PSB) describes government-funded media – but on another level, the term describes an entire philosophy of broadcasting (Reith 1924; Scannell and Cardiff 1991; Tracey 1998; Collins 2004; Curran and Seaton 2010) For commercial media organizations, the audience is a means to the end of making profits from advertising – for public service media organizations, the audience is the end in itself. This is to simplify things, as PSB in different forms is a distinct part of the media environments of different parts of the world and, in the UK for example, terrestrial commercial broadcasters have been subject to public service requirements and regulations on their programming, while being funded by advertising. Moreover, the BBC has been brought steadily within the orbit of markets, competition and demand, competing for the largest audience share as well as catering to the widest range of audiences. But the distinction we draw about audiences as ends or means does capture the PSB ethos (see the debate between Jacka 2003 and Garnham 2003 for more on this). The public service approach has renewed applicability in the convergent media environment. The BBC's public service obligations are set out in its charter, the most recent of which came into operation in 2007. This restated its mission to 'inform, educate and entertain' and also redefined its public purposes as:

(a) sustaining citizenship and civil society;
(b) promoting education and learning;
(c) stimulating creativity and cultural excellence;

(d) representing the UK, its nations, regions and communities;

(e) bringing the UK to the world and the world to the UK;

(f) in promoting its other purposes, helping to deliver to the public the benefit of emerging communications technologies and services and, in addition, taking a leading role in the switchover to digital television.
<http://www.bbc.co.uk/bbctrust/our_work/protocols_policy/index.shtml>.

What is clear from the updated charter is not only the expressed need to expand beyond traditional radio and television services to include online media, but also the idea that new media technologies are developing at a rapid rate and need to be considered as the BBC evolves. By the late 1980s, a range of new technological possibilities had already provoked debates around the possibility of deregulation; the introduction of cable networks and satellite raised the possibility that there were alternatives to broadcast frequency and so there might no longer be a need for government intervention to regulate its scarcity. The 1985 Peacock Report had a different conception of broadcasting. Rather than ground its recommendations in public service, it viewed broadcasting as a marketable commodity, provided for consumers, and argued for 'consumer sovereignty in broadcasting through a sophisticated market system' (Scannell 1989). While the Peacock Report allowed for the special case of public service broadcasting within the market, it signalled a shift in how the BBC might be conceived – one which reflected the reality of emerging cable and satellite delivery technologies and consequential regulatory changes (Küng-Shankleman 2000; Born 2004).

The BBC has been a major driver of digital television in the UK through its creation of the Freeview model, which broke the subscription monopoly on digital delivery. And it has made very significant developments online. Its websites are among the most-visited in the world, it is experimenting with initiatives to digitize and open up its entire archive, and it has made some of the most sophisticated responses to the rise of user-generated content of any established media organization: we discuss some of these in the final section of this chapter. Its creation of the iPlayer – see Chapter 7 for a fuller discussion – and initiatives such as its 'Democracy Live' website show that it is as much a technology organization as a media one. 'Democracy Live' offers live streaming video from both houses of the UK Parliament, from the European and Scottish parliaments, and from the Welsh and Northern Irish assemblies, all within a single page, but its most innovative feature is a speech-to-text tool which allows the user to search for particular words from within its video archive. As Cunningham points out, the role of public service broadcasters like the BBC or the Australian ABC has been crucial in driving such innovation:

> Unlike its commercial competitors, the ABC can experiment and innovate with new technologies in a non- or pre-commercial environment. It is much more difficult for the commercial broadcasters to engage in risk and experimentation without a guaranteed revenue model for any new initiative. (Cunningham 2009: 86)

But to many of those commercial competitors, public service broadcasters have an unfair competitive advantage. In this argument, public subsidy has resulted in entities like the BBC having a significant advantage in media marketplaces the world over. Proponents of this view have long since dismissed any notions that there should be a public service remit in the media marketplace. The most visible recent example of this position has come from News Corporation.

News Corporation

News Corporation is one of the biggest and most consistently audacious media firms on Earth. In its annual report for 2010, it reported revenues of US$32.8 billion. In 2010 it released the biggest box-office movie to date in *Avatar*, launched the hit TV show *Glee*, and saw *The Wall Street Journal* defy the climate for US newspapers and increase its circulation. But in July 2011, News Corporation became embroiled in a scandal over allegations of widespread phone hacking by its flagship UK Sunday paper the *News of the World*. The most damaging of those allegations came when *The Guardian* newspaper reported that the *News of the World* had accessed the phone messages of murdered 13-year-old Milly Dowler after her disappearance but before the discovery of her body. Moreover, it was reported that journalists had deleted some of those messages to create space for new ones, in the process giving false hope to Milly's family that she was still alive and destroying possible evidence for the police investigation. The demonstrated revulsion from the public, from politicians and – perhaps most significantly – from advertisers was so intense that Rupert Murdoch closed down the *News of the World* within the week. In terms of convergence, the abrupt closure of the biggest-selling Sunday newspaper in the UK, a profitable title with more than

160 years of successful publication behind it, is a stark illustration of the current standing and future prospects of the newspaper as a media form. The *News of the World* was sacrificed in an attempt to save News Corporation's bid (since withdrawn) to take full control of the much more lucrative BSkyB broadcasting service in the UK, in which, at the time of writing, it holds a 39% stake. In the logic of convergence, a wholly-owned BSkyB could have been used to bundle cable TV subscriptions with those to other News Corporation properties, exerting commercial dominance across the UK media spectrum, squeezing out other players and so reducing plurality.

The scope and scale of News Corporation's operations make it an exemplar of both senses of convergent media industry. Its roots are in newspapers, in which it still maintains very influential holdings in the UK (*The Sun* and *The Times*), the US (*The Wall Street Journal* and *New York Post*) and Australia, where it owns more than two-thirds of the country's newspapers, including its only national daily and the key metropolitan papers in a majority of its states and territories. News Corporation moved into television and then film as part of its expansion into the US in the 1970s and 80s, and its Fox network controls the top-rating *American Idol* as well as Fox News, the aggressively right-wing rolling news channel it created in 1996 in a deliberate attempt to counter what Murdoch perceived to be the liberal bias of CNN (Chenoweth 2001; Greenwald 2004). It has cable and satellite network interests in the US, Latin America, Asia, Europe and Australia, and a foothold in the Middle East and Africa. Its Twentieth Century Fox is one of the major film studios. It is a major international book publisher through its ownership of HarperCollins. It has a major stake in convergent TV service Hulu. And it has experimented with social network media, buying Myspace for US$580 million in July 2005 only to sell it for just US$35 million six years later.

News Corporation's CEO Rupert Murdoch has now spent almost sixty years building his initial 1952 family inheritance of a struggling Adelaide newspaper into this global conglomerate (Munster 1985; Shawcross 1992; Page 2003). Few figures in the media landscape are so recognizable or so controversial (Neil 1996; Wolff 2010). Both the recognition and the controversy stem from his capacity to use his empire to influence the commercial and regulatory environments in which News Corporation operates. On the first of these points, influencing the commercial environment, Murdoch has a history of initiating aggressive price wars (Doyle 2002), using profitable parts of the business to subsidize losses in another – one reason why initial dismissals of *The Daily* project for the iPad, or perhaps its eventual successor, may turn out to be premature. The second point is much more significant – News Corporation has developed and displayed formidable capacities to have regulatory frameworks adjusted, amended or waived in its favour:

> Over the years, Murdoch has practiced a three-pronged strategy, providing propaganda platforms to those in power, cash to the opposition, and personal favours to a diverse crowd of politicians in need. As a result of this strategy, Murdoch influenced a number of regulatory measures in several countries in ways that greatly benefited his business. (Castells 2009: 429)

Murdoch has, for example, provided a lucrative position at News Corporation to former Spanish Prime Minister José María Aznar, paid very large advances on political memoirs from figures such as Margaret Thatcher (McChesney 1999), and seen political leaders such as Tony Blair implicated in lobbying on the firm's behalf while in office (Chenoweth 2001). News Corporation's aggressive approach to its business has also seen it come into conflict with many competitors in the past. Among the more recent is a software service which moved into the news arena by launching a news aggregator – Google.

Google

Google has become synonymous with web search – indeed, we could perhaps date the moment this happened to June 2006, when 'google' was added as a verb to the Oxford English Dictionary (and if you want to fact-check that date, you can, of course, google it). The word 'google' as equivalent to both 'search' and 'oracle' has leaked into popular culture. The sarcastic abbreviation 'GIYF' or 'Google is your friend' is used in online exchanges in which one party is thought to have asked a question they could have just looked up on Google instead (Halavais 2009: 1). The website 'Let Me Google That For You' offers a similar function, allowing users to create and share a link that shows an animation of the typing of a given question into the Google search box, and the clicking of the 'search' button, above the words 'was that so hard?' <http://lmgtfy.com>. The captain of the 2009 winning team on the BBC's TV student quiz show *University Challenge* enjoyed a week of celebrity as 'the Human Google'. CNN reported on a study into the use of search engines *in general* with the headline 'Most of us Google ourselves, survey finds' (28 May 2010). For better or worse, Google equals search.

But Google is no longer just a search engine. It is a media company. It owns the blogging platform Blogger, the image tool Picasa, and the video site YouTube. It is digitizing millions of books for viewing online, photographing and posting the world's streets, and aggregating the world's news sites into Google News (discussed in more detail in the final section of this chapter). And it provides communications services, through its email, chat and phone products. Unlike the BBC or News Corporation, which have decades of pre-web history, Google is the most powerful example of a convergent media company that is indigenous to the web. And it built its initial success on the most fundamental element of the web – links.

Google's innovation was to treat links in the same way that academics treat references to publications. One way in which academics measure their success is through citation. The more a piece of research is cited by other academics, the more kudos and reputation accrue to the writer. Citations – even hostile ones – count as recommendations. Google's founders Larry Page and Sergey Brin understood how academia works. Not only were they PhD candidates at Stanford in the 1990s, but Page's parents taught computing at Michigan State University, Brin's father taught mathematics at the University of Maryland and his mother was a NASA scientist (Wise 2005: 23–5). So both Page and Brin knew that academic reputations work on a citation system. Their innovation was to view the World Wide Web's use of hyperlinks as analogous to that system. The number of incoming links provide a sense of the importance of a webpage; more than this, as with citations, some links count for more than others. Page and Brin saw that link data was a way to determine the usefulness of a particular webpage, and that the challenge was to come up with a way to calculate the relative importance of those incoming links.

Page and Brin developed a ranking system that privileged highly linked sources by analysing the links into each of the linking sites themselves and adjusting for the popularity or visibility of the linking site (Halavais 2009: 65–8). They called the idea Pagerank and build a basic search engine called 'Backrub' (so called because it dealt with 'back' links to websites) to test their ideas (Wise 2005: 38–9). Backrub was a web crawler which scoured the web, extracting link data from websites. It began operating across the Stanford University network in 1996. Users found that its ranking of results added a useful dimension to the list of sites that those other search engines normally provided. Moreover, the system scaled – it got better as the dataset got bigger (Battelle 2005). Realizing that the project had outgrown its Backrub name, Page, Brin and their colleagues renamed their search engine Google, a misspelling of googol, the number with 100 zeroes, and in 1999, Google the research project became google.com (Wise 2005: 59).

But Google has long since ceased to be just about search, even if that remains its core activity. Google is not just a software service, but a media company. Just as the BBC expands from being a media organization to one which also makes significant technological innovations, such as the iPlayer or 'Democracy Live' projects, so Google is moving from being a technology company to one active across a range of media content and communication areas. In the first decade of the twenty-first century, Google added, among other things, media such as books, blogs, online video and maps to its portfolio. And as clear evidence that the network enables a convergence of previously separate industries, Google also expanded into communications tools such as email and voice. Google also pushed into established computer domains – launching productivity applications (Google Docs), its own web browser (Chrome) and the Android operating system for mobile devices. Some of these came from the firm's own research labs – Gmail, Google Books and Google Maps fall into this category. Others were acquired in the traditional manner of expansionary corporations. Google bought Blogger in 2003 and, when its Google Video service languished in YouTube's wake, bought that competitor in 2006. For the moment, Google's domain is still largely web-based, but it increasingly seeks to expand its presence in the broader Internet domain. Android, its mobile operating system, is becoming a key component of the growing mobile Internet (Wu 2010; Goggin 2011) and with the 2010 introduction of Google TV and its May 2011 launch of a cloud-based music service, it is striving to expand its dominance in information organization and provision.

The clearest alignment with traditional media industries has been in Google's revenue model, which is a twenty-first-century model for linking buyers with sellers. Google's growth has been built on advertising revenue – the introduction of text ads on search results pages, which advertisers only paid for when clicked, was to prove a watershed. By restricting placements to advertisements related to the search phrase and then auctioning placements to the highest bidder, Google managed to create an ecosystem of adwords that worked for both advertisers and Google, and were sufficiently unobtrusive for users. These ads, since rolled out to YouTube videos and Gmail, provide the bulk of its revenues.

News and convergent media industries

News is a collaborative process of making meaning out of events. The news is a representation of social authority, a depiction of who gets to speak and what they get to speak about. In this book, we take news to be not just a genre or a textual system of stories, bulletins, broadcasts and reports, but also to be a set of practices and processes of production, distribution and reception. News is the organized daily production, distribution and use of non-fiction drama. It is an aspect of media that is crucial to everyone – even to those who don't read or watch it – as the news is where decisions about what counts in a society are presented, justified, endorsed or rejected.

Certain key groups are most involved in the processes and practices of news – audiences, journalists, sources and news organizations. Audiences do much of the work of deciding what counts and how it matters (Hargreaves and Thomas 2002; Hartley 2009a). Our daily participation in the rituals of news, from the morning paper through the daily Twitter to the evening TV broadcast, is central to the legitimacy of news. Journalists claim for themselves the role of the Fourth Estate – unelected guarantors of the democratic system (Boyce 1978; Schultz 1998; Curran and Seaton 2010). They are licensed to ask questions on our behalf and to tell stories to us about what they are told in return. Yet much of this work is in channelling the information provided to journalists by high-status sources of information – governments and politicians, the military and the police, corporations and not-for-profit groups among them (Fishman 1980; Herman and Chomsky 1988; Ericson, Baranek and Chan 1989; Lewis, Williams and Franklin 2008a, 2008b). This is the aspect of news into which WikiLeaks crash-landed in 2010, making the role of news sources both more visible and more controversial than at any time since Watergate. And the cultural role of journalists is challenged, as members of 'the people formerly known as the audience' (Rosen 2006) take a more active, participatory role in the news (Hartley 2000; Glaser 2010; Singer 2010). Some specialist bloggers, for example, have increasingly become part of the range of sources upon which the established media rely – specialist bloggers whom Couldry terms 'writer-gatherers' (2010b). Despite these challenges, it is important to emphasize that the Fourth Estate role of journalism remains. For example, the *News of the World* phone hacking story discussed earlier was broken by *The Guardian*, and only emerged due to the persistence of its journalists over several years.

Audiences, journalists and sources are all intrinsic to the production, distribution and reception of news, but in this section we focus on convergent news organizations. News is a product. The news is not a natural category of events that are simply found and presented by journalists. Rather, the news is produced and marketed on an industrial scale by media organizations. And the priorities and imperatives of those organizations have a profound impact on the form and scope of the news. Their institutional requirements and demands lead to news that, in Michael Schudson's estimation, can be summed up as 'negative, detached, technical, and official' (1995: 9). News organizations set the agenda for public debate (McCombs 2004). If they do not quite tell us what to think, in Bernard Cohen's famous 1963 observation, they do tell us what to think about. The commercial orientations and ownership structures of corporate news media can be seen to influence not only the content of the news, but also the contexts – economic, political, regulatory – in which news firms operate (Herman and Chomsky 1988; Bagdikian 2004; Castells 2009). Their industrial organization and publication frequencies have led to the development of the principles of selection and of presentation – often referred to as 'news values' – through which the status of news is conferred on certain events while others remain invisible (Galtung and Ruge 1965; Gans 1979; Hall 1981; Harcup and O'Neill 2001). Their employees (White 1950) or in some analyses the institutions themselves (Shoemaker 1991; cf. Bruns 2005) have been understood as 'gatekeepers', controlling and restricting access to the conceptual arena that Habermas labelled the public sphere (1974, 1989). As James Carey once argued:

> Reality is, above all, a scarce resource. Like any scarce resource it is there to be struggled over, allocated to various purposes and projects, endowed with given meanings and potentials, spent and conserved, rationalized and distributed. The fundamental form of power is the power to define, allocate, and display this resource. (1989: 87)

News organizations, in short, have a substantial claim to defining social reality by determining what counts as news.

But those institutions and organizations are under pressure. More and more people now get their news through convergent media, including on their mobile phones and on the web (OECD 2010). A 2010 Pew survey of US news audiences found that online news had displaced newspapers and radio, and was now second only to TV (Purcell *et al.* 2010). Networked digital media make possible a number of shifts in our experiences of the news, each of which can be seen as a tension between continuity and contestation. This section focuses on three such tensions, each related to the others, and each a consequence of news being both digital and networked. First, the digitization of news leads to tensions between the ideas of news as a coherent package, such as an individual newspaper, and of news as a database of links. Second, digitized news leads to the related tension between distribution and sharing. And third, networked digital media lead to tensions between news as a monologue and news as a conversation.

Each of these trends is enabled by the convergence of content, computing and communications, and each manifests tensions between contestation and continuity. On the one hand, there are elements of contestation and transformation, glimpsed in new possibilities for journalism (blogging, crowd-sourcing, social media tools), new kinds of organization (Google News, Twitter), new kinds of news source (WikiLeaks, specialist bloggers) and reconfigured relationships between the news and its audiences, who are now afforded enhanced opportunities to participate in the news, to discuss it and to share stories that matter to them with audiences of their own. On the other hand, there are also elements of continuity, as established organizations such as News Corporation move to accommodate the possibilities of the convergent media environment into business models and logics that privilege the scarcity of the broadcast model over the abundance of information made possible by networked digital media – the most obvious example of this is the ongoing search for a viable business model in which users will pay for online news.

News as links

The first of these three tensions relates to the fact that news organizations have until now focused on packaging news in coherent objects – a newspaper or a broadcast bulletin, for example. But in the networked digital media environment, the coherence of these news packages is challenged. Rather than a discrete product, the news instead becomes a database through which users can navigate and search (Manovich 2001; Burnett and Marshall 2003). In response, Rupert Murdoch has moved a number of his key newspaper titles behind paywalls (including, as of September 2011, *The Times* and *The Sunday Times* in the UK), a move mirrored in *The New York Times'* re-introduction of a paid-subscription model for its own website in March 2011. Whether subscription income can compensate for the loss of readers (and with them the reduction in advertising rates which his business can charge) remains to be seen, but it is a striking attempt to maintain the websites of these papers as discrete entities, walled off from the rest of the Internet. It is a deliberate attempt to replace the abundance of online news with an artificial scarcity, and to reassert what Peter Horrocks, Director of the BBC World Service, has described as 'fortress journalism' (2009).

Horrocks argues that 'fortress journalism' works through distinct platforms and products – such as a newspaper or a TV programme – but that in the convergent media environment 'all those products are available within a single platform and mental space' (2009: 7). Google News offers a clear example of this. Google News allows the user to personalize their news by selecting and prioritizing topics before viewing. While the default set includes categories such as business, sport and entertainment news, the user can nominate topics as specific, focused or arcane as they wish – entire news sections about vampires, Justin Bieber or kebabs. The random choice of 'kebab' there immediately produced this indelible headline, which very much added to the authors' news experience of that day: 'Thumb That Fell From The Sky Into Car Park Belongs to Missing Kebab Store Worker' (*Daily Mail*, 25 March 2010).

The shift in emphasis made possible here is simple but profound. In the broadcast media environment, we choose our supplier first and then take whatever they have for us. So the choice is to watch CNN or Fox and to view the stories that they have decided matter most, or to buy *The Daily Telegraph* or *The Sun* and only then select from the pre-packaged options they have for us in that edition. But in the convergent media environment, we can choose what we're interested in first, and only then select which supplier suits us best, customizing our news experience in the creation of what Negroponte (1995) dubbed 'The Daily Me' (see also Thurman 2011). 'The reader', as Horrocks points out, 'may never be aware from which fortress (or brand) the information has come' (2009: 7).

Google News updates automatically, so that the most recent story from thousands of sources ranks at the top. This brings with it the need for a new kind of literacy, built around filtering and organizing media material, as we learn how to prioritize and select for ourselves in a media environment in which trust and reputation are being rebuilt (we will return to this point in Chapter 5). It also brings with it the need for new kinds of business model – Rupert Murdoch, for one, has been scathing about Google News, describing it as 'theft' of News Corporation's articles. As a description of the process, this is plain wrong. Google News just offers a link to the article. What Murdoch is objecting to is the way in which this threatens the coherence of the overall news package. Rather than pointing the reader to the front page of, say, *The Times*, Google News will link to an individual story deep inside its website, making it harder for *The Times* to parcel those readers up into a coherent demographic package that it can sell to advertisers, and harder to channel its readers through the pages with the most expensive ads.

News as sharing

A second tension is that between distribution and sharing. All digital media texts, including news, can be copied and shared by anyone. News is no longer simply distributed by media companies *to* audiences – it is now increasingly distributed *by* those audiences, as links, stories, videos and images which are meaningful to particular individuals are recirculated through convergent networks. News has always been just one part of the overall package published as a newspaper – there are also commentaries and opinions, advertising and announcements, entertainment listings and cultural reviews, cartoons and crosswords. All of these can now be found elsewhere – with classified ads better suited to a searchable database environment than they ever were to print – which is just one reason why converting web users to paying for news content appears such an uphill struggle. But as well as this content, the reader was also taking part in a daily ritual (Carey 1989; Anderson 1991; Bird 2010). To read a daily newspaper is to participate in a shared cultural ritual of community, through which stories about 'people like us' call into being or reinforce our senses of the various social groups – neighbourhood, network, nation – to which we belong (Latour 2005). This daily ritual is now challenged by new avenues for sharing, new means for listening, new forms of community, such as those offered by social network media. We discuss social media in more detail in Chapter 3, but for now we will note that they blur the distinction between one-to-one personal communication and public media. In the broadcast media paradigm – in which we include newspapers, as its defining characteristic is that content is provided on a one-way basis to large dispersed groups – news is addressed to nobody in particular. This public quality is the source of many of the most enduring and polarizing debates surrounding the media and journalism – it is the source, for example, of debates about entertainment versus 'hard news' (Postman 1985; Hartley 2001; Zelizer 2009) or about the doctrine of objectivity (Tuchman 1972; Hallin 1986; Lichtenberg 2000). But news in the convergent media environment is *shared* as well as distributed, bringing its public quality and personal communication into new alignments. Sharing what one has heard has always been a key part of the experience of news. As Robert Park once observed: 'The first typical reaction of an individual to the news is likely to be a desire to repeat it to someone' (1967: 42). But convergent media make this possible in new ways and on new scales.

Twitter, for example, gives its users the capacity to reorder and customize flows of public communication. Users can subscribe to updates from established media organizations, filtering and combining their interests. But they can also subscribe to updates from friends and colleagues who share what they find most meaningful or significant at that moment.

> The selection of people one follows on Twitter function collectively as a highly subjective filter that prioritises and re-orders the news agenda as it is understood by a newspaper or a TV network, influencing what is heard, and when. (Crawford 2011: 116)

In this way, the user can outsource the editorial function of gatekeeping to a trusted self-selected network – a 2010 Pew survey of US news audiences found that 51 per cent of those users of social network media (such as Facebook) who use online news sources report getting news items from online Friends on a typical day (Purcell *et al.* 2010: 4). Axel Bruns (2005, 2008b) has described this as the shift from gatekeeping to gatewatching, as users monitor and filter what is being published, and share, link to, annotate and elaborate on this material. Part of the significance of this relates back to our previous point, in which news is disaggregated from the published package, but part of it is also about a challenge to our understanding of the cultural roles of news. To approach the sharing of links through social media as 'citizen journalism' may be a mistake – the sharing of links through social media may instead be better understood as phatic communication (Miller 2008; Crawford 2011), as users find new opportunities for shared feeling and shared listening, relocating news more firmly within Carey's ritual model of communication (1989):

> To a great extent, people's experience of news, especially on the internet, is becoming a shared social experience as people swap links in emails, post news stories on their social networking site feeds, highlight news stories in their Tweets, and haggle over the meaning of events in discussion threads. For instance, more than 8 in 10 online consumers get or share links in emails. (Purcell *et al.* 2010: 2)

News as conversation

The third tension we examine here is that between news as a monologue and news as a conversation. Convergent media are not only digital but also networked, and so in the convergent media environment, viewers and readers are able to respond in more ways than was the case when audience input was restricted to letters to the editor. Dan Gillmor has argued that blogs, for instance, exemplify a major shift in the news: 'from journalism as lecture to journalism as a conversation or seminar' (2004: xiii). The term 'citizen journalism' (Allan 2009; Allan and Thorsen 2009; Deuze 2009a; Bruns 2011) has its problems – journalists, after all, can be citizens too. But members of the public with convergent media devices can generate images and texts that inform the news – committing what J. D. Lasica (2003) has labelled 'random acts of journalism'. Moreover, it is now easier and more common than ever for non-professionals to become key sources for news media, blurring the distinctions between reporter, source and audience.

For example, consider the death of Ian Tomlinson on 1 April 2009. Tomlinson, a 47-year-old newspaper vendor, set out to walk home through central London, his route taking him through riot police deployed to contain demonstrations against the G20 summit. Police at first reported his sudden death that evening as the result of a heart attack, and their information shaped early media reports that spoke of how police officers, trying to assist him, were assaulted by protesters throwing bottles. That narrative came to an abrupt end when *The Guardian* newspaper posted a 40-second video on its website on 7 April. The video shows Tomlinson walking with his hands in his pockets, followed by a group of police in riot gear. One of them, with no apparent provocation, suddenly lunges at Tomlinson, knocking him to the ground. None of the ten or so police officers visible in the video comes to Tomlinson's assistance. An inquest found that he died of the resulting injuries and returned a verdict of 'unlawful killing' on 4 May 2011. The video, the pivotal piece of evidence, was taken by an American visitor to London, who, like Tomlinson, was passing through the protests but not participating in them. *The Guardian* passed the video on to the BBC, Channel 4, Sky and uploaded it to YouTube, from where it spread around the world. In this example, the roles of 'audience', 'journalist' and 'source' converge and become blurred.

The conversational dynamic in which 'the people formerly known as the audience' are able to contribute to the news has been taken up by the BBC. The corporation has been a leading force in the development of ways in which material generated by audiences can be incorporated into its professional output. Stuart Allan and Einar Thorsen (2011) have traced the development of BBC News Online, arguing that it has been shaped by the public service ethos that has always been at the core of the BBC's approach – an ethos which, in Curran and Seaton's estimation, has three primary components: 'serving democracy, generating content that has cultural value and promoting social inclusion' (Curran and Seaton 2010: 380). Of particular importance in the BBC's online news work are the ways in which it has responded to and promoted the rise of user-generated content (UGC), from comments to amateur video. UGC describes a wide spectrum of material, but can be defined as material which is published in some way (excluding instant messages or emails, for example); which involves a certain amount of creative work or contribution (excluding simple copying); and which is created outside of professional practice or routine (OECD 2007: 18, Shirky 2008: 83–4).

The quantity of such material sent to the BBC increased markedly in the middle of the first decade of the twenty-first century, as the number of people online reached critical mass and Web 2.0 affordances became widely adopted. The death of broadcaster John Peel in 2004 prompted over 100,000 emails to the BBC (Thurman 2008: 147). The 2004 Indian Ocean tsunami and the London bombings of 7 July 2005 both brought flows of UGC to the BBC on a new scale – in the case of the London attacks, emails from viewers brought the first challenge to the initial official narrative of the events (Wardle and Williams 2008: 2), to be followed by over 1,000 photos and 20 videos from non-professional contributors, as well as thousands of texts and tens of thousands of emails, such that by 8 July the main evening TV news broadcast led with a package completely edited from UGC video footage (Allan and Thorsen 2011: 30).

The BBC now has a specialist dedicated unit known as the 'UGC Hub', to manage user-generated content – a 24-hour operation staffed by more than twenty journalists, it can receive 12,000 emails and hundreds of videos and images submitted by users on a typical day (Eltringham 2009; Wardle and Williams 2010). Wardle and Williams (2008: 10–12) distinguish between five different types of UGC that the BBC deal with: (1) audience content, which includes breaking news photos and videos; audience experiences, such as case studies offered in relation to news stories; and audience stories, meaning stories generated by audience suggestions or tips; (2) audience comments, which refers to all opinions shared on blogs, radio phone-ins, or in response to a TV presenter calling for views to be emailed in; (3) collaborative content, which describes UGC material produced with BBC input, support or actual training, such as the digital storytelling projects, including Capture Wales (Meadows 2003; Lundby 2008; Hartley and McWilliam 2009); (4) networked journalism, which is a term used within the BBC to describe efforts to involve expert communities to improve the quality of news content; and (5) non-news content, such as wildlife photos or restaurant reviews.

Such a wide range of material means, of course, that UGC plays different roles within different aspects of the BBC's operations and remit. These range from roles which are common to a broader range of news organizations, including commercial ones, such as drawing upon UGC for finding news sources and generating stories; through creating a space for public discussion and in turn building the relationship with audience members; to audience empowerment and skills development, which is a role distinctive to the BBC's public service mission (Wardle and Williams 2008: 24–5).

Established media corporations have embraced to greater or lesser degrees the possibilities of UGC (Thurman 2008; Newman 2009; Singer and Ashman 2009), just as new entities have arisen to provide unprecedented access to media production and consumption possibilities. As the convergence of professional and amateur status continues, so do the debates over what that means for the news. Bruns (2011) argues that citizen journalism can complement what he calls 'industrial' journalism in three main ways – by extending the breadth of coverage (tackling topics that industrial journalists lack the flexibility, inclination or resources to cover), the depth of coverage (opening up debate to include more and different voices) and the duration of coverage (extending the news cycle beyond the deadlines and constraints of the print or broadcast media). Similarly, Beckett (2008: 55–7) offers an example of coverage of a warehouse fire to show how audience input can be incorporated into the professional output at all stages of a single story, from texting reports of the fire leading to a first newsflash, through submitting phone images and videos to be incorporated into the developing story, and on to crowd-sourcing reports of missing people as the story continues.

User-generated content is often celebrated by media scholars and commentators. It is seen variously as a way of making the public sphere more democratic, as a reallocation of symbolic power and as a sharing around of the licence to speak. It is all of those things. But for those who work in the news industry, it also contributes to an ongoing sense of crisis, as journalists – accustomed to a privileged status as the Fourth Estate, the unelected bulwark of democracy – find themselves forced to adjust to an environment in which their professional status and indeed professional existence are questioned on a daily basis (Terranova 2004; Deuze 2007a, 2009b; Lovink 2007; Bird 2009; Mosco 2009). This sense of crisis is not entirely caused by creative audiences. Advertising revenue is falling, there are new forms of competition for news media and the news often suffers from cost-cutting and under-investment in journalism by news organizations (Freedman 2010; OECD 2010; McChesney 2011; Deuze and Fortunati 2011). But the shift from journalism as a monologue to a new environment of news as a conversation, enabled by networked digital media, is a significant reality in the news landscape. We will discuss the roles of creative audiences in more detail in Chapter 5.

Conclusion

The convergent media environment has not suddenly resulted in the overthrow and demise of big media. Indeed, the influence of large corporate entities is still very much in evidence – the global media landscape remains characterized by large corporate entities, both commercial (Google, News Corporation) and non-commercial (the BBC). These organizations still have greater resources of symbolic power, and more opportunities to influence both the content and the contexts of media, than do any other kinds of actors. But this continuity is contested. Established media corporations such as Disney or News Corporation are grappling with the possibilities of the convergent media, resulting in new alliances with partners from computing and Internet backgrounds such as Google, Microsoft and Apple. Such industrial convergence is paired with their experiments in convergent media forms as the so-called mainstream media struggle to find ways to survive, and then thrive, in a networked media space in which previously fundamental principles of media production and distribution have been significantly altered. Our focus on news in this chapter is not to suggest that news is the only area in which these circumstances apply – all other content industries now grapple with the implications of a media environment in which their content can be copied and shared, and in which distinctions between producer and audience blur.

Moreover, there are the additional contests sparked by emerging new companies, without old media baggage, that are sometimes better placed to swiftly take advantage of possibly fleeting opportunities. We should not forget that Google itself is little more than a decade old, or that stalwarts such as Blogger and YouTube are still the equivalent of primary school age. Each of those two sites arose from seemingly nowhere to demonstrate possibilities that were quickly assimilated into now-widespread convergent media practice – and each was assimilated into the political economy of the media giants when purchased by Google. The most significant contemporary contest is the rise of social network media such as Facebook, to which we now turn.

From Broadcast to Social Media

3

Camille has dyed her hair blue. Steve took his dog to work. Emily has finished her thesis. John and Emma have more baby pictures. Elaine is working her way through an enormous bag of nacho cheese-flavoured tortilla chips. What else is on the Facebook news feed? Barack Obama is giving a speech in Cleveland and hopes we'll watch it live. BBC *Newsnight* has an interview later with physicist Stephen Hawking. Aung San Suu Kyi keeps us posted on actions and protests against the ruling Burmese junta. 'Texts From Last Night' sends random messages from the cellphones of unknowable strangers – today's comes from someone in Ohio and reads: 'Those strippers last night smelled great. It was the perfect mixture of vanilla and daddy issues.' And the city of Paris sent us a Facebook message, inviting us to follow it on Twitter. Things are getting weird.

Facebook's news feed mixes personal ephemera, news headlines, party photos, political announcements, attention-seeking, communion and links. These are shared in some cases by people whom we know very well offline, or in other cases by people whom we've barely or never met, or by public figures and media organizations (both established – the BBC – and new – Texts From Last Night). It's a blend of personal communication and public media that manifests a shift in the way we experience mediated communication. Facebook is a complex space, a site of multiple convergences and modes of interaction, and one that offers keys to understanding our converged media environment.

This chapter focuses on the convergence of different forms of communication and interaction, blurring the lines between one-to-one and public communication. Such convergence is what we see going on in our Facebook activities every day, but it is not yet well-understood, and it has important implications – not least for its users' privacy and reputations. This chapter begins by discussing the nature and development of social media tools such as Facebook, before setting these in the wider context of Web 2.0. It then discusses some different modes of communication, before showing how these are converging in social network media.

What are social network media?

On 1 September 2010, Apple CEO Steve Jobs announced that the company was launching a music social network service called Ping. Unlike most popular social networks, Ping had no web presence, but was instead built into version 10 of the iTunes software. Jobs claimed that the iTunes Store had 160 million active accounts, all of whom would be able to activate Ping, which suggested to some that the new network could overnight become a major player in the social media arena – *Wired* pronounced Ping 'already too big to fail' before it had even launched. One million people set up accounts within the first 48 hours, although Jobs himself appeared to deactivate his own after showing it in his public demo. But the early buzz was bad.

Some complained that the options offered when creating a profile were too limited and clunky – profile photos had to wait for 'approval' from Apple, and in outlining their music tastes users were restricted to choosing up to three very broad genres (and no matter what genres you indicated you liked, Ping was likely to recommend that you follow Lady Gaga, Katy Perry or U2). Others complained that it was hard to connect with their friends – there was no option to import contacts lists or link with existing social network profiles, and the email invitations tool was inadequate. And still others complained that there was little to do once they were on Ping – there was little scope to interact with friends, other than commenting on their purchases from the iTunes Store, and unlike existing social music tools like Last.fm or Spotify, it wasn't possible to share playlists or listening histories.

In short, there were perceived limitations with setting up profiles, adding friends and interacting with those friends. These were important flaws because they speak to three basic features of social network tools – (1) creating a profile, (2) adding contacts and (3) interacting with those contacts within the bounded service of the network (boyd and Ellison 2007). The third element of this definition is crucial: boyd and Ellison's exact words are that social network sites allow users to 'view and traverse their list of connections and *those made by others* within the system' (emphasis added). Without this highlighted element, the definition could equally apply to such established networks as the phone system – after all, if we install a landline phone in our house, we can (1) create a profile in the form of a public listing of our name, address and phone number, (2) add contacts to our speed-dial list and (3) interact with those contacts by talking to them on the phone. So the critical difference for social network media is that our interactions may be more or less visible to others. For this reason, we add a fourth criterion to boyd and Ellison's definition, and explore this in more detail below. So as well as sharing the elements of profile, contacts and interaction with those contacts, we define social media tools as those which (4) blur the distinction between personal communication and the broadcast model of messages sent to nobody in particular.

We draw upon this four-part definition throughout this book. We also follow boyd and Ellison's practice of capitalising 'Friends' specifically to refer to Facebook contacts, to distinguish these from the everyday sense of 'friends', and those authors' use of 'social network' rather than 'social network*ing*' – while some social media, such as LinkedIn, are framed around building and extending one's professional network through gaining introductions, users of other social media are more likely to connect with people with whom they already have a shared connection of some kind (Ellison, Steinfield and Lampe 2007). However, unlike boyd and Ellison (or Papacharissi 2011), we do not refer to tools such as Facebook or Twitter as social network *sites*, because those networks are increasingly accessed from mobile devices as well as via websites on personal computers (Goggin 2011), because they are increasingly dispersed across the web itself through 'like' or 'share' buttons on a wide range of other sites, and because it is possible to respond to social media messages from within one's email account or by text message. The actual *websites* of Facebook or Twitter themselves are only part of those networks, and so we refer throughout to social network media or social media tools instead.

According to boyd and Ellison's brief history, the first project to meet their three-part definition was SixDegrees.com, founded in 1997. This site ultimately didn't succeed, as many users didn't yet have a critical mass of friends who were online and there weren't enough ways to interact or share with those friends once they had connected; SixDegrees closed in 2000. But the significance of SixDegrees was that it combined existing features of the Net into a recognizable precursor of contemporary social network media. The creation of user profiles, for example, had antecedents in dating services (Smaill 2004; Arvidsson 2006; Ellison, Heino and Gibbs 2006) and in the presentation of self through personal homepages (Cheung 2007), and contacts lists were features of chat or messaging services, although were not for public display in the way that was so crucial to later social media: one illustration of this last point is that Myspace offers a 'Top Friends' feature, through which users can publicly rank their favourite contacts in order – 'consider it the place to shout out to your BFFs on Myspace', suggests the network's FAQ page, although one teenage interviewee described the politics of this as 'psychological warfare' (boyd 2006). Facebook, similarly, offers the facility to highlight certain contacts on one's profile as 'featured Friends'.

Social network tools require a shift from the ways in which online communities have been understood till now, as being formed around communities of interest (Rheingold 1993; Smith and Kollock 1999; Willson 2007). While Facebook has a 'Groups' function, which allows users to gather around topics of shared interest, the network itself is structured around individual users, with each 'at the center of their own community' (boyd and Ellison 2007). Communities of shared interest emerge through interactions in the network, rather than being the starting point, as users build up a presentation of self that allows others to locate them within shared cultural contexts (boyd 2006).

The first social network to capture wide attention in the UK was Friends Reunited (2000–) (Ofcom 2008), which was bought by broadcaster ITV for £120 million in 2005, when the network claimed 15 million users, but subsequently sold for just £25 million in 2009. The service's decline in popularity coincided with the rise of Facebook; its charging users for full access to contact services may also have contributed to its decline. Friendster (2002–) grew quickly, but alienated many of its early adopters by aggressively deleting profiles they had created for bands, celebrities or fictional characters (boyd and Ellison 2007). Myspace (2003–) was launched in time to capture many of these disillusioned Friendster users, and scored by enabling a focus around bands and music sharing. Its purchase by Rupert Murdoch's News Corporation for US$580 million in 2005 (Dwyer 2010) was the signal moment in making social network media a mainstream phenomenon.

The basic elements of social network media are now integrated into a wide range of online projects, including YouTube, Flickr, Last.fm and Spotify. The capacity to interact through Facebook, Twitter and many other smaller social media services is now also integrated into a wide range of other websites. All of the major convergent media organizations discussed in this book (Apple, the BBC, Google, News Corporation) have integrated social network tools into their services, either by adding proprietary social networks to existing products (Apple's Ping, Google

Buzz), integrating existing networks into their own offerings (as in the BBC's integration of Facebook and Twitter into the iPlayer in September 2010) or by buying a social network outright (as in News Corporation and Myspace). We should also note that social media vary in popularity around the world – Friendster remains popular in some parts of Asia, Orkut dominates in Brazil and India, Cyworld in Korea, Mixi in Japan, QQ in China and Vkontakte in Russia. Hong Kong even offers a social media network for dead people at <http://www.memorial.gov.hk>. However, with 750 million active users as of September 2011 – more than one in every ten people on Earth – Facebook is our primary focus in this chapter.

Facebook launched in February 2004 (later than Dogster, the social media tool for dogs, but beating Catster by a few months). Originally open only to those with an @harvard.edu email address, it quickly expanded to other universities, then high schools and corporate networks, before opening to the wider public in September 2006. It reached a million users in its first year, 5 million by the end of 2005, 12 million by the end of 2006, 50 million by the end of 2007, 150 million by January 2009 and 350 million by the end of that year. As of September 2011, Facebook claims more than 750 million active users, half of whom use the network on any given day. Facebook's own public statistics claim that each month users spend more than 700 billion minutes using Facebook, sharing more than 30 billion links, pictures, videos and other items of content. Moreover, the scale of the network makes it possible for Facebook to absorb successful social network tools from other enterprises – enhancing its photo tools to compete with Flickr (see Chapter 5) and introducing its Places function to compete with location-based services such as Foursquare (see Chapter 6). In the US, 61 per cent of all adults with online access now use social media (Madden 2010: 8). In the UK, people spend more than five times as much time on Facebook as they do on any other site. Ofcom reports that UK Facebook users spent 169 million hours on the network in April 2011; this figure only includes access from a computer, and so excludes the use of phones and other mobile devices – Ofcom's most recent figures for mobile Facebook use are from December 2010, when they reported 42 million hours (Ofcom 2011: 222).

Facebook's extraordinary growth is an illustration of Metcalfe's Law. Not a law so much as a useful observation, this principle states that the value of a communications network increases proportionately to the square of the number of people that are connected to it. If you're the only person with a phone, it's not much use, but once you know three or four people with phones, it becomes much more useful. And once everyone has a phone, it changes from being useful to essential. More than deriving extra benefits if you have one, it becomes a positive disadvantage not to have one. As Fischer describes this process in his history of the early development of the telephone: 'The telephone passed from miraculous in the nineteenth century to mundane in the mid-twentieth century to mandatory by the end of the twentieth century' (1992: 191).

Social network media were not invented by Facebook or Myspace; rather, these players have been among the most successful in refining and combining a set of ideas and tools which have been developing for some years. One analogy would be with the way that Apple achieved commercial dominance in the online music industry by achieving a combination of pricing, interface design and timing, which others had failed to combine before them. The price of an individual song (typically 79p in the UK iTunes Store at the time of writing) was low enough to drive the emergence of a new market and also, by unbundling individual tracks from the album format, gave a huge impetus to the playlist as a cultural form for the convergent media era. The interface was uncluttered and easy to use – almost too easy, as fellow impulse-buyers can attest. And the timing was crucial – the iTunes Store arrived at a moment when illegal downloading of music was more difficult and off-putting than it had been in the heyday of the original Napster – competitor services such as Kazaa were less reliable and brought concerns about spyware (Goldsmith and Wu 2006) – and before broadband penetration was sufficiently great to enable the widespread sharing of music through BitTorrent or services like RapidShare. Moreover, with the launch of the iPod, Apple had itself given new impetus to the hardware market for MP3 players, endorsed by the major record companies in response to the threat manifested by Napster (David 2010).

Facebook, by analogy, got the price right (the sign-up page reads 'It's free, and always will be') and it's worth recalling that some earlier high-profile social network services such as Friends Reunited charged users for full access to the service. The interface is, as with iTunes, simple and uncluttered – creating a profile and interacting with Friends is a matter of filling in text boxes and forms, and the overall look of the network is uniform and neutral. This contrasts with Myspace, part of the culture of which is pimping out profiles in often garish colours and designs – attractive to many users, but not, as it turned out, able to cross the kinds of demographic boundaries that Facebook has. The price to be paid for this, as Lanier argues, is that the idiosyncratic personal homepages of the early web era or the lurid stylings of many Myspace profiles are replaced by 'multiple-choice identities' (2010: 48), a presentation of self built around the bureaucratic organizing principle of the standardized form and its deliberate elimination of nuance (Beniger 1986). The third key element in Facebook's rise was that the timing, again as with iTunes, was crucial – by the time of its ascendancy, the basic principles of social network media had become more familiar to many users, the rise of other Web 2.0 services had lowered the barriers to creating and sharing content, there was a critical mass of devices on which users could access the service, and, quite simply, enough people were now online for everyone to be able to connect with at least some people with whom they would want to be Friends.

Social network media and Web 2.0

The rise of social network media needs to be set within the wider context of so-called Web 2.0. This term is credited to Tim O'Reilly (2005; cf. Meikle 2002 for a related distinction between 'Version 1.0' and 'Version 2.0' of the Internet). The Web 2.0 idea is rooted in the observation, around 2003, that although the first dot.com bubble had burst with the fall of the NASDAQ technology shares index after March 2000, there were still successful new Internet firms continuing to emerge. In searching for what these new firms had in common, the term 'Web 2.0' became fixed in the lexicon from 2005, and had an iconic moment of mainstream acceptance in *Time* magazine's 2006 cover story which identified 'you' as the Person of the Year (Grossman 2006).

A recurrent objection to the idea of Web 2.0 is the '2.0' part, which can seem to be uncomfortably implicated in the commercial logic and language of software upgrades – more features, fewer bugs, further obsolescence. It can also seem to suggest a linear progression that is not matched by reality, and a certain teleology. Moreover, in its usage to describe participatory web cultures, it describes a vision which was actually fundamental to Berners-Lee's original conception of the web, making it perhaps a more fully-achieved Web 1.0 (Berners-Lee 1999). But the term is useful in reminding us of change and development, that the web is never static, but is always in constant movement and reinvention, as discussed in Chapter 1.

The Web 2.0 concept is most often applied to online participatory culture, and to the rise of blogging, photo and video sharing, music filesharing, collaborative writing and editing, and social network media in the first decade of the twenty-first century (OECD 2007). But we should note that in O'Reilly's usage it describes business models for convergent media firms, built around database management, customization, personalization, automation and participatory affordances for users: 'Web 2.0 is the business revolution in the computer industry caused by the move to the internet as platform, and an attempt to understand the rules for success on that new platform' (O'Reilly 2006). This is an important distinction because it places a much-needed emphasis on the corporate imperatives that drive Web 2.0 projects. It is not just that many people can now create, collaborate and share online, and it is not just that 'we are the web' as ex-*Wired* editor Kevin Kelly has it (2005). Web 2.0 is also a shift to new kinds of business model for convergent media firms, in which the users do the unpaid work of building and promoting the business, creating its content, and generating advertising material through using the service. Novelist William Gibson, as ever, is one of the sharpest commentators on this aspect of online life:

> Google is not ours. Which feels confusing, because we are its unpaid content-providers, in one way or another. We generate product for Google, our every search a minuscule contribution. Google is made of us, a sort of coral reef of human minds and their products. (Gibson 2010)

We are the web, perhaps – but we're not getting paid for our labour in building it (Terranova 2004; Ross 2007; Lanier 2010).

The tensions between, on the one hand, the appeal of self-expression and sharing in online participatory cultures (Gauntlett 2008; 2011) and, on the other hand, the commercial logics of Web 2.0 firms is captured in YouTube's slogan – 'Broadcast Yourself™'. Kylie Jarrett (2008) points towards how the invitation (or imperative) to broadcast yourself, with its connotations of a do-it-yourself ethos and of the presentation of personal identity, is positioned within discourses of intellectual property through the superscript trademark identifier™. Setting aside the question of intellectual property, to which we return in Chapter 8, the juxtaposition in 'broadcast yourself' also speaks to what we identify in this chapter as the central tension animating social media, that between the personal and the public, between the message shared one-to-one and the message sent to nobody in particular.

O'Reilly's first definition of Web 2.0 (2005) was a list of examples, including Google, Flickr, blogs, Wikipedia and BitTorrent (which is not, strictly speaking, web-based, although users do use websites to locate files to exchange using BitTorrent). From this, the term developed to describe a loose set of principles. A central one is the observation that successful convergent media firms were being built around providing services rather than packaged software. Netscape had been emblematic of the first dot.com boom, and built its business on distributing copies of a desktop browser application; in contrast, we do not download, license or buy access to, far less a copy of, Google – we just use it. A second principle is an 'architecture of participation', through which users add value to the system just by using it – think of Amazon's recommendation engine, which is able to provide more accurate recommendations the more people use its system. Another key principle of Web 2.0 is that firms develop software services which can be used across multiple devices – think of Facebook on your iPod and your phone as well as your desktop. And a fourth is an emphasis on the database as the key to market dominance: 'Every significant internet application to date has been backed by a specialized database: Google's web crawl, Yahoo!'s directory (and web crawl), Amazon's database of products, eBay's database of products and sellers, MapQuest's map databases, Napster's distributed song database' (O'Reilly 2005).

The question of 'who owns the data?' then becomes central. A social network such as Facebook is a colossal database of the personal information of hundreds of millions of users – their contact details, their photos and videos, their likes and dislikes, their friends and networks, their biographies and behaviour, their allegiances, aspirations and secrets. But who owns this data? Facebook does. By 2010, a degree of public anxiety about this was visible in constant media coverage of privacy issues and problems with social network media; researchers found an increase in users modifying their privacy settings, perhaps linked to this coverage (boyd and Hargittai 2010, Madden and Smith 2010). Much of this coverage and anxiety starts from an implicit assumption that Facebook's 750 million users are its customers and should be afforded the respect this suggests. *But Facebook's users are not its customers – the users are the product.* Facebook's commercial operations are instead business-to-business, grounded in advertising and partnerships. Its business is selling uses of its database, made up of the daily lives of hundreds of millions of users, who add value to that database with every friend request, status update and poke. At the time of writing, O'Reilly's 2005 prediction that this explosion of proprietary data would lead to a 'free data' or 'open data' movement (paralleling the emergence of open source software in response to proprietary commercial systems) was being realized in the attempted launch of open alternatives to commercial social networks, such as Diaspora. However, as of this writing it is far too early to tell whether this will succeed on any scale, and the challenges of establishing a database of a size and comprehensiveness to rival the established Web 2.0 giants suggest that those with the biggest databases – Google, Amazon, YouTube, eBay, Wikipedia, Facebook – will be hard to supplant.

Who do you think you're talking to?

This chapter argues that Facebook manifests a convergence between personal communication (to be shared one-to-one) and public media (to be shared with nobody in particular). In his book about social media *Here Comes Everybody*, Clay Shirky discusses the apparently banal everyday nature of much online interaction. For example, why would you, as a stranger browsing a social media network, want to bother reading about Camille's blue hair, Steve taking his dog to work, or John and Emma sharing pictures of their baby? 'It's simple', writes Shirky, 'They're not talking to you' (2008: 85). The broadcast model trained us to expect publicly shared material to be addressed to an audience of nobody in particular, whereas social media allow everyone to address a specific audience of their own selection. But is it that simple? The blurring of the distinction that Shirky suggests is so clear is in fact the key thing that characterizes the social media environment. Broadcast media, Shirky also points out, are good at creating very large groups (usually called audiences), whereas personal communications media such as the telephone are good at facilitating conversations. Convergent media bring these two together (Shirky 2009; Baym 2010: 4). But rather than being a third form of communication, social network media create a tension between broadcast and personal communication, between messages intended for someone in particular and messages intended for whoever comes across them. This is the point at which we diverge from Castells, who describes the convergent media environment as one characterized by 'mass self-communication':

> It is mass communication because it can potentially reach a global audience, as in the posting of a video on YouTube, a blog with RSS links to a number of web sources, or a message to a massive e-mail list. At the same time, it is self-communication because the production of the message is self-generated, the definition of the potential receiver(s) is self-directed, and the retrieval of specific messages or

content from the World Wide Web and electronic communication networks is self-selected. (Castells 2009: 55)

Castells argues that this is a new and distinct mode of communication. We argue instead that the social media environment is characterized by unstable shifts between two much older modes of communication – between mediated personal communication (as in email, letters or phone calls) and mass communication in the broadcast media paradigm (as in TV, newspapers or radio).

To explain this we draw in this section on work by Thompson (1995) and Scannell (2000), each of whom offers valuable distinctions between modes of interaction. Thompson distinguishes between face-to-face interaction, mediated interaction and the kinds of interaction we have with broadcast media, which he terms 'mediated quasi-interaction'. This third mode of communication is characteristic of the broadcast model of media. By this we refer to a media framework in which information is distributed in a one-way fashion from a central provider of some kind to dispersed audience members who do not have the capacity to respond through the same medium.

First, consider daily conversation – the kind of interaction you had at the café yesterday. This kind of interaction is two-way, involves people who are present in the same location at the same time, and affords certain cues to enhance communication – things like tone of voice, body language, gesture and facial expression. Because we are in the same space at the same time, we can draw upon this shared context to help establish meaning. Second, compare this with the different kinds of interaction we can have through means such as email, phone calls, text messages, letters, instant messaging or online chat. Such mediated interaction is also two-way, but is different in that the participants are not present in the same location, and there may be a time difference too. We can answer your email when we feel like getting round to it, and that might take days or weeks; it's harder to get away with that in face-to-face conversation. This second kind of interaction also makes use of a technical medium of some kind, such as paper or phones or computers. And it gives us fewer cues to understanding tone and attitude, which means we need to provide extra information for context – things like: Dear Sir/Madam, ☺, 'Hi, it's me', and so on. 'Not even a telephone company publicist', observes Fischer, 'could assert that telephone calls capture the intimacies conveyed by eye contact and physical touches' (1992: 239). Moreover, in this kind of interaction we may not always be sure of with whom we are communicating; this is particularly the case with online media, where cues such as handwriting and voice are removed (Marinucci 2010).

Scannell (2000) points to some important aspects of such mediated interaction. Some kinds of communication, some kinds of message or media text, are only meaningful to particular people, to a special someone – the love letter, the family holiday snap, the birthday party video. These are messages that are not intended for the wider world but for our most intimate family or friends. Each of us has photos, perhaps videos, perhaps letters, which we treasure because of the relationship they express, the moment they capture, the aspect of our self to which they contribute. They are intelligible to others – anyone who can read could make some sense of your most intimate emails, so make sure you have a strong password – but they are only really *meaningful* to the intended recipient. Only certain people would ever *treasure* these messages. Scannell calls these 'for-someone' messages. On an unremarkable, everyday basis, we all exchange 'for-someone' messages – a phone call, an email, a text. These are messages sent one-to-one; they are messages 'for-someone' in particular.

In this, they are distinct from the kinds of communication we have with TV. This is the kind we all learned to think of as 'media' back in the twentieth century – TV, cinema, newspapers, recorded music, radio, magazines. These send messages in one direction only – you can yell at that guy on the news, but he can't hear you. The really striking thing about such interaction, and yet the thing we most often take for granted, is that this kind of communication is made up of messages that are addressed to *nobody in particular*. Thompson's (1995: 23–31) analysis of such communication identifies five key characteristics. First, it involves the mutual development of media industries and communications technologies. Industries exploit the potential offered by technological innovations, and shape the ongoing development of the technology, while the affordances of the technology itself in turn contribute to the directions in which the industry can go. Second, mass communication involves what Thompson terms 'the commodification of symbolic forms' as texts, ideas and images, stories and songs, information and entertainment are assigned an economic value. Third, mass communication involves a 'structured break' between media production and media reception – for the most part, media texts within the broadcast paradigm are produced in a certain place by certain people but are consumed in different places by different people (see Chapter 5 for our discussion of how this structured break is challenged in the convergent media environment). Fourth, mass communication extends the availability of

information in both space and time – 'Every owner of a radio or television set possesses both a time machine and a teleportation device for
alien personages', in John Durham Peters's striking image (1999: 247).
And fifth, the products of mass communication are, in principle, available to anyone. To again draw on Peters, the implicit addressee of a
broadcast media message is 'To whom it may concern' (1999: 206). This
public quality of mass communication is at the root of many of the central debates surrounding the media – questions of standards and taste, of
impact and influence, of ownership and control.

When we watch *Inception* or *Mad Men*, when we listen to LCD Sound-
system or the BBC news, we are clearly not sharing in messages that are
intended only for us personally as special someones. So are messages in
the broadcast media model 'for-anyone'? Not exactly. Scannell argues
they are instead best thought of as 'for-anyone-as-someone' messages,
and explains this by contrasting them with the products of industrial
mass production as artefacts that are really 'for-anyone' – any tooth-
brush will do for millions of potential users; a certain pair of jeans
will fit anyone with a 32-inch waist; anyone who knows how to drive
can drive that car over there. These are not objects designed with a
special someone in mind. They're made 'for-anyone'. However, while
some influential and pessimistic readings of the media (Adorno and
Horkheimer 1995 [1972]; Schiller 1989; Herman and McChesney 1997)
have indeed seen media texts – TV programmes, films, popular songs –
as being standardized, mass-produced objects, intended 'for-anyone',
Scannell argues that we don't experience these in the same ways as
toothbrushes, jeans or cars. Instead, we experience them as speaking to
us directly. They address us as *someone*:

> I find, when I turn on the news, that I am spoken to while knowing
> that millions of others are watching at exactly the same time and
> seeing and hearing exactly the same things. In each case the experi-
> ence is the same. In each case it is 'for me'. This is the characteristic
> effect of a for-anyone-as-someone structure. The news is, in each
> case, appropriated by me as an aspect of my experience and yet at
> the same time this experience is shared by countless others. (Scannell
> 2000: 11)

This is a feature of the characteristic mode of address of, for example,
television. Think of Ryan Seacrest opening the show on *American Idol*
or Dermot O'Leary on *X Factor*: 'Thanks for joining us. Don't go away,
don't touch that remote, because tonight *you're* in charge, *you* get to

decide who stays in the competition and who goes home this week.' They're talking to you. Except they're not. They're talking instead in a conversational manner that addresses multiple, dispersed listeners as though directly, but is in fact addressed to no one in particular. They're looking straight into the camera, outwards towards an implied other – 'you'. It is this combination of a way of talking and a way of looking, argues Scannell, that helps to create 'a public, shared and sociable world-in-common between human beings' (2000: 12), or what Benedict Anderson calls an 'imagined community' (1991). Peters describes how such strategies were devised by early broadcasters to compensate for the perceived lack of real human content – direct address, conversational tone, a cultivated sense of intimate connection:

> Media culture is a lush jungle of fictional worlds where "everyone knows your name," celebrities and politicians address audiences by first names, and conversational formats proliferate. The conventional concept of "mass communication" captures only the abstract potential for alienation in large-scale message systems, not the multiple tactics of interpersonal appeal that have evolved to counter it. (Peters 1999: 217)

With social network media, it is no longer always clear whether we are being addressed as 'someone' or as 'anyone'. It is no longer always clear to what extent messages are intended to be shared one-to-one and to what extent they're intended to be available to a much wider public. There are historical antecedents for this, the resolutions to which suggest we are now in a similar transitional phase, as we work out the cultural boundaries around social media. Writing of developments in the postal system in the nineteenth century, Peters notes that the idea of the personal letter as *private* communication was slow to develop, and that for some time there was a public dimension to the post:

> personal letters in the United States at least could be raided for publication in the newspaper or at least for postmaster-led discussion. Some postmasters in the colonial period apparently freely quoted in their newspapers from love letters and personal correspondence. (1999: 165)

It took the development of the postage stamp, the sealed envelope, and the public post-box to give letters their private dimension, as each of these innovations removed the need to interact with a postmaster directly. And as Peters observes, mislaid, intercepted or lost letters 'manifest the ways that person-to-person communication, once recorded and transmitted, can break free of its senders and receivers' (1999: 176). The example of the letter shows how norms and standards develop in social use of media forms – they are not imposed from the start by the technical properties of those media. So the rise of social network media demands a public conversation about what those norms and standards are to be.

Some interactions we may have through Facebook are one-to-one and some are open to all our Friends; depending how we've set our privacy, they may be open to everyone on Facebook. But other interactions are less clear-cut. Think about the way that Facebook publicizes our activities to everyone on our Friends lists through the 'news feed' function. You might do something that's not really intended for public distribution, only to find that Facebook has told everyone you know. You may think a particular comment that you make on a Friend's status is restricted from others whom you might not want to see it, only to find that her profile is open to everyone, and so your remark has been redistributed to every one of your Friends as 'Top News'.

One reason why Facebook is so fascinating is that it mixes up the personal message with the message sent to nobody in particular. In this chapter's opening examples, the messages from Barack Obama, BBC *Newsnight*, Aung San Suu Kyi, Texts From Last Night and – sadly – the city of Paris weren't sent to us personally. They were instead being sent to everyone who had 'liked' those pages: to nobody in particular. But our other examples – Camille's blue hair, Steve's smuggled dog, Elaine's doomed tortilla chips, and the others – are not quite personal messages either. As of September 2011, Facebook states that the average user has 130 Friends; each of the people included here has considerably more than that. So to whom are their status updates addressed? Here again the personal and the public are blurred. Status updates are most commonly personal, informal, quotidian, perhaps banal messages. A Facebook status update, suggests Jodi Dean, 'marks the mundane by expressing it, by breaking it out of one flow of experience and introducing it into another' (2010: 98). It is phatic communication, as Miller (2008) argues, intended to maintain relationships, rather than the actual exchange of information. Status updates most commonly address us directly, as though they were 'for-someone', for us. But, depending on the privacy settings imposed by their authors, they are received by all of those authors' Friends. Is this personal communication? Or is it a message sent to no one in particular? It blurs this distinction; it can oscillate between the two. A status update is not 'for-anyone-as-someone' in the ways that *American Idol* is. It doesn't try to address an unknown audience of millions, making each feel they're included. It is for a self-selected audience, and even if your profile is entirely without elective privacy settings and open to the 750 million people using Facebook, most of them will not see it. Instead, it addresses your own list of Friends, which may number in the dozens or the thousands, and will be restricted to those with whom you have established this small reciprocal relationship. It is at once 'for-someone' in particular (only one's Friends) and 'for-anyone-as-someone' (any of one's Friends).

This convergence of the personal message with the message for nobody in particular is characteristic of other kinds of interaction Facebook offers. For example, a basic tool offered by Facebook is the ability to exchange one-to-one messages with Friends, in a format essentially identical to web-based email services such as Gmail, if rather more limited. This is a straightforward example of two-way personal communication – except that it's not unusual to send someone a message in this way only to have them reply by writing on the 'wall' area of your page, thus opening up the conversation to what may be a much wider audience, depending on what privacy settings are applied to the wall in question.

This convergence also manifests itself in wall posts and items that a user might choose to post on their wall or share with specific Friends, such as YouTube videoclips, links to other websites or photographs. Sharing a music video on your wall may be to share that video with all of your Friends, any of your Friends, no Friend in particular, but can draw comments from specific individuals that again blur the distinction between one-to-one interaction and messages addressed to no one in particular, opening up a conversational dimension to what is otherwise a broadcast presentation or performance of personal taste. What's more, the capacity for Friends to contribute to one's profile means that the Facebook user doesn't have total control over their presentation of self (Baym 2010: 112; boyd 2011).

Moreover, the Friends with whom you are interacting are likely to be more than just a list of offline friends, relatives, classmates and colleagues. It's very often considerably more complicated than that, not least because 'friendship' is an elusive concept in other areas of life as well. boyd notes that it lacks the firm sense of shared responsibilities of 'family' and the bounded sense of 'colleague'; the line separating 'friend' from 'acquaintance' or 'contact' can shift in specific daily use, and can vary across cultures and age-groups (2006). On Facebook, 'Friend' means something different again – it means 'other Facebook user with whom I am connected on Facebook'. Many users are likely to have many Facebook Friends whom they have never met outside Facebook, but with whom they share a connection of some sort. There may even be Friends whom we might actually *dislike* – it often seems more diplomatic or politic to accept the Friend request than to ignore it. On Facebook, then, 'Friend' is a metaphor.

But once a Friend is added, they're added. Unless we hide them from our news feeds – a crude binary option: in or out? – then what we see on Facebook doesn't distinguish between someone we'd trust with our lives and someone we wouldn't recognize in the street. They all converge on the news feed. Is this personal communication? Or is it the sending of messages to nobody in particular? How do we negotiate these distinctions in a convergent media environment? This matters, because the convergent media environment is an area in which people's private lives can become public instantly. It is not always clear, even to ourselves, how public we intend our interactions through social network media to be – and other people might take that decision on our behalf, with what can sometimes be unexpected consequences.

Some examples: Britain's top spy, the head of MI6, was compromised when his family holiday photos appeared in newspapers after his wife posted them on her Facebook page – 'You know he wears a Speedo swimsuit', the Foreign Secretary told the BBC, 'that's not a state secret' (BBC News, 5 July 2009). Or consider Amanda Knox, the American student convicted of the murder of British student Meredith Kercher in Italy – Knox is now known the world over as 'Foxy Knoxy', after reporters mined details, including that nickname, from her online profiles (*Newsweek*, 14 July 2008). Or consider Dartmouth professor Reiko Ohnuma, who made the mistake of posting on Facebook that she was writing her lecture on modernity for the next day using Wikipedia as her main source – a student took a screenshot and posted it to the college newspaper website, from where it circulated very widely (*Chronicle of Higher Education*, 6 February 2009). Or consider Ms Ashley Alexandra Dupré, an aspiring singer-songwriter who was outed as a prostitute implicated in the scandal that claimed the career of former New York governor Eliot Spitzer. As part of their coverage of the Spitzer story, the UK *Guardian* newspaper actually assigned their rock and pop critic to review some songs Ms Dupré had written and posted on her Myspace page, and published his review in the main news section of the daily paper – he awarded her tunes only two stars out of five, in a redefinition of the expression 'adding insult to injury' (*The Guardian*, 15 March 2008).

These examples illustrate how communication that we may think is intended for a particular, self-selected audience can, in the convergent media environment, become available instead to a much wider audience of nobody in particular. boyd (2011: 45–8) points to four specific affordances of networked digital media that are salient in thinking about how social network media enable and constrain their users' actions. First, what we write in the convergent media environment is *persistent* – it is recorded and archived by default, however ephemeral we may imagine an interaction to be. Second, these interactions are *replicable* – digital messages can be copied and shared across networks with people we had never imagined when we wrote them. Third, our interactions are *scalable* – the potential audience for any online interaction is huge and unknowable, as the examples in the previous paragraph indicate; the convergent media environment doesn't ensure a readership for what one writes online, but it does enable it, and so questions of visibility are ever-present (see Chapter 6). Fourth, online interactions are *searchable* – each interaction contributes to a networked database which others can explore, and this ties in to the previous three points, in that what searchers find is persistent, can be copied, and may be scaled up to a larger public.

This blurring of public and personal raises enormous ethical dilemmas. Two groups of people who are having to face these dilemmas already are employers and job applicants. There have been widely reported cases of people losing jobs because messages they had intended to be private turned out to be more public than they had assumed. In a remarkable innovation, the City of Bozeman, Montana attempted in 2009 to carry out background checks on job applicants, which involved requiring them to supply not only the usernames for their social network profiles but also their *passwords* (*Boing Boing*, 17 June 2009). There are reports that some US employers have taken to asking applicants to log in to their social network profiles *during their job interview* (*Sydney Morning Herald*, 2 January 2011). University applicants, similarly, are reported to be increasingly adopting pseudonyms for Facebook, to prevent college admissions officers scrutinizing their profiles and so jeopardizing their chances of entry (*The New York Times*, 23 April 2010).

Such dilemmas also confront journalists. To what extent is it allowable to mine details of people's lives from social media profiles for use if those people suddenly become noteworthy? How public are such details intended to be? Even if a user may recognize that they are potentially viewable by anyone on Facebook, they may not expect this visibility to extend to publication in the *Daily Mail*. When the former Pakistani leader Benazir Bhutto was assassinated in December 2007, and her son Bilawal agreed to assume a political role within the Pakistan People's Party, details of his personal life quickly appeared in UK newspapers, which obtained those details, including photos of him at a Halloween party, from his Facebook page. This in itself was ethically questionable, but was further complicated when the political party claimed his Facebook profile was a fake (BBC News, 3 January 2008).

Some news organizations now have ethical guidelines for the use of material found on social network media, including Australia's public broadcaster, the ABC; the BBC College of Journalism also offers training in social media tools for staff. But others, such as the Scottish *Sunday Express* newspaper, have treated private individuals' profiles as equivalent to press releases. In March 2009, this paper led with a front-page story headlined 'Anniversary Shame of Dunblane Survivors' (8 March 2009). The article revealed personal details from the social media profiles of teenagers who had survived the 1996 mass-shooting in which Thomas Hamilton murdered sixteen small children and one adult at a primary school in the Scottish village of Dunblane. The *Sunday Express* story – a new low for tabloid journalism, in our assessment – implied that the normal teenage behaviour of those in the story (chatter about parties, drinking, boyfriends and girlfriends, the occasional fight) somehow made them unworthy of having survived the massacre.

Conclusion

In September 2010, 14-year-old Rebecca Javeleau of Harpenden in the UK posted an invite on Facebook to fifteen friends to her fifteenth birthday party. She created an 'event' page for the party, and included her home address and mobile number. 21,000 people replied to say they were coming (*Telegraph*, 20 September 2010). Personal communication and public media converge with unpredictable consequences. The roles that social network media play in our daily lives – connecting people, enabling information flows – expand and augment activities that used to happen using older technologies such as telephones, letter-writing and coffee shops. They allow us to reach out across time and space at a speed, scale and level of complexity that were not previously possible, blurring our social connections as 'Friends' augment 'friends' (Miller 2011). But they also bring with them new kinds of visibility that allow our lives to be recorded and searched, to be scaled up to larger, unknowable audiences, as Rebecca Javeleau can attest. Social media can allow any-to-any communication just as easily as one-to-one and the mechanisms for controlling who gets to see are substantially different from those of the broadcast paradigm. The responsibility for content, once the domain of media corporations and governments, is now distributed across all participants. As both sources of information and networked distribution systems, how social media tools are used is still contested.

Social network media, then, challenge much of what we thought we understood about media and communication, about questions of privacy and visibility, about the distinctions between mass communication and personal communication. Social media demand that we think through an ethics of online communication. Who gets access to the material that we generate when we use Facebook? What are they allowed to do with it? How do we as individual users treat the material created by our Friends? These are questions that are not going to go away – if anything, they will become ever more pressing, as the principles of social network media tools spread beyond the bounded services of a password-protected service like Facebook across the wider convergent media environment.

Never Ending Stories

4

On 19 March 2011, Israeli remix artist Kutiman uploaded to YouTube a new video called 'My Favorite Color'. It was an original piece of music and of video art, a benchmark of remix creativity, created by adding 22 pre-existing videos of instrumental tracks to a vocal by YouTube user Tenesan1, a young woman singing her own unaccompanied composition 'Green' to her webcam. Like the vocal, the instrumental tracks were also all found-videos of musicians playing by themselves to camera before posting on YouTube – three separate piano videos and three French horn parts; a professional sax solo, a rain stick demonstration, a triangle part from an instructional video on Cajun music. Underpinning these was a loop of an organ part played by a middle-aged Texan mum, from a home movie recorded by her daughter. As each instrumental layer entered the song, a thumbnail of its YouTube clip would appear within Kutiman's video window, building up a new collaborative work created by bringing together separate texts in a way that their originators could never have imagined.

Kutiman's videos show the changing nature of media texts in the convergent environment. In a broadcast media environment, different textual forms rely on different modes of delivery and reception. Newspapers are printed on paper and land with a thump on your doorstep. Books are printed and bound, and sold in shops. Movies are watched in cinemas and television on TV screens. Radio programmes are tied to a device in your car or in your bedside clock. In short, different kinds of text are aligned to particular media systems and platforms. Connections between separate texts operate through intertextuality – 'Any text that has slept with another text [...] has necessarily slept with all the texts the other text has slept with' (Stam 2000: 202). In a broadcast media environment, intertextuality occurs within the same system of texts (books referring to other books, for instance) or between systems of texts (newspapers referring to television shows, for example).

But in the convergent media environment, with what Negroponte (1995) has labelled the shift from atoms to bits, the direct link between texts and a particular physical system of delivery and consumption is broken, and intertextual relationships can become more complex and diverse. Because all media forms can now be digitized and transmitted across global communication networks, there are new possibilities for textual convergence; indeed there is no *technical* reason why established media forms need remain separate, although of course, technical considerations are not the only factors – there are also cultural expectations and enormous global industries predicated on existing media forms.

This chapter explores the continuities and contestations involved by examining three models of converging texts. In each case, we trace historical precursors, see emerging new combinations of media texts and forms, and explore the tensions that arise as both media industries and creative audiences exploit the possibilities of networked digital media. First, we consider the mash-up model illustrated by Kutiman's 'My Favorite Color', through which texts of the same form, never intended to converge, are brought together in ways that their original authors might not have considered, in order to complement, counterpoint or subvert these texts. Technologies of production and distribution are now more accessible, making possible new combinations of existing texts in the creation of new media objects. Such convergence demonstrates the shift that is reconfiguring the relationships between professional and amateur, and challenges the industrial systems of production and the associated assumptions of copyright on which the monetization of media production has been predicated.

Second, there is the multimedia model – the textual convergence that occurs when previously distinct media forms are combined in ways that blur established understandings of both a media institution and the activity with which it is associated (viewing, reading, listening, playing). In the multimedia model, producers combine previously separate media experiences into a single media object, designed to engage users in different modes within a single activity on a particular platform. It can be seen, for example, in the website of a major newspaper organization, where text, audio, video, graphics and animation may all be used to present aspects of a single story. In such examples, convergent multimedia forms provoke important questions about the future shape of cultural institutions and industries, such as newspapers and television, as core activities are supplemented in the process of creating entirely new coherencies.

And third, there is the convergence of textual forms *across* platforms, which Jenkins (2008) terms 'transmedia storytelling'. Here, a common text is spread across the widest possible range of media forms and exists as a brand of intellectual property that has elements in both established (television, books, cinema) and convergent (web, videogames) media as well as in ancillary industries (toys, t-shirts) and an expanded range of locations, both physical and virtual. The affordances of networked digital media make such convergent multimedia texts both more accessible and more diverse, and again challenge established approaches to storytelling, whether fictional or journalistic.

Mash-ups

In November 2010 US artist Girl Talk (Gregg Gillis) released his fifth album *All Day*. The album comprised 372 samples from other artists' records – from Black Sabbath to Miley Cyrus – blended into a single 71-minute mix. A timeline at <http://mashupbreakdown.com/all-day> identifies each sample for the listener as it appears, while the music plays, tracking the moment when Lady Gaga, the Beastie Boys and Iggy Pop converge. *All Day* illustrates the mash-up approach to creating music, which became increasingly visible throughout the first decade of the twenty-first century. Some of the most influential mash-up tunes were illicit, such as Freelance Hellraiser's 2001 'A Stroke of Genius', which put the vocals from Christina Aguilera's 'Genie in a Bottle' over the music from The Strokes' 'Hard to Explain'. Others gained legal clearance for their samples, such as the 2002 album *As Heard on Radio Soulwax Pt. 2* by 2 Many DJs. And still other examples came from established artists, such as the Sugababes' 2001 version of Adina Howard's 'Freak Like Me' which replaced the original music with Tubeway Army's 'Are Friends Electric', or Kylie Minogue's performance of a 2 Many DJs mash-up of her own 'Can't Get You Out of My Head' and New Order's 'Blue Monday' at the UK BRIT music awards show in 2002. On YouTube you can find an inspired 7-minute mash-up in which every track on Billy Joel's *Greatest Hits* album is played at the same time.

While much of this music is novel and exciting, the artistic strategy of the mash-up is long-established. It builds on sampling, which in turn, as Paul D. Miller (aka DJ Spooky) points out, 'is a new way of doing something that's been with us for a long time: creating with found objects' (2004: 25; see also Eshun 1998; Chandler and Neumark 2005; Miller 2008). Creating with found objects informed the work of some of the major artists of the twentieth century – Picasso, Duchamp, T. S. Eliot – and some of its most important creative movements, from Dada to hip-hop, from Cubism to punk, from pop art to postmodernism. The uses of new technologies have often been crucial in such movements. Henry Jenkins (2003: 286) traces historical antecedents which paved the way for the participatory culture in which we find the contemporary mash-up aesthetic – the photocopier, whose adoption by small presses, alternative media groups and fanzine publishers enabled a broadening of sub-cultural expression; the VCR, which allowed audiences to exploit broadcast material (building personal libraries, editing their own amateur productions); the camcorder, which enabled amateurs to create footage for their own productions; portable music players, from the Walkman to the mobile phone, which allowed users to customize their environment with a personalized soundtrack; videogames, which fostered a sense of immersion, participation and engagement with media stories; and digital cameras and photo manipulation software, which, as with music sampling and editing programs, made possible still more new forms of production.

As an aesthetic strategy, the mash-up approach is increasingly central to creative production, both by amateurs and the established media industries. Copyright scholars point out that commercial creative works have always been built on the shoulders of others and that large media corporations have long used the mash-up aesthetic by appropriating older works and reconfiguring them. Disney's classic cartoons were often constructed by repurposing traditional folk and fairy tales, creating apparently original works from the combining of older texts with newer sensibilities (Lessig 2004: 133). So Disney's animated *Cinderella* from 1950 is a re-telling of 'Cendrillon' by Charles Perrault, itself a version of a story with many historical antecedents. Similarly, their 1937 *Snow White and the Seven Dwarfs* cartoon drew heavily from a story about Snow White by the Brothers Grimm.

These examples are first and foremost marketing strategies, which draw on both the recognition factor of the earlier work, and their prior track-record as successes. From movies through music (think cover versions), the creative industries have always drawn on the act of repurposing older material. The incorporation of the mash-up aesthetic can be seen in examples of established recording artists turning the component tracks of songs over to users to remix (Nine Inch Nails, David Bowie) or doing the same thing with their music videos (REM, Radiohead). In a recent example from book publishing, Seth Grahame-Smith combined period fiction with modern horror in his book *Pride and Prejudice and*

Zombies, a novel which mashes-up Jane Austen's original text with Grahame-Smith's scenes of zombie mayhem ('It is a truth universally acknowledged that a zombie in possession of brains must be in want of more brains'). The book sold well and its publisher followed up with a range of similar mash-up titles such as *Sense and Sensibility and Sea Monsters, Android Karenina* and *The Meowmorphosis*, a remix of Kafka for the web era, in which his Gregor Samsa awakes to find himself transformed not into a gigantic insect but a cute cat.

The approach has also been used in more complex ways by non-commercial media organizations such as the BBC, which ran its 'Backstage' project from 2005 to 2010. This encouraged and supported mash-ups drawing on a range of BBC data – users could produce amalgams of BBC travel news, BBC London traffic cams, local weather, geotagged Flickr photos and UK speed cameras; a retrospective book of these projects titled *Hacking the BBC* can be downloaded from <http://backstage.bbc.co.uk>. Driven by its public service imperatives, the BBC had the resources to enable a range of potentially useful user-generated mash-ups. Others have also experimented with such initiatives for non-commercial reasons. For example, Lawrence Lessig's commitment to Creative Commons included a 'remix this book' contest for his 2009 book *Remix*, through which users were invited to download the book from his publisher's website and remix it in any way they chose.

Convergent technologies dramatically increase access to these practices – mash-ups are now easier to make, and to make visible. Creators no longer require the resources of a Hollywood studio to remix, repackage and redistribute mashed-up material. The almost ubiquitous personal computer provides users with all the necessary production tools, and the Internet enables instantaneous global distribution and access to potential audiences. For example, a 2007 survey of 'most-viewed' content on YouTube saw around 50 per cent of material fit into a category that the authors defined as 'user-generated' (Burgess and Green 2009: 43). And professional content on YouTube comprises decades of TV, film and music video clips that has given new impetus to the mash-up method. Of course, not all user-generated material is mashed-up, but YouTube clearly contains a large quantity of material that is.

Our opening example of Kutiman illustrates an approach in which clips are mashed together in order to *complement* each other by bringing together discrete texts which share complementary elements or themes. Some examples of this kind of mash-up can be remarkable feats of creativity and effort – one recreates Spike Jonze's music video for the Beastie Boys' 'Sabotage' (itself a pastiche of seventies cop shows such as

Starsky and Hutch) by remaking it shot-for-shot using only images and sequences from *Battlestar Galactica*. But the approach can also focus on texts which *counterpoint* each other, juxtaposing often radically different texts to exploit the possibilities of their incongruous realignment. Clips of the Muppets have been mashed-up to have Miss Piggy perform 'Fuck the Pain Away' by Peaches or the entire ensemble cover 'Closer' by Nine Inch Nails. Dialogue from movies and TV shows can be mashed-up with contrapuntal clips – a sequence from the animated *Peanuts* TV series takes on a whole new aspect when Joe Pesci's menacing dialogue from the 'I'm funny? Funny how?' scene in *Goodfellas* is added, as does a sequence from *Toy Story* with dialogue added from *The Wire*, or an existentialist version of *Star Wars* with subtitles drawn from the writings of Jean-Paul Sartre. The obscene rants allegedly made in phone messages from Mel Gibson to his girlfriend have been mixed with video of *Dora The Explorer* or with the trailer for Gibson's own film *The Beaver*, in which they're spoken by the eponymous beaver hand-puppet. And there are 'YouTube Doubler' experiments, in which two video clips are played at the same time in side-by-side windows – Nickelback versus a noisy rooster, or Usher against a goat, with the recording artists coming off second-best in both cases.

Remix creativity can also be used to *subvert* existing texts. A mash-up aesthetic is sometimes deployed towards political ends, often discussed as *culture jamming* (Dery 1993; Meikle 2002, 2007). Culture jamming is the reworking of existing media images and texts to make a political or cultural statement. Very often jamming is self-reflexive media activism, in that it uses the media to address a media issue – the influence of advertising, for example (Lasn 1999) – and it is often intended to draw media attention to that issue. The term 'culture jamming' was coined by the experimental rock group Negativland, who used it on their 1984 record *Jamcon '84* (Dery 1993; Joyce 2005). Negativland are perhaps better known for their legal disputes with U2's record company than for their own music – the group were sued for using an uncleared sample and for releasing a single in a cover that made it appear to be a U2 record (Negativland 1995). In Craig Baldwin's film about the U2 affair, one of Negativland defines culture jamming as 'going in where you're not supposed to be on the airwaves and screwing everything up' (Baldwin 1995). From this perspective, jamming is obstruction and this is one way to think about it – culture jams turn regular signs into stop signs. But the musical sense of 'jamming' is also important here. From this perspective, jamming also suggests collaborative creation around an existing theme – experimental, exploratory and, above all, playful (Meikle 2008a).

For Negativland, culture jamming is what happens 'when a population bombarded with electronic media meets the hardware that encourages them to capture it' (1995: 251). Culture jamming is the practice of taking familiar signs and trying to change them into question marks.

Mark Dery places culture jamming in a historical context, which includes covert underground publishing and radical journalism, satire and sabotage, and literary experiments such as William Burroughs's 'cut-up' collage method of composition (as Burroughs himself explained this, 'Cut-ups establish new connections between images, and one's range of vision consequently expands' 1982: 264). There is also a direct link to the theoretical positions of the small group of writers, artists and theorists the Situationist International, who were active from the mid-1950s until the early 1970s (Knabb 1981; Gray 1988; Sussman 1989; Plant 1992; McDonough 2002; Wark 2011). The Situationists sought to undermine what their key theorist Guy Debord called the *spectacle*: the integrated, commercialized cultural space in which, in Debord's words, 'Everything that was directly lived has moved away into a representation' (1987: section 1). One of their key tactics was the practice of *détournement* – 'to detour, to hijack, to lead astray, to appropriate' (Wark 2011: 35). *Détournement* involves lifting an image from its original context and setting it in a new one, creating a synthesis that calls attention to both the original context and the new result.'Any sign or word', suggested Debord and Wolman, 'is susceptible to being converted into something else, even into its opposite' (1981: 13). For Greil Marcus, this could be understood as 'a politics of subversive quotation, of cutting the vocal cords of every empowered speaker' (1989: 179).

One example of a Situationist-inspired remix is DJ Spooky's touring video project *Rebirth Of A Nation*, in which he performs a live remix of Griffith's film *The Birth of a Nation* – a film which, on the one hand, maintains its status as one of the foundational works of cinema while, on the other hand, it operated as a Ku Klux Klan recruiting film until the 1960s, if not beyond (Miller 2004: 84). DJ Spooky's project of reworking Griffith's film to subvert its racist dimension was itself the key example of the Situationists, who used *The Birth of a Nation* to explain *détournement* in 1956 (Debord and Wolman 1981 [1956]). This Situationist idea has also been used very explicitly by Adbusters, who organize the annual Buy Nothing Day event each November. But gestures of this sort are easily absorbed into the vocabulary of their targets. Advertisers now commonly launch knowing guerrilla ad campaigns that pre-empt subversion, which neutralize satire by satirizing themselves first. And there appears to be no anti-commercial gesture which cannot be commercialized – even

Negativland have been invited to provide the soundtrack for a beer commercial (Klein 2000: 330). Adbusters themselves, we would note, market a hefty range of products for the sponsors of Buy Nothing Day – at one point they even sold Buy Nothing Day t-shirts, but have moved on to marketing their own range of sneakers 'for kicking corporate ass' <http://www.adbusters.org/campaigns/blackspot>.

Contemporary contests surrounding the use of mash-ups are generally concerned with the 'legitimacy' of the activity, and the ownership of the intellectual property involved. The convergent media environment allows new engagements with textual forms, with the intersection of digital mash-up with Internet distribution resulting in provocations from 'amateurs' and 'professionals' alike. An example that drew wide attention was DJ Dangermouse's *The Grey Album* in 2004. This remixed Jay Z's *The Black Album* with The Beatles' *White Album*. EMI, owners of rights to the Beatles' music, moved to block *The Grey Album*'s distribution, but Dangermouse's creation gained both notoriety and critical acclaim, sparking a debate over the nature of creativity and originality, as well as an activist action on 24 February 2004 called 'Grey Tuesday' in which supporters posted the mash-up for download from hundreds of websites in defiance of EMI (Ayers 2006; Andrejevic 2007: 31; Wikström 2009: 156–9).

Such tensions between copyright holders and other users remain unresolved with ongoing disputes as owners of intellectual property seek to constrain such activity. Jane Austen novels and Grimm's fairy tales are, of course, in the public domain. But their commercialized reconceptions are not, and established media content corporations have demonstrated that their enthusiasm to mash-up is matched only by their desire to prevent others from doing so without their permission. As media convergence develops, distribution companies become increasingly implicated in disagreements over rights, sometimes with absurd results. For example, in 2009, reacting to disputes with Viacom and Warner Music, YouTube inadvertently created a brand-new genre of silent music videos by disabling the audio on fan-created videos and mash-up clips (Campbell 2009). Among the silenced music videos on the site is a performance of John Cage's '4'33"', which even before YouTube's intervention was itself, of course, a performance of four-and-a-half minutes of silence.

Multimedia

On 11 March 2011, one of the most powerful earthquakes on record struck the east coast of Japan's main island. A tsunami caused by the event surged inland, leaving tens of thousands dead or missing, millions more without electricity or water, and triggering a crisis at the nuclear power station in the coastal town of Okuma in Fukushima prefecture. The next day's newspapers were filled with reports and images, with commentary and speculation about what was to come, in textual styles that would have been familiar to a reader from the nineteenth century – key reports were written in the long-established inverted-pyramid style, in which all key information is presented within the first paragraph, with each subsequent paragraph judged by its writer to be less important than the one before (Bird and Dardenne 1997; Pöttker 2003; Meikle 2009: 53–5). But online, coverage drew on a wider range of media forms. For example, the website of *The Guardian* newspaper included a live blog updated constantly throughout that day and for many days afterwards, incorporating video clips, screen shots of Twitter posts, and audio clips from Japan. Written stories incorporated video of the tsunami engulfing towns and villages. And opinion and reaction from the paper's commentators could be augmented with, in some cases, hundreds of comments posted by readers, many linking to other material elsewhere. As the humanitarian and nuclear crises continued to unfold, a dedicated section of the paper's website grew to include interactive applications through which users could explore the range of expert solutions to the Fukushima reactor crisis, compare before-and-after photo galleries of affected areas or listen to audio podcasts of commentators and experts discussing the crisis. This kind of web-based convergence of different elements – the coming-together of text, image, video, audio and animation – is now commonplace, confirming the personal computer as a key *multimedia* platform.

Of course, the combination of media forms has always allowed new engagements to occur. Long before digitization, artists found ways to blur the blunter distinctions between particular textual forms in the analogue realm – the written word, photography, illustrations and graphics, audio and video – and combine them to create innovative new forms: from Richard Wagner's 1849 vision of the *Gesamtkunstwerk* as a vehicle for 'uniting every branch of Art into the common Artwork' (2001: 4), to Dada's 1916 Zurich events mixing music, performance, poetry and confrontation (Richter 1965). In the Futurist Cinema manifesto, also of 1916, Marinetti and his collaborators declared that their Futurist cinema would free words from the fixed pages of the book and painting from its frame. It would comprise 'painting + sculpture + plastic dynamism + words-in-freedom + composed noises + architecture + synthetic theatre' (Marinetti *et al.* 2001: 15). This vision recurred throughout the twentieth century, from the networked experiments and events of Fluxus, which see 'all works as literary, musical, visual, and performative rather than just as one of these forms' (Smith 2005: 126), to the Acid Tests of Ken Kesey and the Merry Pranksters (Wolfe 1968), and Andy Warhol's *Exploding Plastic Inevitable* show built around the music of the Velvet Underground (Goldstein 1995). Rock shows continued to incorporate multimedia elements – Pink Floyd's *The Wall*, U2's *Zoo TV*, tours by Gorillaz or Flaming Lips – while theatre companies like La Fura dels Baus drew on elements of rave culture and video art. Separate textual forms were reconfigured and repurposed for delivery in any number of ways. Books were illustrated, soundtracks were added to silent movies, and those moving images allowed the animation of still illustrations.

So, as William Gibson declares: 'Multimedia is where we have always been going. Geeks and artboys, emerging together from the caves of Altamira, have long been about this great work' (Gibson 2001: xii). And in the late 1960s, at around the same time as the Velvet Underground were confronting audiences with their multimedia mix of music, cinema, dance, lighting and whips, computer pioneers such as Douglas Engelbart (2003), Ivan Sutherland (2003) and Alan Kay (1999) were laying the foundations for the graphically enabled multimedia personal computer. Engelbart created the oNLine System (NLS) which introduced the world to the idea that computers could be used by laypersons to manipulate information for personal purposes. In a famous 1968 demonstration, of which video is widely available online, Engelbart introduced such concepts as the mouse, windows, hyperlinks and a range of computer-mediated communication tools that prefigured email and video-conferencing. Sutherland's prototypical graphical user interface 'Sketchpad' had allowed users to create and manipulate images and objects on a computer screen as early as 1963. Introducing their concept of the 'Dynabook', Alan Kay and Adele Goldberg wrote in 1977 that 'Although digital computers were originally designed to do arithmetic computation, the ability to simulate the details of any descriptive model means that the computer, viewed as a medium itself, can be *all other media*' (1999: 112, original emphasis).

Digitization and the development of the networked personal computer expanded the idea of multimedia, and convergent technologies force us to reconsider apparently settled distinctions: 'In a digital art-work words can lead to virtual architectural spaces, in which gestures may trigger images, which may in turn evoke sounds' (Jordan 2008: 245). The emergence of the personal computer as a media device is central to more recent understandings of multimedia. Lev Manovich's (2001) 'new media' attributes of numerical representation, modularity, auto-mation, variability and transcoding (as discussed in Chapter 1) are now central to many contemporary multimedia forms. In particular, modu-larity is fundamental to this type of textual convergence. In contrast to mash-ups, multimedia texts retain distinctive parts: 'Media elements, be they images, sounds, shapes, or behaviours, are represented as col-lections of discrete samples [...] These elements are assembled into larger-scale objects but continue to maintain their separate identities' (Manovich 2001: 30).

Just as still images were animated and combined with sound to create the talkies, so digitized media types, forged into different combinations, have become something quite new. One example is the idea of enhanced books – an idea which itself has a prehistory. In 1985 the first version of Grolier's CD-ROM encyclopedia was released. It pioneered the mul-timedia encyclopedia genre, common in the 1990s, and which marked the demise of the printed encyclopedia. These were early examples of digital multimedia – products such as Microsoft's *Encarta* combined rela-tively lengthy articles with embedded pictures, audio and video mate-rial. CD-ROMs were the distribution mechanism for, by the standards of the day, vast quantities of large audio, video and graphical resources that could be displayed on then-powerful multimedia computers. Even governments were persuaded by the possibilities. In 1994, the Australian Government's cultural policy included funds for the 'Australia on CD' project which saw the development of multimedia CD-ROMs for schools covering topics from indigenous history to Australian rock music his-tory (Australian Government 1994). Book publishers embraced the idea that multimedia personal computers could prove to be a large market for their content, and many established new media divisions. However, by 1996, most had withdrawn from the multimedia market as losses became common. By then it was clear that there was no mass market for multimedia CD-ROM titles (Roper 1995; Clark and Phillips 2008: 30).

With hindsight, CD-ROMs were a limited transitional approach whose inflexibility was superseded by the increased bandwidth of modern broad-band and the usability of the graphical web browser. However, embold-ened by the success of Apple's iPad, with its clear interactive possibilities and simple distribution options, book publishers are again exploring new ways of combining textual forms. Rick Perlstein's *Nixonland*, published by Scribner, is an early example of what some are dubbing 'enhanced' books. Telling the story of Richard Nixon's presidency, the iPad version of the book includes 27 video clips from the CBS archive, providing contemporary context for the story being told in prose. Enhanced iPad versions of T.S. Eliot's 'The Waste Land' and Jack Kerouac's *On The Road* saw critical and commercial success in 2011. Hilary Mantel's 2009 Booker Prize-winning historical novel *Wolf Hall* has an enhanced edition, including a video of the novelist discussing the period of the book with historian David Starkey, while *Alice for the iPad* incorporates animations which respond to tilts and shakes of the device into the text of Lewis Carroll's classic. Songwriter and novelist Nick Cave's 2009 book *The Death of Bunny Munro* also has an iPhone app version, which includes not only the electronic text of the novel, but also an audiobook version, videos of the author reading sections, and an original sound-track by Cave. Another example is *The Elements: A Visual Exploration*, which combines textual information from the sister hardback book with interactive 3D representations of each element, video clips of relevant chemistry experiments and live data from the WolframAlpha search engine (Jardin 2010).

Those same live data feeds exemplify Manovich's ideas of automa-tion, variability and transcoding (2001: 32–45). The provision of APIs (application programming interfaces) for common tools such as Google Maps, combined with the relative ease of programming and publishing websites, has resulted in multimedia forms which incorporate computer code as textual elements, the execution of that code resulting in new combinations of data and presentation to provide newly useful informa-tion. One of the earliest examples was a mash-up of Google Maps and Chicago crime statistics into the Chicago Crime Data Map, an example of a new textual form made by combining two or more separate com-puter data-sets in a graphical manner. A similar example from the UK is *The Guardian*'s Crime Map which allows users to graphically compare the incidence of crime in a number of British cities. Other examples include a Google Maps flight simulator; a NSFW Celebrity Sexy Video Finder; Battlecell, which turns maps of the world into a giant game of *Risk*; the Rap Map which connects sites from hip-hop history on a Google map; or Sad Statements, which pulls in unhappy-sounding tweets from Twitter feeds and illustrates them with morose photos. The 'History of Jazz' iPad app produced by 955 Dreams offers a graphical timeline drawing upon live links to Wikipedia articles, YouTube performance videos and iTunes Store purchasing options to repurpose those modular elements in a single space. Such experiments represent the type of new media attributes that Manovich identifies, without raising the political tensions and conflicts of control apparent in mash-ups.

Networked digital media allow the data involved to be drawn from multiple sources, generated by other users or crowd-sourced. Again, book publishing provides examples. Amazon's Kindle allows users to high-light sections of the book they're reading, something that many readers find extremely useful. More controversially, highlighted sections are sent back to Amazon and combined with information from other users to create a Popular Highlights feature for each Kindle book. So while reading Kindle titles, users can see sections of their books which have been highlighted by other readers. The feature has prompted questions over privacy and necessity but other publishers are exploring this model for different ends. For example, educational textbook publishers are exploring network potentials. As well as the combination of multimedia elements that sees a reinvention of late 1990s CD-ROMs, albeit with a more sophisticated presentation, publishers are investigating how the new technologies can create what some call 'learning networks'. The 'Inkling' iPad app, for example, allows users to post notes onto their texts – which then appear to other users as they are reading. These can take the form of notations, or even questions to which users can respond – combining the possibilities of social network media with the central text in question.

Such social media information adds a critical new dimension to the multimedia mix. For example, *Gourmet* magazine's *Gourmet Live* tries to combine social network media elements with traditional publishing content. In fact, this Condé Nast magazine is no longer available in print – its masthead is exclusively electronic, currently focused on an iPad app. *Gourmet Live* asks users to log in with their Twitter or Facebook account details and, as they read and respond to the magazine content, they simultaneously share their experiences with their friends or fol-lowers and are rewarded with extra content as they further engage. The example of *Gourmet Live* evokes Clay Shirky's suggestion that 'The web didn't introduce a new competitor into the old ecosystem, as *USA Today* had done. The web created a new ecosystem' (2008: 60). This media ecosystem now includes social media, which add a new curato-rial dimension to the multimedia mix by expanding the range of people who get to make those combinations. The editorial and gatekeeping processes (Shoemaker 1991) that have been the domain of publishers and broadcasters can now be distributed to draw upon the input of users – a redistribution of editorial judgment that can be seen both as a flattening of hierarchies (Shirky 2008) and as an exploitative encroach-ment of unpaid labour (Terranova 2004). We discuss such changing audience roles in more detail in Chapter 5.

Digg, for example, is a website that provides its users the opportu-nity to share, discuss and rank news stories of their choice. Digg users submit stories from around the web, which end up in the Digg queue. Registered members of the community (Digg reviewers) examine the queue's contents, and 'digg' content they like by clicking on the appropriate link. Once an article receives sufficient Diggs, it is 'promoted' onto the Digg homepage. The site's popularity is such that a place on the homepage will result in a large number of views for the original article. Digg is one of many services – others include Slashdot and Reddit – that exist as recommendation engines. While they each take different approaches, they all provide an alternative to the editorial priorities of traditional media institutions. Axel Bruns calls this approach 'gatewatching' and argues that 'despite the networked, open-access nature of hypertext on the World Wide Web, there still remains a need and a desire amongst its users to see news in context as they search for information'. For Bruns, gatewatchers provide a 'variety of pointers to a range of alternative ways of seeing and interpreting the news that are slated to different user needs' (2005: 19).

Facebook and Twitter also act as recommendation engines, the wisdom of like-minded crowds ensuring that their recommendations are more commonly 'liked'. An important distinction is that, unlike Digg recommendations, social network recommendations come from people that users have self-selected – the suggestions come from Friends, rather than strangers. For example, Facebook allows users to embed links within their pages, and clicking the 'like' button is a simple act of recommendation. The combination of those curatorial roles with the new multimedia possibilities is emerging as a new type of media form. *Gourmet Live* is one example of such innovation, driven by a traditional print publisher. Another is the 'Flipboard' iPad app which utilizes the user's social networks to curate media content into a 'personal social magazine'. Rather than relying on a web interface for Facebook and Twitter recommendations, Flipboard recompiles recommendations into a lush visual representation, presenting the content as a coherently designed magazine-style publication populated by material curated by the user's Friends.

Such textual convergence is predicated on the existence of a media platform which affords the presentation of different media types simultaneously. To date, that platform has been the Internet-connected multimedia personal computer – a platform which has the technical potential to deliver all media forms. More recently, increased processing power and portability have enabled that platform to become a mobile one, which allows location to be added to the multimedia mix. GPS (Global Positioning System) technologies built into mobile devices provide accurate latitudinal and longitudinal information that can be easily mapped against a variety of other data elements. At the most basic level, information sources can localize news, weather or traffic information. So, travel guides can display relevant site information, banks can display nearby branches and ATMs, and restaurant reviews can provide information to potential diners based on proximity.

More innovative applications are also emerging. Sydney's Taronga Park Zoo has released its 'Monkey Mayhem' iPhone application, which combines location-based activities with an interactive narrative and simple gameplay. Users are asked to use the iPhone's camera and GPS to navigate around the zoo, and to take photos of selected animals to unlock secret content, in order to replace missing pages in a fictional 'Zoo manual'. Moreover, location is used to connect people rather than to connect people to information. Location-based social media tool Foursquare is an example of an application that asks its users to 'check-in' wherever they are and to comment on businesses that they frequent, information which is shared with social network Friends. That information can be used to locate nearby Friends and issue invitations. As well as leveraging location technologies, it introduces gaming elements by rewarding users for particular activities and encouraging them to become 'mayor' of a particular restaurant or park. But the trade-off for this is allowing an increased degree of visibility, an issue which we discuss in more detail in Chapter 6.

There are obvious tensions in the developing multimedia mix. Our examples interrogate accepted ideas of what a particular media form is, what it could be or what it should be. For example, book culture, so strongly rooted in the idea of a printed object, is slowly shifting to the screen (Young 2007) and as it does, simple remediation (in the form of ebook representations of a printed book on a Kindle screen) becomes only one possibility; a networked multimedia future becomes a likely alternative, as the technologies of engagement become even more compelling. Books aren't the only print-based medium being reinvented. Other print publications such as newspapers and magazines have embraced the World Wide Web. But having struggled to make a profit in that space, publishers are exploring more self-contained possibilities – electronic magazines and newspapers that integrate multimedia elements in a manner that the web doesn't allow. *Wired* magazine introduced an iPad edition in the middle of 2010, combining audio, video, animation and interactivity as well as words and images in a self-contained package. It was quickly followed by a range of other titles from *Popular Mechanics* to *Esquire* magazine, each experimenting with new multimedia forms.

In each of these cases, print publishers are changing platforms, from paper to screen, and any such transition will be contested. Manovich points out that what he calls 'new media' involves a convergence of media and computing histories, which 'changes the identity of both media and the computer itself' (2001: 20). In the media realm, publishers and broadcasters struggle to reconcile their traditional roles with the new possibilities, while simultaneously grappling with the technological affordances which have damaged their previous business model of scarcity. In the computing domain, contests over platforms continue – the particular shape, the protocols and capabilities of specific media devices vary from manufacturer to manufacturer, and market dominance is a struggle through uncertainty with moments of relative stability. As the contests in each of those domains play out, new multimedia forms continue to develop.

Transmedia

In August 2009, Justin Halpern opened a Twitter account to record his father's pithy observations on life. Things like: 'Tennessee is nice. The first time I vomited was in Tennessee, I think' <http://twitter.com/shitmydadsays>. Shared initially with his friends, Halpern's Twitter feed quickly found its way onto Jon Stewart's *The Daily Show* and gathered over 1.7 million followers. Halpern then signed with HarperCollins publishers in October of that year, and the book *Sh*t My Dad Says* was released in May 2010, reaching *The New York Times* bestseller list. A spin-off television sit-com, *$#*! My Dad Says*, starring William Shatner as the dad, began broadcasting in September 2010 on the CBS network. *Sh*t My Dad Says*, in its various incarnations (so far) as Twitter feed, book and sitcom, is an example of the third type of textual convergence – the spread of a common piece of intellectual property or brand across a range of media; and it is also representative of the expansion of this type as convergent media forms – in this case Twitter – develop.

Twitter is not the only online source which has spawned spin-offs in other media. A more common example is that of the *blook*, a hybrid text that begins as a blog, before becoming a printed book. Salam Pax, the pseudonymous blogger from Baghdad whose daily musings on life in that city in the build-up to the 2003 Iraqi conflict became a book, was one of the first. The publication of his blog 'Where Is Raed?' in book form as *The Baghdad Blog* sparked the emergence of the blook. In recognition of this category, print-on-demand publishing website Lulu created the Blooker Prize, and its 2006 winner of the non-fiction prize was *Julie and Julia: 365 Days, 524 Recipes, 1 Tiny Kitchen Apartment*. That book started as a blog in 2002, created by Julia Powell to tell the story of her attempt to cook all of Julia Child's recipes. The blog developed a wide audience and was published as a book by Little Brown, selling more than 100,000 copies, before becoming a 2009 movie starring Meryl Streep. Other blook examples include *Things My Girlfriend and I Have Argued About* by Mil Millington and *The Intimate Adventures of a London Call Girl* by a research scientist writing as 'Belle de Jour', later made into a TV series starring Billie Piper.

These examples illustrate just one type of textual convergence – a fairly straightforward reconfiguration of a brand for different media forms, beginning from the web. And the convergence has also happened in the other direction. Harry Potter's origins in print eventually moved to film and new media properties such as videogames, as well as toys, clothing and coffee mugs. The multi-platform adventures of the BBC's 2005 reboot of *Doctor Who* are well-documented. The television show's expansion across a range of platforms – mobile phone mini-episodes, podcasts, video blogs, websites ostensibly run by characters – was hailed as a success by both audiences and the BBC, while also building upon decades of novelizations, radio dramas, films, records and comics about the Doctor's travels in space and time since the show's first appearance in 1963 (Perryman 2008; Evans 2011).

There is, of course, a prehistory to this – novelizations, for instance, have accompanied movies for decades (George Lucas himself wrote one of the early *Star Wars* spin-off novels); videogames have been spun off movies since *E.T.* (Wu 2010); and the music industry has long had parallel recorded versions and published sheet music, with separate rights. The expansion of a franchise to include everything from plastic dolls to comic books was a common phenomenon with television shows as far back as the 1960s. For example, the Adam West *Batman* TV series spun off a movie, a 45 rpm single, comic books, trading cards, action figures, toys, Viewmaster slides, puzzles and cut-out dolls and models (Cane 2010). In addition to the expected film, television, book and graphic novel releases, today's examples are more likely to include officially licensed videogames (across a range of console, handheld and computer platforms), clothing, theme park rides (or even complete theme parks), Lego, fast-food meals and crockery. And as Wu points out, with the exception of *Avatar*, the top ten most expensive movies of the first decade of the twenty-first century were all sequels or remakes built around established properties such as Spiderman or Harry Potter, with the actual films functioning as advertisements for the brand (2010: 228–9). In the same vein, we see the blurring of content types – what might once have been identifiably advertising is now part of a more complex media presence. For example, it's hard to tell whether Lauren Luke's successful YouTube make-up tutorials are marketing material for her line of beauty products, or the other way round.

As well as the clear economic imperative driving this activity, as media corporations seek to profit from a well-known character or brand, convergent media technologies have enabled a broader range of what are now termed transmedia possibilities. The conflation of production, consumption and an accessible means of distribution have added Web 2.0 properties to the media mix. As well as the official merchandise, we can now expect fan-driven websites, social networks and collaborative fiction. This textual convergence is now more elaborate, more widespread and more central to the business models for exploiting media content, as the digitization of content brings different platforms closer together and as the increased integration of media firms makes more kinds of synergy possible.

Despite an evolving technical convergence – as devices such as the iPad combine the affordances of radio, television, print publishing and the Internet – discrete media platforms remain the usual practice. As we explained in Chapter 1 Henry Jenkins rejects what he calls the 'black box fallacy' which proposes a world in which 'all media content is going to flow through a single black box into our living rooms (or, in the mobile scenario, through black boxes we carry around with us everywhere we go)' (2008: 14). Jenkins suggests that convergence is more likely to happen 'across devices'. So a user would begin by watching a television show, switch to their mobile phone to interact with the show's producers by SMS and then switch to their personal computer to discuss the results of that interaction on a website, where additional video material would also be available. There are many examples. NBC's *Heroes* series situated its actual TV content within a complex context of mobile phone alerts and puzzles, online graphic novels, and the options to receive emails or read blogs purporting to be written by the show's fictional characters. Twitter users who enjoy the show *Mad Men* can subscribe to updates from the daily lives of its fictional characters. The Showtime cable network promoted the fourth season of its serial killer drama *Dexter* by producing a videogame app for the iPhone and publicizing this through a YouTube video circulated on Facebook. *Battlestar Galactica's* show-runner Ronald D. Moore recorded commentary podcasts to accompany episodes of the show and distributed some mini-episodes through YouTube, extending the narrative between seasons (Leaver 2008; Kompare 2011). The BBC used online games to extend the narrative world of its TV spy drama *Spooks* (Evans 2011). And reality contests such as *Big Brother* or *American Idol* extend the audience's engagement across a range of media platforms beyond the TV broadcast (Turner and Tay 2009; Kavka 2011).

Such approaches go beyond the marketing opportunities afforded by simple adaptations across platforms. The BBC, for example, has experimented with incorporating such approaches into its specific public service mission (Bennett and Strange 2008). Geoff Long suggests that 'Retelling a story in a different media type is adaptation, while using multimedia media types to craft a single story is transmediation' (2007: 22). Jenkins dubs this more complex textual convergence 'transmedia storytelling':

> A transmedia story unfolds across multiple media platforms, with each new text making a distinctive and valuable contribution to the whole. In the ideal form of transmedia storytelling, each medium does what it does best – so that a story might be introduced in a film, expanded through television, novels, and comics; its world might be explored through game play or experienced as an amusement park attraction. Each franchise entry needs to be self-contained so you don't need to have seen the film to enjoy the game, and vice versa. Any given product is a point of entry into the franchise as a whole. (Jenkins 2008: 97–8)

Jenkins uses the example of *The Matrix* universe, which consists (in part) of three movies, a ninety-minute collection of animated shorts called *The Animatrix*, comics and videogames, all of which contain storyline elements necessary to an understanding of the whole. So the animated 'Final Flight of the Osiris' short features a protagonist, Jue, who sacrifices herself to send a message to the crew of the ship, the *Nebuchadnezzar*, an event referred to in the opening scenes of *The Matrix Reloaded* movie when the characters discuss the last transmissions of the *Osiris* (Jenkins 2008: 104). In that same film, Morpheus and Trinity are rescued by Niobe, who seems to appear from nowhere – but players of the console videogame would have encountered a mission designed to get Niobe to exactly that rendezvous point (Jenkins 2008: 105).

> The filmmakers plant clues that won't make sense until we play the computer game. They draw on the back story revealed through a series of animated shorts, which need to be downloaded off the Web

or watched off a separate DVD. Fans raced, dazed and confused, from the theaters to plug into Internet discussion lists, where every detail would be dissected and every possible interpretation debated. (Jenkins 2008: 96)

The Matrix was not simply an exercise in film-making, but one of world-building (Sconce 2004). Creative energy was spent in developing an *environment* within which narratives take place – an environment that can span a broad range of media forms and texts. This is less about marketing or promoting a central text, as Evans argues in her analysis of the transmedia adventures of *Doctor Who*, and more about 'creating a coherent, deliberately cross-platform narrative experience' (2011: 20). This kind of transmedia storytelling predates convergent media. Peter Greenaway had argued for such an approach in 1993 (Bordwell 2009) and before that David Lynch had created a fictional world for *Twin Peaks* in which various books provided the background of major characters and a travel guide to the fictional location of Twin Peaks. These filled in the narrative of the television series, which itself was complemented by a later feature film. The convergent media environment amplifies those transmedia possibilities, and provides the mechanisms for creators to expand their canvas across a range of media forms. The potentials for user engagement on the various platforms are different, and increasingly, transmedia approaches allow both users and creators to play in new spaces – the fictional world can now converge with the real world.

Such convergence between mediated and real-world experiences is illustrated by a form of transmedia storytelling known as alternate reality games (ARG). The earliest major example is *The Beast,* staged as a pre-release marketing campaign for the 2001 Spielberg movie *A.I.* (Örnebring 2007; Dena 2008; Jenkins 2008). In the game, cross-referenced clues were planted across a variety of media as hooks to propel fans to engage with a range of media. *The Beast*'s cue for action was a curious credit for a robot therapist planted in pre-release publicity posters for the movie. A Google search for this character's name led players to fictitious websites from the future – which in turn led to an intricate web of further baffling and suspicious artefacts related to a murder investigation. The maze of clues unearthed as the game progressed enabled fabricated histories and non-player characters to masquerade as real through fake email accounts, phone numbers, faxes, ads, videos and web sites. Because the game posed as real, there were no rules or instructions as such, just problems that challenged the audience to find solutions any way they could.

The ARG convergence approach provides opportunities in the broader social and political realm, as marketers, lobby groups and political actors use the range of media possibilities to tease out the various parts of their chosen narrative, drawing on the co-creative possibilities of creative audiences. For example, to promote their A3 model, Audi launched *The Art of the Heist*, a three-month-long advertising campaign across multiple platforms that included online elements, live participation at dealerships and auto shows and a complex narrative whose components included emails, voicemail recordings and videos. According to the advertising agency involved, half a million people participated in the campaign, which generated 10,000 leads and nearly 4000 test drives (Leavitt 2005).

But Jeff Gomez suggests that the power of transmedia has potential beyond the directly commercial – he argues that:

> Transmedia storytelling is quickly becoming the single most powerful way to convey messages and narrative to a mass audience. We're seeing this most prominently (if awkwardly) in the interaction between politics, media and the American people right now. It doesn't seem to matter how accurate the information is, so long as you are building a compelling narrative around it and taking advantage of television's omnipresence, the Web's interactivity, the soap box of radio, or the intimacy of town halls. While it's debatable how much of this is being done according to some master plan, you can't argue with its efficacy. (quoted in Dinehart 2009)

While examples of overt transmedia strategies are rare in the political domain, the approach has been used by non-government organizations. The *Conspiracy for Good* project incorporated the use of convergent media technologies and mixed/augmented reality approaches in an innovative combination of fact, fiction and social activism <http://www.conspiracyforgood.com>. It was the brainchild of Tim Kring, creator of the NBC television series *Heroes*, who described it as 'the pilot project for a first-of-its-kind, interactive story, that empowers its audience to take real-life action and create positive change in the world. Call it Social Benefit Storytelling'.

According to its website, *Conspiracy for Good* is 'an inaugural movement that blends online and real-world tasks to effect social change through audience participation'. The project's concept is of a secret global, historical 'conspiracy for good' whose members have decided to go public in order to address the very real and dire circumstances facing the planet. London in the summer of 2010 was the chosen venue for action – and the project asked users to join well-known artists and musicians in participating in an evolving storyline leading up to the summer climax. Kring partnered with Finnish mobile phone company Nokia, which provided the connective technologies for the project through a series of phone apps, games, songs and physical events designed to 'blur the links between the digital and real world'. The project revolved around a four-part interactive online TV series, designed to engage users in fund-raising activities for specific charities. Musicians contributed their music and played roles in the fiction – Jamaican singer Nadirah X was a key character in the series, which outlined an intricate fictional backstory involving resisting the intentions of an evil corporation. Participants were then invited to take part in a series of activities, consisting of a number of Internet-coordinated events – or missions – linked by the common theme and documented across the web.

Both *The Art of the Heist* and *Conspiracy for Good* combined traditional media elements with real-world experiences in the form of an ARG – contemporary incarnations of older explorations. Japanese media cultures, for example, have a rich tradition of combining media objects with real-world engagements. Mimi Ito describes the Japanese manga and TV series *Yugioh*, which created such an effect using trading cards as a web of narrative mirrors to effectively cross-reference fantasy narrative with real-world enactment:

> *Yugioh* is similar to the media mixes of Pokemon and Digimon in that they involve human players that mobilize otherworldly monsters in battle [...] the monsters in *Yugioh* inhabit the everyday world of Yugi and his peers in the form of trading cards, which the players carry with them in their ongoing adventures. The "other world" of the monsters is in intimate relationship with the everyday; the human players in the manga mobilize monsters in their everyday world, and kids in "real life" mobilize these same monsters in their play with trading cards and game boys [...] Scenes in the anime depict Yugi frequenting card shops and buying card packs, enjoying the thrill of getting a rare card, dramatizing everyday moments of media consumption in addition to the highly stylized and fantastic dramas of the duels themselves. (Ito 2005: 186–7)

Beyond these engagements, a more recent phenomenon has seen the use of convergent technologies to augment reality. For example, trading cards become augmented reality artefacts – when viewed through digital

cameras they appear to be inhabited by interactive, animated characters. Early, if relatively crude, versions of the ability to transplant fantasy
images upon real-world objects appeared in mobile phone scavenger
hunt games like *Mogi*, in which players using the World Wide Web command mobile players working in a team effort to collect virtual creatures
and hidden objects that appear at different times of day. Nearby users
also exchange virtual creatures in order to complete their collections.

British art group Blast Theory was another early creator of ARG
experiences. Their 2001 production *Can You See Me Now* was a chase
game, played online and in the streets of a real city simultaneously.
Online players pursued actual runners, equipped with hand-held
devices, who had to deal with the challenges of pursuit in both real
and virtual spaces. Mobile devices expand the depth and breadth of
such experiences, and entrench location as a dimension in the transmedia activity of mobile gaming (Goggin 2011: 99–115). The 2004
game *Pac-Manhattan* reimagined the streets of New York as a game
of *Pac-Man*, combining players interacting on the street with others
coordinating the game through GPS and mobile devices (Hjorth 2011:
85–101). More recent ARG explorations such as Jeff Watson's 2010
Games of Nonchalance incorporate more sophisticated storylines. Designed
as a transmedia experience 'woven into the fabric of San Francisco', the
game hooks players through online rabbit holes (mysterious websites)
or physically embedded clues (such as posters on telephone poles or
actual live events). Once hooked, the game unfolds as a story world
that reveals the city in a new light. Jane McGonigal's 2011 game *Find
the Future* recruited hundreds of participants through Twitter, the web
and YouTube, to spend the night inside the New York Public Library,
exploring the collection to solve puzzles and collaborating on writing
a book to be added to the library's collection.

Of course, transmedia approaches have their critics, particularly among
those schooled in the formal differences between media types. David
Bordwell (2009) has pointed to a number of objections to the idea of
expanding the world of a film:

> Most Hollywood and indie films aren't particularly good. Perhaps it's
> best to let most storyworlds molder away. Does every horror movie
> need a zigzag trail of web pages? Do you want a diary of Daredevil's
> down time? Do you want to look at the Flickr page of the family
> in *Little Miss Sunshine*? Do you want to receive Tweets from Juno?
> Pursued to the max, transmedia storytelling could be as alternately
> dull and maddening as your own life.

Bordwell goes on to argue that viewing a film is *already* an active participatory process in the co-creation of meaning and that some limits are a
desirable part of this process, as clear boundaries contribute to a story's
power. In his words, 'There's a reason that pictures have frames.'

Such objections exemplify the challenges raised by transmedia
approaches; in such projects, previously discrete media industries must
come together to create fictional worlds across their various platforms –
often requiring different skills and practices. Questions arise over the
privileging of a particular media form, and conflicts might emerge over
the tensions between, for example, narrative and gameplay elements.
Convergent media affordances draw those contests into stark relief as
producers, critics and audiences alike are confronted by possibilities
they may not wish to embrace.

Conclusion

We argue in this chapter that textual convergence is not a new practice –
artists have long combined otherwise distinctive media elements, and new
media industries are often forged from previously discrete forms (think
music videos). But convergent media technologies change the scale and
scope of such activity; the digitization of media objects and the ease with
which they can be cut up and recombined has the potential to reconfigure
our media cultures and industries. In each of the cases above, the textual
convergence highlights the contested nature of new media formations.
Mash-ups suggest that media texts can no longer be considered fixed
artefacts, but need to be thought of as elements in a continuing, dynamic
process of invention and reinvention; they also demand a new emphasis
on the user as the creator of not only their own media meanings but also
their own media texts, however small-scale or rudimentary. Multimedia
modes require producers and consumers to understand the affordances
of all textual forms, and challenge them to create media which transcend
traditional specificities. And cross-platform or transmedia convergence
expands the canvas across which creative production can occur. No longer
are media confined to the pages of print, or the constraints of the screen –
transmedia opportunities allow expression across a canvas that includes
a variety of traditional media platforms, and the reality of location. Each
of these aspects of convergent media texts points to new kinds of literacy,
and to altered relationships between our understandings of 'producers'
and 'audiences'. It is to these that we now turn in the next chapter.

Creative Audiences

5

Fire up Google Earth and click on its Sightseeing Tour. The camera descends from space to the Eiffel Tower in Paris, before pulling back and travelling down over North Africa, then across the Atlantic to the statue of Christ in Rio. It heads north to the Grand Canyon, across the Pacific to the Sydney Opera House, west to St Peter's in Rome, to the London Eye, before plunging deep into the North Atlantic to the under-sea remains of the *Titanic*, and then east to the Forbidden City in Beijing and Mount Fuji in Japan before ending, with a certain remorseless logic, at Google's own headquarters in Mountain View, California. At each of these destinations – with the *Titanic* excepted for now – the scene is dotted with tiny icons, each linking to a photo, a YouTube video, a 360° panoramic image, or some other piece of content created and tagged by other users of Google Earth. The aerial view of Paris, for instance, is dusted with a layer of icons to YouTube videos – tourist clips of the city illuminated on Bastille Day, someone's friend jumping with excitement at the sight of the Tower, a bus being pulled from the Seine, shots of Paris taken by a camera attached to a bunch of released balloons.

This Google Earth tour is a complex example of convergent media. From one perspective, viewing the tour fits with our experiences of the broadcast model – it's possible to just click the 'play' button, sit back and watch, as the application flies you from one side of the globe to another. But from another perspective it illustrates how it is also possible to interact with convergent media in far more complex ways, as the many icons linking to UGC items show – tagging landmarks, adding layers of content from your own photo collections, linking to videos; and once the tour is over, you can use Google Earth to record your own tour of places that are most meaningful to you and to share them with your friends. The Google Earth tour illustrates one of the most important phenomena we can observe in the convergent media environment – the blurring of distinctions between producers and audiences. In the broadcast media paradigm, there is a clear distinction between producer and audience. Certain people are doing the producing but other people are doing the receiving. Production and reception happen in different places and at different times. But more and more we see new possibilities for production and also for reception, which make possible new kinds of collaboration and exchange, new kinds of engagement and creativity. We now have to recognize audiences as *creative*, rather than imagining them as faceless blobs, sprawled on the couch.

This is in part the result of the widespread availability of simple tools for the creation of all kinds of texts and images – the Web 2.0 trend, as discussed in Chapter 3. Lawrence Lessig has argued that the convergent era can be different from the 'read-only' media world of the broadcast model – 'It could be both read and write' (2004: 37). But while the 'write' component of a 'read-and-write' culture connotes certain kinds of new media forms, such as blogs (Rettberg 2008) or digital storytelling (Meadows 2003; Lundby 2008; Hartley and McWilliam 2009), convergent media make possible other shifts in behaviour as well as what we may think of as writing. We can now also *access* more kinds of material (a 'read-more' culture), we can *organize* media content in new ways for ourselves and others (a 'read-tag' culture), we can *remix*, remake and reimagine digital media texts (a 'read-remix' culture), we can *collaborate* on all of the above (a 'read-and-write-together' culture) and we can *distribute* or *share* what we've found or made (a 'read-share' culture). This chapter discusses each of these kinds of behaviour in turn, after first situating them in the larger context of concepts of media audiences and examining how these should be reframed from 'understood as consumption' to 'understood as creativity'.

Who are you calling an audience?

Audiences have been, and continue to be, thought of in many different ways and from many different research traditions. One reason why there are so many ways to understand – and misunderstand – audiences, is that both media industries and media scholars have to create them before they can study them. To do so, we might choose to emphasize geography (metropolitan newspaper readers, local-radio listeners, global box-office), or medium (smartphone users, CD buyers, TV news viewers), or content (consumers of horror films, financial news or online amateur porn), or time (the prime-time TV audience, breakfast show radio listeners) or demographic factors such as gender, income, ethnicity, sexuality or age (pre-teen videogamers, Chinese news viewers, LGBT moviegoers) and so on (McQuail 1997). In each case, we are focusing not only on a different kind of group but on a particular relationship of power, in which meanings are being negotiated on different terms (Ross and Nightingale 2003).

A further reason for the difficulty of understanding audiences is what Thompson calls the 'structured break' (1995: 29) that separates the industrialized production of media content from its localized, dispersed reception. The ways in which audiences respond to media content, and the meanings that they make from it, have been largely invisible to the producers of that content, who have turned instead to finding new ways to emphasize the claimed aggregate size of a given audience as an index of popularity and as a simulated currency to be traded in the advertising marketplace (Ang 1991). But as Gitlin (1983) points out, such claims can only really be about the number of TV sets, for example, that are believed to be turned on, rather than about any actual responses or meanings produced by any actual viewers.

But perhaps the key reason why audience research is one of the most contested areas of media analysis is that how audiences are imagined and understood is a question of power. To think only of communicative effects, as Terranova observes, is to elide 'the struggle over meanings' (2004: 10). As Raymond Williams once pointed out, while we speak of 'mass media' and 'mass communication', there are in reality no masses – 'there are only ways of seeing people as masses' (1961: 300; see also Hartley 2003: 34–7, and the published dialogue between McKenzie Wark and Geert Lovink in Lovink 2002: 314–25). So how we imagine users of media is not only of absolute importance in understanding communication, but also has a political dimension.

This political dimension is clearest in research into the 'effects' of the media on their audiences. Much of this research starts from an explicit or implicit assumption that certain kinds of media constitute 'dangerous reading' or 'dangerous writing'. There is a long history to this, stretching back past the web and videogames, past broadcasting and cinema, past magazines and comics – one media history points to sixteenth-century controversies over the risks of teaching women to read because, if they could read, they might be sent love letters (Briggs and Burke 2005: 51). And as Camille Paglia and Neil Postman once observed in a published discussion, even the Ten Commandments can be seen as an early response to perceived media effects, with their injunctions against using certain kinds of words and making certain kinds of images (Postman and Paglia 2007). Dangerous reading, dangerous writing.

In the twentieth century, with the rise of broadcast communication media, such controversies took on new force. The broadcast model of media which underpinned both media regulation and media analysis assumed a one-way delivery of meaning – 'who says what in which channel to whom with what effect?' in Harold Lasswell's famous formulation of communication (1995 [1948]: 93). This was the media environment described by James Carey in which 'Some get to speak and some to listen, some to write and some to read, some to film and some to view' (1989: 87). This one-way conception of media communication continues as the starting assumption of much research to this day, imagining audiences only as recipients and not as producers of meanings. Its influence is clear in controversies about media effects and dangerous viewing, about censorship and standards – controversies which see the media as the source of obvious and predetermined meanings from which their users have to be protected. And yet, as Castells notes, 'Communication is the sharing of meaning through the exchange of information' (2009: 54). *Sharing, meaning, exchange* – these are key words, which highlight how users of media bring their own contributions to the creation of meanings from stories, whether presented as true or as fiction.

When analysts write about media effects, they do not generally mean everyday and uncontentious media influences such as taking an umbrella if the weather forecast predicts rain or staying up too late playing Xbox Live games (Barker 2001: 37, McQuail 2010: 454). Rather, they mean research that tries to establish direct negative effects of certain kinds of media content which the researcher sees as likely to be harmful – *Batman* not Bergman, Public Enemy not Puccini, and Tarantino not Shakespeare, even though more characters meet spectacular violent ends within the plot of *Hamlet* than do in *Pulp Fiction*, including being stabbed with a poisoned sword. Research into such media effects has incorporated a range of approaches and methods (Ruddock 2001), but these share certain assumptions about the causal role of media in our behaviour. They also share a history of poor results: 'The history of audience research is littered with the corpses of studies that have tried and failed to demonstrate, once and for all, a cause and effect relationship between media message and receiver behaviour' (Ross and Nightingale 2003: 9; see also Carey 1989: 91–2). Many scholars of media and culture are scathing about effects research: 'an entire research tradition is based on thin air' (Barker 2001: 43; see also Gauntlett 1998), and have long since moved 'from the analysis of what texts *do* to the audience to what texts *mean* to them' (Ruddock 2001: 116, original emphasis).

A key moment in taking seriously the role of audiences in the creation of meaning was Stuart Hall's 'encoding/decoding' model (2006). Hall's analysis, first circulated in 1973, argued that while media producers will have a particular point-of-view they wish to get across in a story – 'encoding' this in their construction and presentation – individual audience members may make something quite different in 'decoding' the story. Hall suggested that users of media might produce three broad kinds of possible meaning: a *dominant* one, in which the position most clearly foregrounded in the story is broadly accepted; a *negotiated* one, in which the individual's situation, interests and background are brought to bear on the story, producing a meaning which is in some way qualified; and an *oppositional* meaning, in which the individual rejects the premises and assumptions of the dominant perspective encoded in the story.

Hall's model was enormously influential, paving the way for landmark studies such as David Morley's focus-group study of how viewers from different social backgrounds interpreted TV current affairs items (1980), and opening the door for many subsequent studies within what is now thought of as the 'active audience' tradition (Fiske 1989; Morley 1992; Ang 1996). With the rise of identity politics from the 1970s on (Castells 2004), and increased attention within media and cultural studies to questions of gender and sexuality, ethnicity and the body, much of this diverse work has explored how media are used and interpreted within particular cultural groups. Landmark examples include the study of cross-cultural readings of US television (Liebes and Katz 1990), and Marie Gillespie's (1995) ethnographic observations of media use in diasporic communities.

One important approach here has been the study of groups of fans (Hills 2002; Ross 2008). Fan studies have made visible the ways in which some media users make meanings from content that they are deeply attached to (Ang 1985), and can in some cases become immersed in communities of interest around their chosen texts (Radway 1984; Baym 2000), and in creating and circulating their own media content (Penley 1991; Bacon-Smith 1992; Jenkins 2006b). Henry Jenkins describes self-organizing communities of fans who variously share songs they have written about *Star Trek* characters (1992) or short films they have made to add to the *Star Wars* canon (2006a). In one impressive case study, he writes about *The Daily Prophet,* an online newspaper for the fictional Hogwarts school from the Harry Potter novels, created and overseen by a home-schooled teenage girl managing submissions by scores of kids from around the world, some of whom developed specialisms in particular aspects of J. K. Rowling's imagined world. In Jenkins's description: 'A girl who hadn't been in school since first grade was leading a worldwide staff of student writers with no adult supervision to publish a school newspaper for a school that existed only in their imaginations' (2008: 179).

Jenkins is right to argue that these young people were developing the skills needed to live in what he stresses is a participatory media environment – sharing and collaborating, making connections, expressing interpretations and emotions, and circulating DIY media creations (2008: 185). But it is worth noting that Jenkins's case studies of fan cultures focus on groups with unusual degrees of interest in, and attachment to, their chosen favourites, and so their behaviour is not necessarily analogous to more everyday media use (Ruddock 2001: 153–6). For example, Jenkins devotes considerable attention to an online community of hardcore fans of the reality TV show *Survivor*. How hardcore are they? They have hacked into CBS computers to look for clues about a series winner, studied satellite photos cross-matched against demographic maps of Africa to try to identify the precise location of a then-forthcoming season, and tried to predict winners by stalking contestants to take pictures that can be compared against publicity photos – the more weight lost, the longer the contestant may have stayed in the game (Jenkins 2008: 25–58). It is safe to say that such fan activity is in no way typical of everyday media use in most other groups that we could isolate for discussion, and so we should be careful not to generalize too much from such work.

Other work on fan cultures deals with more everyday forms of engagement with media texts (see the essays collected in Gray, Sandvoss and Harrington 2007, for example). As those authors argue, fan activity has become more mainstream and accepted — even taken for granted — as audiences have become both more fragmented and more focused, and as much media industry strategy has become centred around cultivating attachment and engagement from audiences. Convergent media have also multiplied the means by which all of us can communicate about our favourite media texts, and the concept of the fan has become less exceptional as a result — clicking the 'like' button on the Facebook page of a favourite TV series requires less investment and perhaps less involvement than the kinds of fan activity discussed in Jenkins's *Convergence Culture*. But this does not mean it is less important.

In the following sections, some of the examples of convergent media audience activities fit with the more hardcore end of the fan activity spectrum (such as the *Star Wars Uncut* project discussed below), while others are examples that would not usually be considered as aspects of fan behaviour (such as commenting on news items). What these examples share, and where they intersect with some of the literature on fans and fandom, is their concern with the media as something that people *do*.

One thing that everyone does with media is to make meanings. The creation of meaning can be thought of as the exercise of *symbolic* power (Thompson 1995). This, for Pierre Bourdieu, is 'a power of constructing reality' (1991: 166). It is the capacity to influence others by the creation of meaning, by the defining of reality, by the naming and endorsement of what counts as true, real and important. Symbolic power is exercised in the creation and circulation of stories and images, of entertainment and information, and in the selection and description of the issues of the day. For many, audiences continue to be thought of as the more or less helpless victims of the exercise of symbolic power – we read and believe, we hear and absorb, we see and are swayed. But the history of media audience research (Ruddock 2001; Brooker and Jermyn 2003), dating back to the middle of the twentieth century, can also be seen as a long, gradual recognition that audiences are participants in the creation of meanings – that while our resources of symbolic power are not equal to those of an enormous global communication firm such as News Corporation, we nevertheless make meanings as well as take them. Symbolic power is not only exercised in the creation and circulation of stories, but in their reception and interpretation as well. To understand media in the convergent era, we have to think of their users as dynamic and active, even if operating within constraints imposed by other actors. And, as this chapter explores, we now not only make meanings for ourselves, but we also make and remake media.

Questions of media industry and production, and questions of media audiences and consumption, can now be brought together (Hartley 2009c). Indeed, there is an opportunity to move beyond metaphors of consumption and to rethink our behaviour in relation to media texts in terms of *creativity*. Consumption is an inadequate metaphor for what we do with media texts, which 'remain alive for indefinite reconsumption' (Hartley 2009c: 233), unlike, say, a consumed chicken. The broadcast media paradigm is built around such agricultural metaphors, which are no longer fit for purpose in the twenty-first century convergent communications environment (Deuze 2007b: 258–9). The word 'broadcasting' itself originally described a method of sowing seeds by hand in wide arcs:

> The metaphor, in other words, relies on the existence of a bucket of seeds – that is, centralized resources of information, knowledge, creative and technical competence, and the like – that is to be distributed as

widely as possible in a certain "field" or territory. "Broadcasting" is thus an optimistic, modernist metaphor: successful sowing will, given the right conditions of growth, yield a rich harvest some time in the future when universally distributed information, education, and entertainment (the classic formula for John Reith's public service broadcasting at the BBC) results in an enlightened, socially and culturally empowered, and presumably quite happy, population. (Gripsrud 2004: 211)

Much of our activity in the convergent media environment seems a long way from the conception of the audience as spectator or listener. For Jay Rosen, we are now 'the people formerly known as the audience' (2006). When you chat on MSN, tag a photo on Facebook, or find that last hidden package in *Grand Theft Auto*, are you part of an *audience* as such? Is 'audience' then the wrong word for our contemporary media environment? There are other contending terms – citizens, publics, readers, consumers, users, 'produsers' – but none captures a fuller sense of media use or connects so clearly with existing traditions of media research. 'Citizens' (Carey 1989: 4; Rodriguez 2001) or 'publics' (Higgins 2008) might seem attractive alternatives, but each connotes only certain more public-sphere-oriented media activities – the news rather than porn, for instance, while that latter example reminds us that, as McQuail notes, not all media use should be thought of as public at all (2010: 400). 'Readers' can be used in a broad sense to include viewing of images, films or websites, but obviously underemphasizes writing – which can similarly be used in a parallel broad sense. 'Consumers' locates audience behaviour only within a particular sphere of one-way media use while, as with 'users', it also suggests interaction with an already-finished product of some kind, which omits the possibilities of co-creation. And as Livingstone notes (2003: 45), the term 'user' is not specific to communication either, as one can just as easily be a user of a microwave oven. Bruns (2008a) offers 'produser' to describe collaborative processes of content creation and development, but this useful term is not portable into other dimensions of our media lives. So 'the people formerly known as the audience' (Rosen 2006) will probably continue to attract that label, as the best available term. The necessary move is to see them not as consuming audiences but as creative audiences.

Access

When the authors were undergraduates in the 1980s, music could be hard to find. Record-shop shelf-space was limited, and labels would delete music from their catalogues if it didn't sell well. In 1984, UK independent label 4AD released *It'll End In Tears,* an album recorded under the umbrella name This Mortal Coil by a collection of their artists. It included several cover versions of songs by then-obscure cult figures Tim Buckley and Big Star, and sparked interest in both, with the version of Buckley's 'Song to the Siren' sung by Liz Fraser going on to become something of an indie standard. But key albums by both Buckley and Big Star were unavailable in those days – if you wanted to hear the originals, you had to hunt around second-hand shops or record fairs, or find someone who could make you a copy using the cutting-edge file-sharing technology of the cassette tape. As is customary, the recording industry of the day was loudly concerned with piracy – 'Home Taping is Killing Music' was its slogan of the time. But if anyone was killing music, it was the recording companies themselves, by deleting albums that sold in only modest numbers, such as those by Tim Buckley or Big Star.

By contrast, in 2011, extensive selections by both those artists are available from the iTunes Store, along with 12 million other tracks. Their key albums can be streamed for free from the 10 million-song library of Spotify. Scores of music blogs offer illicit downloads of the complete catalogues of both acts, including rarities unavailable elsewhere. YouTube offers clips of both, which would have been impossible for most fans to see only a few years earlier, including the unlikely spectacle of Buckley performing the delicate 'Song to the Siren' on an episode of *The Monkees* TV show. Mobile phone app Shazam can identify tunes from even these artists' more minor albums, and offer the user links to discographies, biographies, online videos and Facebook fan pages.

The online availability of Tim Buckley and Big Star illustrates what Chris Anderson calls 'the Long Tail' (2004, 2007). In the broadcast media paradigm, content industries were built around hits, with a widely held rule-of-thumb suggesting that 20 per cent of media content would be responsible for 80 per cent of sales. Niche content would be dropped when it failed to become a hit. The broadcast model, Anderson points out, was good at delivering a single item to a million people, but not good at delivering a million different items to one person each (2007: 5). The economics of scarcity in production, distribution and consumption helped fuel a culture built around blockbusters and top-ten lists. But in the convergent media environment, it becomes possible to cater for limitless niches. And all those niches can add up to a market whose size rivals that of the blockbuster content. Firms such as Amazon, YouTube, eBay or iTunes, unconstrained by shelf-space, can afford to supply the most arcane content to audiences in the low single-figures. It all adds up.

The Long Tail idea reminds us that size doesn't always matter. It's a mistake, for example, to dismiss a blog with a small niche readership as unimportant, as Hindman does (2009). In his analysis, the only blogs that matter are those which can compete for readership size with the established media. The broadcast media paradigm trained us to think that only large audiences count, but a blog can be worthwhile, meaningful and important to a readership of only half a dozen people. The Long Tail concept also highlights the need for new kinds of media literacy. In an information environment characterized by abundance and potential overload, rather than by scarcity, there's a corresponding need to develop new skills in filtering our media intake. Audiences need to find ways to hierarchize, categorize and filter infinite choice into accessible and desirable media flows. In short, we need tools and skills to help us *organize* media content, as discussed in the next section.

Organize

As well as accessing more material than ever, audiences in the convergent media environment have new opportunities – and new imperatives – to organize the material we find. We can, for example, organize material for ourselves, through time-shifting technologies such as digital video recorders or podcasts or online services like the BBC iPlayer or the US Hulu, and so customize our media schedules away from the industrial timetable of the broadcast model (see Chapter 7 for more on this). We can also organize our personal intake of material through filtering tools such as RSS feeds (Rich Site Summary or Really Simple Syndication, depending who you ask), which automatically filter and forward stories from certain websites or blogs, or through aggregators such as Google News.

We can also organize media material *for others* through tools such as playlists on YouTube or Spotify (Rizzo 2007; Burgess and Green 2009), social bookmarking and recommendation sites such as Delicious or Digg, and *tagging*. To tag a photo, or any other item of media content, is to add a small piece of metadata – a label – to that content. We can tag text, audio, images, video or entire websites that we've either found or made for ourselves. If the link is the defining characteristic of the web, the tag is a key characteristic of Web 2.0, enabling users to categorize, organize and publicize media content, and in so doing to create social connections and potential relationships and communities.

As of September 2011, the photo-sharing website Flickr offers more than 35,700 images tagged 'Narnia' – a place, it's worth recalling, that doesn't actually exist. There are pictures of lions that remind someone of the character Aslan, screenshots of the various films and TV versions of the Narnia books, snapshots of kids reading them, red-carpet photos of lead actors, landscape shots of locations that remind someone of a place in the stories or that were used in a Narnia movie, fan-art, cosplay and private jokes. This is a remarkable feat of collaborative organization by fans of C. S. Lewis's imaginary world – a rich example of how audiences can both adopt and adapt media material into their own imaginations, remaking and recirculating it as they go. It's also an illustration of collaborative organization of the media landscape made possible by tagging. When you tag your lion picture 'Narnia', it becomes automatically linked to other pictures with the same label. And you can add the tag to relevant pictures uploaded by others as well. Other Narnia fans on Flickr in turn can find and tag your pictures, opening up these photos to search-driven audiences. Moreover, as Shirky points out, there is an inherently social dimension to this kind of bottom-up collaborative organization, as tagging pictures creates a connection between the users, as well as between the photos (2008: 33).

Tags are particularly powerful on Twitter, where users can add a hashtag to their tweet (such as #iPad) and so become part of the stream of Twitter monologues and dialogues open to anyone interested in iPads that day. Hashtags can add a layer of extra information or perspective to a tweet. They can identify a topic to which the tweet is related or can offer ironic counterpoint on it. They are fundamental to the difference between what David Silver has termed 'thin' and 'thick' tweets (2009). In this distinction, 'thin' tweets offer a single piece or layer of information. These may be trivial – on the authors' Twitter feeds today, people we follow have variously posted 'bacon', 'karaoke it is' and 'I'm on the wrong bus'. But they may not always be trivial, as in the tweet by bystander Janis Krums which became the first news that US Airways Flight 1549 had landed in New York's Hudson River: 'There's a plane in the Hudson. I'm on the ferry going to pick up the people. Crazy.' (Crawford 2010: 117). 'Thick' tweets, in contrast, offer several layers of information in 140 characters or fewer, by for example including a link, a comment on that link, and a hashtag that complements both, while also helping to situate the tweet within a larger conversation. So again, the tag helps to connect not just the content but the users.

Remix

In *Downfall*, the 2004 film about the final days of the Third Reich, Bruno Ganz gives a towering performance as Adolf Hitler. No one who has seen the film will forget the pivotal scene in the Berlin bunker when Hitler is briefed on the latest developments by his generals and key aides and builds into a vast rage, unable to absorb the news that Oasis have broken up before he has the chance to see their Berlin concert. Or the news that he has been kicked off Xbox Live. Or that Lady Gaga has been screening his calls, that Michael Jackson has died, that Pokemon characters aren't real. Scores of parodies of the original *Downfall* scene are posted on YouTube, using the original film video and German-language audio, but changing the subtitles. There is even, inevitably, one in which Hitler's outburst is provoked by hearing about the *Downfall* parodies.

Changing subtitles, adding captions – in the previous chapter we discussed such practices as part of the mash-up model of convergent texts. In this section, we shift our focus to the various audience activities involved in remixing texts such as *Downfall*. As Manovich (2006) argues, the remix aesthetic has become a fundamental logic of cultural production. Lessig (2004) describes it as 'Walt Disney creativity', in a provocative observation that much of Disney's fiercely copyrighted output has involved recombining and remaking stories and elements from the wider culture – Cinderella, Snow White, Beauty and the Beast – and in so doing re-inscribing these public domain stories within regimes of intellectual property (see Chapter 8). John Hartley, also, has argued that editing and manipulating existing media material is the key practice in the contemporary media environment:

> Is it possible to tell a society by how it edits? Is redaction a symptom of the social? [...] Are we in a period where it is not information, knowledge or culture as such that determine the age but how they are handled? (Hartley 2000: 44)

To sample and remix, to annotate and combine – each of these is to actively intervene in the symbolic environment that we inhabit, even if in a tiny way:

> Sampling allows people to replay their own memories of the sounds and situations of their lives. Who controls the environment you grew up in? Who controls the situation with which you engage? At the end of the day, it's all about reprocessing the world around you, and this will happen no matter how hard entertainment conglomerates and an older generation of artists tries [*sic*] to control these processes. (Miller 2004: 28–9)

Creative audiences can manipulate media texts in the convergent environment in a range of ways. They can *juxtapose* texts, as in the Keyboard Cat meme, in which videos of mishaps, accidents or epic fails are spliced with the same clip of a cat playing the organ. They can *combine* multiple texts into a new hybrid object, as in the remarkable 'The Mother of All Funk Chords' video by Kutiman, which edits together multiple YouTube clips of individuals playing musical instruments by themselves into a single tune. They can *revise* existing texts, as in Wikipedia entries (the 'Toast' page, for instance, to which someone has added a helpful before-and-after image of a slice of singed bread). They can *adapt* texts from one form to another, as in the 2011 online version of *The Great Gatsby* reimagined as a 1980s Nintendo game or the re-telling of Homer's *Odyssey* as a Twitter feed ('Wrecked the boat. Totaled. Everyone dead. FAIL'). And they can *remake* texts – a phenomenon popularized to some extent by Michel Gondry's film *Be Kind, Rewind,* and visible in many YouTube videos, such as one in which both parts of Tarantino's *Kill Bill* movie are re-enacted in one minute. And, at the simplest possible level, they can add a deliberately misspelled caption to a picture of a cat and share in the global lolcat joke.

Lolcats (from Laughing Out Loud) began at 4chan.org, but developed into a popular culture phenomenon through the popular blog 'I Can Has Cheezburger?', started in early 2007. Named after an image of a grey cat asking this pivotal question, Cheezburger has spawned an empire of related blogs built around single concepts (the many flavours of FAIL, for instance), and dozens of memes and riffs – invisible bicycle, cheez: ur doin it rong, the spiritual struggle between Ceiling Cat and Basement Cat, and so on and on. The process of making a lolcat is automated on the site, requiring minimal technical skills. And the site's founders are having the last laugh – in January 2011, the Cheezburger network announced it had attracted investment funds of US$30 million (*The Guardian,* 21 January). 'Web 1.0 was invented to allow physicists to share research papers. Web 2.0 was created to allow people to share pictures of cute cats' suggests Harvard Internet researcher Ethan Zuckerman (2008). For our purposes in this chapter, though, the significance of lolcats is that they are something which creative audiences don't simply look at, but make and share for themselves:

> Let's nominate the process of making a lolcat as the stupidest possible creative act [...] Yet anyone seeing a lolcat gets a second, related message: *You can play this game too.* [...] On the spectrum of creative work, the difference between the mediocre and the good is vast.

Mediocrity is, however, still on the spectrum; you can move from mediocre to good in increments. The real gap is between doing nothing and doing something, and someone making lolcats has bridged that gap. (Shirky 2010: 18–19, original emphasis).

To make a lolcat is indeed to make *something*, however trivial and arcane. Note how Shirky's perspective emphasizes the value of creating a text, even a crude one, for the creator. It emphasizes creative audience behaviour as a learning experience. This is something that critics of remix creativity often miss. Jaron Lanier, for example, dismisses mashups with this distinction between what he calls first-order expression (high-level creative art works) and second-order expression:

First-order expression is when someone presents a whole, a work that integrates its own worldview and aesthetic. It is something genuinely new in the world. Second-order expression is made of fragmentary reactions to first-order expression. A movie like *Blade Runner* is first-order expression, as was the novel that inspired it, but a mashup in which a scene from the movie is accompanied by the masher's favorite song is not in the same league. (Lanier 2010: 122)

But to compare a professional text like *Blade Runner* (1982) with a non-professional mash-up video is not to compare like with like. *Blade Runner* is a major Hollywood feature production, whose director Ridley Scott had already established himself with the critical and commercial hit *Alien*. It is based on the 1968 book *Do Androids Dream of Electric Sheep?* by Philip K. Dick, who had already published more than 30 other novels before this one. These, then, were established professionals, not beginners learning to express themselves. And they were also both working in mature media forms – by the time of *Blade Runner*, there had been films for eight decades, and by the time of Dick's book, there had been novels in a recognizable modern form for more than 250 years. In contrast, the creator of a home-made mash-up posted on YouTube is in an emerging media environment and may not have any thoughts of competing with Ridley Scott. The experience may or may not lead to further creative production or may be a one-off to share with a few friends. But the crucial thing is that the experience of creating something – even a 'second-order expression' – will make that person a better reader and viewer, a more engaged respondent to other media texts. Rather than dismissing the mash-up text as not being on the same artistic level as a major feature film, we should recognize the ways that its creator is developing their media literacy. As Benkler puts it: 'The practice of producing culture makes us all more sophisticated readers, viewers, and listeners, as well as more engaged makers' (2006: 275).

The lolcat concept has spread to many variations – the epic quest of the lolrus for his bukkit, for instance. There is even a Loltheorists page devoted to making images of social, cultural and media theorists <http:// community.livejournal.com/loltheorists>, combining references to their lives and work with references to established lolcat tropes. We're quite fond of the photo of Chomsky, captioned 'noam noam noam' – you'll either get this or you won't, which is, we suggest, the point. Is this the popular culture of the convergent media environment? It may make more sense to describe a project like the Loltheorists page as *unpopular* culture. To say this would be to note first that it is literally unpopular, in that it appeals to a small niche audience – although this is also the case with many media products from within the broadcast paradigm. But it would also be to note that the content of the Loltheorists page trades in in-jokes which actively work to restrict the audience further by narrowing the scope of those who might get the joke. A staring picture of Foucault, for instance, with the caption 'ALL UR SUBJEKTIVITIES ARE BELONG 2 DISCURSIVE REGIMES UV POWR', rules out anyone unfamiliar with Foucault's work, the 'all ur base are belong to us' meme, and, indeed, who the guy in the picture actually is. But it's also a community with no real separation between producers and audience. It's organized around regimes of audience production rather than regimes of consumption. As Shirky says, anyone viewing this page gets the extra message that they can join in. From one perspective, a community built around in-jokes and specialist references could be seen as one built around exclusion. But as Baym argues, successful performance in such a forum is also a way of building recognition and of presenting an aspect of oneself in an environment in which others can respond:

> As people appropriate the possibilities of textual media to convey social cues, create immediacy, entertain, and show off for one another, they build identities for themselves, build interpersonal relationships, and create social contexts [...] Performing well can bring a person recognition, or at least lead to a sense that there is a real person behind otherwise anonymous text. Our expressions of emotions and immediacy show others that we are real, available, and that we like them, as does our willingness to entertain them. Our playful conventions and in-jokes may create insider symbols that help groups to cohere. (Baym 2010: 62)

So, once again, the importance of user-generated content is that it is fundamentally social.

Write

In the broadcast media environment, writing was something that most of us only did in private, if at all. Content industries were built around scarcity, with gatekeeping practices in place to filter out all but a handful of professionals:

> This is where journalists have had the upper hand for so long: they can "write" in public. But now, worryingly for them, anyone can join them; readers are transforming into writers in the interactive media. (Hartley 2000: 42–3)

Writing in public is now something anyone can do. At the entry level, anyone with access to networked digital media can now add a comment to the published output of major media organizations. The *Guardian* news website, for example, maintains more than 50 blog sections to which readers can contribute. The largest of these, 'Comment Is Free', is an online extension of the newspaper's op-ed page, opening all its opinion columns up to moderated comments from readers, and augmenting these with additional columns and featured debates. Users must register in order to post comments, but these are moderated after posting, not before. As Shirky (2008) observes, the gatekeeping principle of the broadcast media paradigm is 'filter, then publish', but with the repositioning of scarcity, the principle of the convergent media paradigm can become 'publish, then filter'. This basic principle attracts very significant numbers of contributors. As we write this, it's 10.30 a.m. on Tuesday, and this morning's featured *Guardian* piece by Polly Toynbee has already drawn 600 comments – the active audience made visible.

The BBC's 'Have Your Say' forums can draw as many as 10,000 comments in a single day (Wardle and Williams 2008: 21). Not all of these will offer an original perspective or draw on any personal experience or expertise (a thought-provoking blog called 'spEak You're bRanes' collects examples of intemperate, off-topic, bigoted or howling-mad comments from BBC forums). But many do, and the BBC has acknowledged the value of these comments in various ways – they can influence the coverage of a developing story, for example, offer journalists leads to pursue and possible contacts, particularly in countries where access to locals can be difficult, and can contribute an emotional dimension not present in impartial coverage (Wardle and Williams 2008: 20–3). For the contributors, it is a straightforward and simple way of writing in public.

Creating a blog of one's own is no more difficult – to create a blog at Blogger.com involves three clicks. And millions of people have done this – when Blogger marked its tenth anniversary in 2009, it was reported that the site drew 300 million unique visitors per month, that 270,000 words were written on its blogs every *minute,* and that around 250 billion words had been published on the platform since it launched (Naughton 2009). The website Technorati indexes more than a million blogs and ranks these according to how many other blogs link to them. Its 'State of the Blogosphere' report for 2010 surveyed 7200 bloggers and found them optimistic about the future of the form, even as the lines between social network use and blogging blur. More are blogging from mobile devices (25 per cent), more have been blogging for a significant length of time (81 per cent for more than two years), and more than a third believe that blogs are being taken more seriously as sources of information and opinion (Sobel 2010).

Blogging is social. Blogs are often compared with personal journals, but a journal points inwards towards its author, while a blog points outwards towards other blogs, other media material and other people. This is because, as a form indigenous to the web, blogs are built around links. Blogs often comment on other material, linking to it, and in so doing establishing a connection between the material and also between the blogger and the author of that other material (although this connection is very often not reciprocal). This social dimension, which as with tagging situates the user within networks of other users, is an important dimension of blogging (Bruns and Jacobs 2006).

Writing is also a term that we can apply to a broader spectrum of creative activity than blogs and comments – it offers a distinctive perspective on videogames, for example. Newman (2008) shows how videogames are the vehicle for often unexpected creativity from their players – not in playing the games as such, but in playing *with* the games, in writing and creating new expressions and experiences catalysed by the relationship with the games. There is fan art, fan fiction, fan music and cosplay; there is the writing of often extremely detailed and elaborate FAQs and step-by-step walkthrough guides for others to master the game (Consalvo 2003); there are the competitive activities of speedrunning and sequence-breaking, in which gamers not only complete a given game as rapidly as possible but also increasingly record these virtuoso displays and share them on YouTube; and there is the creation of new gameplay elements, levels, maps, and indeed new games, drawing upon toolsets shipped with some games or included as part of the actual gameplay, as in the case of *Little Big Planet*.

Collaborate

In July 2009, Casey Pugh created a website for a project he named *Star Wars Uncut*. He broke George Lucas's original *Star Wars* film – *Episode IV: A New Hope* – into 473 segments, each 15 seconds long, and threw open the doors to anyone and everyone who wanted to choose a segment and remake it in their own style, with the best versions to be combined together into a full-length remake of the original film. The remake was finished by April 2010, and the whole thing can be viewed on the site <http://www.starwarsuncut.com>, as a continuous sequence of the highest-rated versions of each tiny scene – some acted out by kids running around, some made with Lego, some animated drawings, some slick re-enactments, others hopelessly crude, most filled with humour and an infectious enthusiasm; hundreds of different approaches to interpretation and reimagination. The project went on to win an Emmy for 'outstanding creative achievement in interactive media' (*The New York Times*, 27 August 2010).

Star Wars Uncut is just one of many innovative convergent media projects built around creating a space for users to collaborate – the Johnny Cash Project, to which users have contributed more than 250,000 drawings, which are collated online into an ever-changing music video for his final recording 'Ain't No Grave' <http://www.thejohnnycashproject. com>; the In B Flat website, which combines 20 specially submitted YouTube videos of individuals playing melodies in the key of B ♭, which the visitor can combine as they wish <http://inbflat.net>; the Tate Movie project, in which UK schoolchildren submit ideas for an animated film involving the collaboration not just of the kids but also of the Tate galleries, the BBC and Aardman Animation <http://www. tatemovie.co.uk>; or the film of Radiohead's Prague concert on 23 August 2009, which was compiled from mobile phone and camcorder footage pooled by more than 60 fans, with the band sharing their own audio recordings of the show <http://radiohead-prague.nataly.fr>.

Networked digital media tools simplify processes of creation, manipulation, submission and combination, and make collaboration significantly easier than in other media. Such projects mark a shift from DIY media (do-it-yourself), the animating principle of punk and its parallel subculture of zine-writing, and of many cultural movements since (Dery 1993; Duncombe 1997; McKay 1998; Knobel and Lankshear 2010), to what Hartley (2009a) calls DIWO media – Do It With Others. Deuze (2007b) points out that producers and users have long collaborated in creative production – artists and patrons, newspaper letters pages, TV news opinion polls and vox pops, while Lievrouw (2011) observes that most aspects of social organization by definition are collaborative. Sociologist Marc A. Smith, interviewed by Howard Rheingold, points to the big picture here:

> Whenever a communication medium lowers the cost of solving collective action dilemmas, it becomes possible for more people to pool resources. And "more people pooling resources in new ways" is the history of civilization in [...] seven words. (Marc A. Smith, quoted in Rheingold 2002: 31)

Convergent media, then, are not facilitating some unlikely new turn in human affairs – rather, they are enabling us to extend our natural impulses for collaboration, cooperation and sociability into the networked digital media environment. What *is* new is the scale and scope of possibilities afforded to users, who can now find common ground and common purpose with remote, dispersed others whom they might not otherwise have encountered at all.

Such developments illustrate what Tim Berners-Lee, creator of the web, has termed 'intercreativity' – collaborative creative work made possible through the adoption of networked digital media technologies (1999: 182–3). The open source software movement, for example, has demonstrated the power of dispersed networked collaboration for years (Raymond 2001; Stallman 2003 [1985]). For Berners-Lee, the web was never intended in the first place to be about delivering content to passive audiences, but about shared creativity – which is one reason why the Web 2.0 label can be frustrating to many:

> We ought to be able not only to find any kind of document on the Web, but also to create any kind of document, easily. We should be able not only to follow links, but to create them between all sorts of media. We should be able not only to interact with other people, but to create with other people. *Intercreativity* is the process of making things or solving problems together. If *interactivity* is not just sitting there passively in front of a display screen, then *intercreativity* is not

just sitting there in front of something 'interactive'.(Berners-Lee 1999: 182–3, emphasis in original)

The most impressive example of intercreativity is Wikipedia. Launched in 2001, by its tenth anniversary on 15 January 2011, Wikipedia had more than 3,500,000 articles in English alone, while the site's 'About' page reports that the German and French versions each contain more than a million articles, and that more than thirty other language versions – including Russian, Chinese and Indonesian – have each passed the 100,000 articles mark. The Pew project reports that 42 per cent of all American adults (not just those with Internet access, but all adults) use Wikipedia (Zickuhr and Rainie 2011). The origins of Wikipedia have been widely documented, and the site itself offers exhaustive details on its origins and evolution (see also Shirky 2008; Bruns 2008a; Zittrain 2008; Lievrouw 2011). To some, Wikipedia exemplifies the public sphere online (Gauntlett 2009); to others it appears as a harbinger of 'digital Maoism' (Lanier 2006). As Lawrence Liang observes, the Internet divides into 'those who swear by Wikipedia and those who swear at it' (2011: 51).

We don't enter into the debate here about the reliability of knowledge as represented in Wikipedia, other than to note in passing that an active, questioning approach to the reliability of material on Wikipedia is something we should all extend into our other media use as well. Rather, we are interested in what Wikipedia illustrates about the changing nature of audience behaviour in the convergent media environment. The key point for our purposes is that Wikipedia both enables and depends upon collaboration among its users – every article is also a discussion, every edit can be traced in the visible history of the article, and status in the network accrues from participation. The 'edit' link at the top of every page is a direct challenge to the viewer-as-reader to become reader-and-writer. Moreover, as Gauntlett (2011) points out, collaboration on Wikipedia is at the micro-level of contributors editing each other's sentences, in contrast to the larger-scale units of modular collaboration that make up a project like *Star Wars Uncut*. Not everyone is a contributor, though. 'Collaboration is always accompanied by conflict and struggle', observe Lovink and Rossiter (2011: 289), and Wikipedia edit wars can be confronting, with the most active users those most willing to contribute to such an environment. Sue Gardener, the head of Wikimedia, the parent body that administers the Wikipedia project, told the *Guardian* 'Tech Weekly' podcast on 4 January 2011, that of Wikipedia's 408 million worldwide users, in any given month only around 100,000 of those comprise their 'core editing community', defined as making more than five edits a month; of those, 87 per cent are male, and the average profile of a core editor is a 25-year-old male postgraduate who is keen on technology and very confident in expressing themselves.

Pierre Lévy's concept of 'collective intelligence', through which 'No one knows everything, everyone knows something' (1997: 13–14), is illustrated in Wikipedia. And the 'something' which 'everyone' knows results in an extraordinarily wide range of articles – a list of cats with fraudulent diplomas, a detailed biography of a rabbit named Oolong ('famous for his ability to balance a variety of objects on his head'), and a dauntingly comprehensive list of fictional squirrels among them. We point to these examples not to diminish or ridicule Wikipedia, but rather to indicate our admiration for the way the site enables the collaborative expression of even the most arcane ideas. To us, the process of writing, editing, rewriting and revising each of these millions of articles is a vivid illustration of conversational interactivity, of distributed collaboration, of the convergent media environment as populated by creative audiences.

Share

A blog called the Post Punk Progressive Pop Party offers a huge archive of music, links and information about the music of the early eighties. On the day of writing, it tells us that Joy Division released 'Atmosphere' as a single on this day in 1980, and offers links to a Joy Division fan website, their Wikipedia page, a YouTube video of the band performing the song, and an illicit download of their best-of album as a single zipped file. Another blog, Blaxploitation Jive, hosts exhaustive links to downloads of recordings by early seventies funk artists, ranging from complete discographies of the well-known (Curtis Mayfield) to hard-to-find albums by the more obscure (Betty Davis). Numerous blogs share MP3s of radio shows presented by the late BBC broadcaster John Peel, including one he made on 10 December 1976 dedicated to an emerging phenomenon called punk rock. We are told that all of these activities should be thought of as piracy. But it's worth thinking about the extent to which they can also be seen as curation. The impulse to *share* material that some people find precious, to share the meanings and interpretations that this material inspires, and in the process to connect with others, is behind the transformations and the contestations that surround creative audiences.

Creative audience behaviour is fundamentally social. In the broadcast model, we watch, we listen, we read. In the convergent media environment, we do all of these things, with access to more content than ever, but we also organize, manipulate, write, collaborate and share media content – sometimes with 'invisible audiences' (Andrejevic 2007: 40; boyd 2007), sometimes with a self-selected network of maybe a few thousand or maybe a few people. 'In the economy of ideas that the web is creating, you are what you share', argues Charles Leadbeater, 'who you are linked to, who you network with and which ideas, pictures, videos, links or comments you share' (2008: 6). But there are contests around the word 'share', as there are around every important term in this book. On the one hand, the word appears as a link under every BBC web story, every YouTube video, every Facebook post. 'In our society,' writes Castells, 'the protocols of communication are not based on the sharing of culture but on the culture of sharing' (2009: 126).

In this vein, Joshua Green and Henry Jenkins propose the term 'spreadable media' to describe the active ways in which audiences choose to share and connect:

> Choosing to spread media involves a series of socially embedded decisions: that the content is worth watching; that it is worth sharing with others; that the content might interest specific people we know; that the best way to spread that content is through a specific channel of communication; and, often, that the content should be circulated with a particular message attached. [...] As we listen, read, or view that material, we think about not only what the producers might have meant but also what the person who sent it our way was trying to communicate. (Green and Jenkins 2011: 113–4)

On the other hand, the word 'share' is mobilized by content industries as a threat to their survival, as users copy and circulate their material through peer-to-peer networks and blogs (Dean 2007). This is the 'criminalization of sharing', in David's evocative subtitle to his book about online music (2010). Both senses of the word can be seen in BitTorrent. As Kelly (2005) observes, BitTorrent protocols for sharing files are built on an assumption of sharing – the user uploads simultaneously to downloading; BitTorrent is also a key mechanism for the illicit sharing of copyrighted material. And in a further tension, BitTorrent has legitimate applications for collaborative work and for curation and sharing. When the BBC announced plans to axe more than 170 of its websites in January 2011, one anonymous user quickly archived copies of all of them and posted the complete package online, encouraging others to copy and circulate them for posterity through BitTorrent (Goldacre 2011). There was no monetary incentive to this act, only a cultural one. Sharing connects audiences that were previously imagined as dispersed consumers. Social connection is much of the point of UGC – as Shirky points out (2010), nobody would bother to make a lolcat to keep only for themselves. And as Cory Doctorow of popular blog *Boing Boing* puts it: 'Content isn't king [...] Conversation is king. Content is just something to talk about' (2006).

Conclusion

Web 2.0 platforms have empowered creative audiences; they also, how-ever, implicate their users within regimes of intellectual property. The Web 2.0 'architecture of participation' means that we *collaborate* on building our Friends' profiles on Facebook, with each post or comment on their Wall, each tag and invitation, contributing to building up their presentation of self. But, as Andrejevic notes, this collaborative activity is privatized by Facebook in the act of publicly sharing it:

> When we explore what people do on Facebook or MySpace and the forms of community such sites enable, we must also keep in mind what gets done with the products of this activity, who controls its use and re-use, who profits from its transformation into commercial commodities and marketing campaigns, as well as who is targeted by these campaigns and to what end. Contrary to conventional wisdom, social networking sites don't publicize community, they *privatize* it. Commercial social networking sites are ostensibly collaborative productions, except when it comes to structuring terms-of-use agree-ments, and, of course, allocating the profits they generate. (Andrejevic 2011: 97)

Similarly, Jarrett (2008) points out that the full slogan of YouTube – 'Broadcast Yourself™' – includes the superscript trademark symbol and reminds us that audience creativity becomes other people's private property. The authors used to joke that 'Monetizing Lolcats' would be a good chapter title for this book, but that was long before Cheezburger's US$30million investment. But as we have emphasized throughout this chapter, creative audience behaviour is social – it connects people who organize, write, manipulate, collaborate upon and share media texts – and it allows people to develop their media literacies in new and creative ways, becoming more engaged, active and critical viewers, readers and listeners. Andrejevic and Jarrett are right to point out that audience creativity can be commodified by convergent media businesses, but Green and Jenkins are also right when they observe that 'Not all of the value is produced for the companies' (2011: 126). Audiences find value in these processes too, can make and share meanings and interpretations, and in the process establish and maintain social relationships. Audience creativity, then, is one more catalyst of cultural contest in the convergent media environment.

Making the Invisible Visible

6

In February 2010, Google launched a new social network service called Buzz, which it attached to the accounts of its email service, Gmail. With Buzz, users can share status updates, links, photos and videos, and comments with their Gmail contacts; these can also be tagged with the user's location when shared through smartphones. To kick things off, Google automatically created a list of 'followers' for each Gmail user – whether they wanted this or not. These lists were generated by identifying the Gmail contacts that a user emailed or chatted with most often. But one problem with this was that frequent email with, say, one's boss doesn't necessarily mean that one wants to share drunken party photos or funny cat videos with that boss.

Moreover, this list of most-frequent contacts was automatically made visible to others through the user's Google profile. Unlike Facebook, where Friends are self-selected, Google decided on each user's behalf who were to be their followers, and then announced them publicly. But what if you were a journalist whose confidential sources were revealed? Or a whistleblower or a dissident whose contacts were exposed? Or a client who frequently emails a divorce lawyer, gynaecologist or addiction counsellor? Or what if you just don't want your boyfriend to know that you still chat all the time with your ex? These were not hypothetical concerns – one widely circulated blog post described how its pseudonymous author's abusive ex-husband had been given access through Buzz to her contacts list and to comments she'd shared on links with her new boyfriend (Harriet J, 2010). Many others shared their anxiety or outrage online, and the official privacy agencies of ten countries wrote to Google to express their concerns. Google moved quickly to tweak its default settings and offer opt-outs. Six months later, Google's then-CEO Eric Schmidt suggested to *The Wall Street Journal* that he anticipated a solution to the problem of people needing to distance themselves from their social media profile histories – we can just change our names and move on (17 August 2010).

Schmidt drew some ridicule for this suggestion, such as this response from novelist William Gibson writing in *The New York Times*:

> If Google were sufficiently concerned about this, perhaps the company should issue children with free "training wheels" identities at birth, terminating at the age of majority. One could then either opt to connect one's adult identity to one's childhood identity, or not. Childhoodlessness, being obviously suspect on a résumé, would give birth to an industry providing faux adolescences, expensively retro-inserted, the creation of which would gainfully employ a great many writers of fiction. So there would be a silver lining of sorts. (Gibson 2010)

But Schmidt's suggestion has also been floated seriously by Internet legal theorists. 'As real identity grows in importance on the Net', argues Zittrain, 'the intermediaries demanding it ought to consider making available a form of reputation bankruptcy' (2008: 228). With the rise of convergent spaces that demand real names (such as Facebook), as email transactions are increasingly mined for advertising keywords (Gmail), as photos can be tagged by others and found online, and as our online traces are increasingly persistent and searchable, Zittrain suggests there should be a mechanism for erasing one's digital past and relaunching one's life online.

If this sounds paranoid, ask yourself what you did on your last really big night out. What were the highlights? Think about how you would describe the night to your best friend – which parts would you emphasize, which would you skip over? What kind of language would you use? Now think about how you would describe that same night to your grandmother. Would you emphasize the same parts? In the same words? What about describing the night to your boss? Your girlfriend's mother? The police? It would be very surprising if you told the story of your big night out in exactly the same way to each of those different people. This doesn't mean that you are dishonest. It means that our identities work through presenting ourselves in subtly different ways in different situations – some formal, some less so; some intimate, some remote; some serious, some not. We choose to make certain elements of ourselves visible to certain people in certain situations, and we choose to reserve other elements of our identity from others in other situations

(Goffman 1959; Meyrowitz 1985; Solove 2007; boyd 2008). Each of us manages, maintains and protects our own reputations as best we can.

In contrast, consider these 2009 remarks by Facebook CEO Mark Zuckerberg:

> You have one identity.... The days of you having a different image for your work friends or co-workers and for the other people you know are probably coming to an end pretty quickly.... Having two identities for yourself is an example of a lack of integrity. (quoted in boyd 2010a)

In the convergent media environment, as Zuckerberg's comments make clear, balancing our multiple self-presentations can be much harder (Livingstone 2008). Our various offline networks and situations can converge in the same online space. Your much older or much younger relatives might want to Friend you on Facebook. Your boss or professional colleagues might follow you on Twitter. Your lecturer might read your blog (and might take a screenshot of that post where you vent about her class).

This chapter is about the ways in which such *visibility* affects different aspects of our daily lives in networked digital environments. We emphasize visibility in this chapter rather than the more common frame of privacy. Not all aspects of these issues can easily be accommodated under the umbrella of privacy, as mediated visibility has further dimensions through which people perform and display themselves, and connect with others, in ways which may not be intended to be private. Media extend the availability of information across time and space, making it visible to new observers in new contexts. And new developments in media make possible new kinds of visibility, including making us visible in the same online space to members of our multiple offline networks. Convergent media make the invisible visible.

In this chapter we address three related aspects of this. First, the idea of the many made visible to the few, most commonly discussed through the concept of Foucault's Panopticon. Second, the few made visible to the many, as in our capacity to scrutinize politicians, celebrities or reality TV contestants; here we are concerned less with surveillance as such and more with the ways in which people choose to perform through convergent media – or are required to perform. Third, we turn to the idea of any-to-any communication online – the many made visible to the many – and the parallel idea of the few made visible to the few, as communities of interest come together through convergent media, and users find new ways to connect with others who are now visible to them in new ways and to whom they are now visible in turn.

Every breath you take

In April 2007, the UK government's 'respect tsar' Louise Casey announced that new CCTV surveillance cameras had been introduced in the English town of Middlesbrough and were to be rolled out in twenty other areas. This in itself was not news. Only a few months earlier, a report for the UK Information Commissioner's Office had estimated that Britain already had 4.2 million CCTV cameras, a number equivalent to one camera for every 14 people (Ball and Murakami Wood 2006: 8). It has been claimed that 20 per cent of the world's CCTV cameras are located in the UK (Lyon 2007: 39). 'One Nation Under CCTV' as graffiti artist Banksy put it, in letters three storeys high, on a London building in 2008 (without being caught by the surrounding cameras). But the new cameras announced for Middlesbrough were different. These cameras were special. They would not just film you going about your business. These cameras would shout at you as well.

Hundreds of thousands of pounds had been spent on adding loudspeakers to cameras and employing a staff of 12 who could yell at miscreants to pick up their litter in the street. The then-Home Secretary John Reid justified the introduction of the shouting CCTV cameras by saying 'it's interactive' (BBC News, 4 April 2007). He also moved the story far beyond the reach of satire by announcing that competitions would be organized in schools, for children who wanted to become the voices of the shouting surveillance cameras.

Here was a vivid reminder that in a convergent communications environment each of us is visible to new people in new ways every moment of every day. We drive to work along roads equipped with cameras that can record and read our licence plate numbers. We pass through public spaces under the gaze of cameras linked to facial recognition software. We may work in offices that record the keystrokes on our computers or which can only be accessed with electronic key cards. Our shopping and banking transactions feed linked databases. Our email, web search histories, telephone call logs and text messages are all recorded on multiple distant servers, open to search, copy and analysis by distant others. These are the visible – but sometimes unnoticed – manifestations of enormous political and economic infrastructures built upon mechanisms of surveillance: 'purposeful, routine, systematic and focused attention paid to personal details, for the sake of control, entitlement, management, influence or protection' (Ball and Murakami Wood 2006: 3). Such surveillance is increasingly comprehensive and pervasive. In May 2011, London's Metropolitan Police confirmed the purchase of a security programme called GeoTime, which collates information from mobile phones, social network services, web network log-ins, financial transactions and satellite navigation tools in order to build up a high-resolution image of an individual's communications, location and movements (*The Guardian*, 11 May).

But what does this have to do with *media*? In the convergent environment of networked digital communications, we need to consider more aspects of mediation than are commonly included in the broadcast paradigm. A very useful analysis here comes from Bordewijk and Kaam (1986), who distinguish between four 'information traffic patterns' which they term allocution, conversation, consultation and registration. The four together form a matrix which maps the possible combinations of information transfer depending on who or what is producing the information and who or what is distributing it. In an allocution pattern, information is produced and distributed by a centralized provider: a broadcast model. In a conversation pattern, information 'consumers' both produce and manage the distribution of their own information, as in an online chat session. In a consultation pattern, information is produced by a centralized provider, but accessed on request, thus affording the user a degree of control over its distribution, as in web browsing or catch-up TV (see Chapter 7 for more on this). And in a registration pattern, information is generated by individual users but is distributed by a centralized provider, affording the user no say over what is subsequently done with the information they have created, as in texting one's vote to a reality TV contest.

Bordewijk and van Kaam note that most work in media research has traditionally been within the paradigm they term allocution, and argue that developments in the media environment demand greater attention to the others. Their emphasis is on the application of this model in policy debates. They suggest, for instance, that privacy issues are most relevant in systems which adopt the registrational and conversational patterns, while intellectual property concerns are largely relevant to the other two patterns. But the networked digital environment of the convergent era demands more attention to all the patterns they identify, moving away from an exclusive focus on the broadcast media paradigm. Our daily surveillance illustrates the importance of what they call 'registration' – the inverse of the broadcast model, in which information is generated by dispersed individuals and sent to some central authority. Each of us is hard at work all day long, generating information to be registered by central (if networked) others. And what they do with it is not always knowable.

The most influential concept in discussing such surveillance is Michel Foucault's Panopticon. This is a model of power based on visibility. Foucault describes a transition from a model of political power built around public spectacles, making the few visible to the many (public executions are his most dramatic example) to a model of power exercised through making the many visible to the few. 'Visibility', he writes, 'is a trap' (1977: 200). Foucault builds his analysis on the figure of the Panopticon, derived from a prison building proposed in the late eighteenth century by Jeremy Bentham:

> The principle was this. A perimeter building in the form of a ring. At the centre of this, a tower, pierced by large windows opening on to the inner face of the ring. The outer building is divided into cells each of which traverses the whole thickness of the building. These cells have two windows, one opening on to the inside, facing the windows of the central tower, the other, outer one allowing daylight to pass through the whole cell. All that is then needed is to put an overseer in the tower and place in each of the cells a lunatic, a patient, a convict, a worker or a schoolboy. The back lighting enables one to pick out from the central tower the little captive silhouettes in the ring of cells. In short, the principle of the dungeon is reversed; daylight and the overseer's gaze capture the inmate more effectively than darkness, which afforded after all a sort of protection. (Foucault 1980: 147)

In Foucault's analysis, this becomes a general model for the exercise of power though the visibility of the many to the few (1977: 205). We are aware of being observed, or of the potential to be observed at any time – in the street, at work, in class – and so we modify our behaviour accordingly. We internalize the work of surveillance, monitoring ourselves, in 'a machine in which everyone is caught' (Foucault 1980: 156). This is a model of power which took deep root in popular culture through the figure of the ubiquitous telescreen in George Orwell's novel *Nineteen Eighty-Four*:

> The telescreen received and transmitted simultaneously. Any sound that Winston made, above the level of a very low whisper, would be picked up by it; moreover, so long as he remained within the field of

vision which the metal plaque commanded, he could be seen as well as heard. There was of course no way of knowing whether you were being watched at any given moment. How often, or on what system, the Thought Police plugged in on any individual wire was guesswork. It was even conceivable that they watched everybody all the time. But at any rate they could plug in your wire whenever they wanted to. You had to live – did live, from habit that became instinct – in the assumption that every sound you made was overheard, and, except in darkness, every movement scrutinised. (Orwell 1949: 4–5)

The Panopticon is an arresting image and a productive concept, but it is not without its limitations and criticisms. Deleuze (1992) argues that this disciplinary model of surveillance organized around institutions of modernity such as the school, factory, hospital or prison gives way to a society of control, organized around networked electronic registration. In the former, the individual was identified by a signature and a number that indicated their location within a 'mass' (payroll, passport, student numbers). But for Deleuze, social organization no longer depends on enclosed institutions, but on dispersed electronic networks and data-bases: 'what is important is no longer either a signature or a number, but a code: the code is a *password*' (1992: 5, original emphasis).

Richard Grusin's book *Premediation* (2010) also moves beyond the panoptic model, drawing upon Foucault's work on governmentality to discuss *securitization*. This is a complementary perspective to that of sur-veillance, through which rather than aiming to inhibit or restrict behav-iour, authorities aim to let that behaviour play out in order to gather data: 'Concerned less with individuals than with populations, securitization works not by restricting travel and mobility but by making it easier to move, travel, or cross borders (understood broadly as spatial, cultural, or temporal)' (Grusin 2010: 123). This is not about surveillance in the Panopticon model, but about the gathering of data which can then be analysed to reveal 'suspicious' behaviour:

> securitization not only depends upon but also encourages the prolif-eration of transaction and other data so that its algorithms can con-nect the dots. Premediation operates in the current security regime to ensure that there will always be enough data (enough dots) in any par-ticular, potential, or imagined future to be able to know in advance, before something happened, that it was about to happen – enough transaction data to prevent (or pre-empt) future threats to national or international security. (Grusin 2010: 124)

But the most striking omission from Foucault's analysis is that of any reference to the media (Meyrowitz 1985; Thompson 1995; Mathiesen 1997). As Mathiesen points out, this is all the more remarkable given that the period Foucault discusses in *Discipline and Punish* as that in which panopticism emerged (the late eighteenth and nineteenth centuries) was also a crucial period for the development of communication media, with the emergence of newspapers on a recognizable modern scale followed by photography, telegraphy, telephony, recorded sound, cinema and, subsequently, broadcasting. Mathiesen argues that the Panopticon, in which the few watch the many, is paralleled by the development of the media, which he terms the Synopticon, in which the many watch the few (politicians and celebrities, for example).

It is important to note that in this analysis, panoptic and synoptic viewing are reciprocal; one does not replace the other – look again at the excerpt from *Nineteen Eighty-Four* and recall that Orwell's telescreen worked both ways, showing Winston to the Thought Police but also displaying Big Brother to Winston. Lyon gives the September 11 attacks on the US as an example of this reciprocity – for most of the world, this was a TV event, a synoptic event in which the many watched the actions of the few, above all in New York. But it was also an event which continues to be used to justify increased panoptic surveillance, in which the few watch the many, fuelled by fear of further political violence by non-government actors such as Al-Qaida (Lyon 2007: 140).

What you see is what you get?

28 April 2010. The UK general election is just eight days away, and incumbent Labour Prime Minister Gordon Brown is on a walkabout in the northern English town of Rochdale. On camera, he meets Gillian Duffy, a 65-year-old life-long Labour voter, who asks him about immigration numbers. Brown is polite and makes a mild and reasonable point in response, before smiling and chatting about her grandchildren's future education plans and her red jacket being in Labour's colour. Then he climbs into his car, neglecting to remove his Sky TV microphone, and vents his infamous temper to his aide: 'that was a disaster ... should never have put me with that woman ... whose idea was that? [...] ridiculous ... she was just a sort of bigoted woman.'

The incident, which dominated the campaign for days, dramatized many of the rumours about Brown's temper. It worked to confirm suspicions about the disparity between his public positions and his private thoughts about his core voters. And it exposed the contrivance in the staging of the election campaign itself, with Brown's remarks about an aide organizing Ms Duffy's participation undoing the intended image of the impromptu walkabout with unscripted and unplanned voters. It was a stark example of how, in John Thompson's terms, 'mediated visibility is a double-edged sword' (2005: 41). The many can also watch the few, opening up ever-more opportunities for very visible figures such as politicians to undo themselves through gaffes or to be undone by others through smears, leaks and scandals (Thompson 2000; Castells 2004). As Umberto Eco commented on the WikiLeaks Cablegate events: 'The state has its eye on every citizen, but every citizen, or at least every hacker – the citizens' self-appointed avenger – can pry into the state's every secret' (2010).

As prime minister, Gordon Brown struggled to present an attractive version of himself on screen, coming across as grim and dour, unable or unwilling to articulate ideas in the kinds of brief and immediate sound-bites demanded by a media environment built around rolling TV news updates and complemented by 140-character tweets. His exposure in the Gillian Duffy incident contrasted his onstage persona ('it's very nice to see you') with his backstage one ('bigoted woman'), making both visible for viewers to compare. Brown's three-year tenure as prime minister was marked again and again by his failure to *perform* the role in an appropriate fashion for our screens, most cruelly in the release of an excruciating YouTube video in which he pulled unlikely smiles at inappropriate moments, apparently in response to off-camera urgings from aides. Brown's media presence illustrated what Joshua Meyrowitz has described as television's tendency to 'lower the political hero to our level' (1985). It also illustrates how increased mediated visibility brings with it not only questions of privacy and surveillance, but also of performance and display.

Television brings not only the communications *given* by politicians but also those inadvertent communications that they *give off* (Goffman 1959: 14). It is, as Meyrowitz puts it, 'a secret-exposing machine' (1995: 42). The more we see of our leaders, the less we respect or trust them. Campaigns attempt to combine the presentation of an impressive public figure, commanding the stage, with appealing images of the politician's family or domestic life. David Cameron's first 'Webcameron' public video post as UK Opposition leader showed him chatting to the camera while washing the dishes – an example of the construction of the 'ordinary' that Graeme Turner calls 'the demotic turn' in media and culture (2004, 2010). Political communication further blurs these onstage and backstage personae through informal yet staged events – photos of the politician in meetings, TV interviews in the family home. But the resulting visibility and exposure can be wielded as political weapons, as in the undermining of a staged photo of David Cameron demonstrating his green credentials by cycling to work through the release of a different view of the scene which showed his large official car following him with his suit in it. Carefully crafted images are now regularly subverted as private asides more easily enter the public domain, leading to self-inflicted damage, as in the example of former Australian Prime Minister Kevin Rudd, ousted by his own party in June 2010, who went some way towards sabotaging his own image, two pillars of which were his background as both a diplomat and a fluent Mandarin speaker, when he was heard to comment of the Chinese delegation at a major conference that 'Those Chinese fuckers are trying to rat-fuck us' (quoted in *The Sydney Morning Herald*, 7 June 2010).

Politicians are not the only public figures who trade in visibility and yet are vulnerable to it. In March 2006, New York celebrity gossip blog Gawker added a new feature, the Gawker Stalker map: 'Today we're launching the next step in inane celebrity drooling [...] in which we try visually [*sic*] pinpoint the location of every stalkworthy celebrity as soon as they're spotted.' This feature allowed anyone to text or email details of a celebrity sighting in the city, which could be tagged on a Google map embedded on the blog, identifying not only the celebrity but their actual location. While the map itself is no longer part of the page in 2011, the Stalker updates are. As we write this, *Harry Potter* star Emma Watson has been spotted outside Starbucks at 72 Spring Street, *Star Wars* actor Hayden Christensen has bought toenail clippers from a shop at 59th and Park, and Chelsea Clinton has entered the Flatiron building 'accompanied by guys in suits'. The Gawker Stalker is not a metaphor – it *is* stalking.

Celebrity media coverage works through dramatizing fault lines between the ordinary and the extraordinary (Wark 1999). Those celebrated in the media may take their place for extraordinary attributes of some kind – musical, sporting or acting skills – but are most likely to be written about for their ordinary behaviour, such as visiting Starbucks or buying toenail clippers. More than this, exposed are their relationships, their transgressions, the day-to-day failings that puncture their public image of enviable success. Indeed, as Turner points out, one key condition of contemporary celebrity is that the most visible will attract greater attention for their private than their professional lives (2004: 3). This too is a consequence of mediated visibility, and of the blurring of the lines between their onstage persona (Oscar-winning actor) and their backstage self (alcoholic multiple-divorcee). It is also a consequence of the requirements of certain media industries – Angelina Jolie may make only one film a year, but a magazine may want her in their issue every week.

What complicates this still further is the machinery of promotion through which the celebrity industry pursues visibility by trying to emphasize the 'ordinary' or backstage elements of a public figure's life in order to capture media attention. As one of Gawker's editors wrote in a *New York Times* op-ed piece, the banalities recorded on the Stalker page can seem quite trivial and harmless when compared with the up-skirt shots of starlets engineered for blogs such as Perez Hilton with the complicity of those celebrities and their publicists (Gould 2007). Celebrity is an industrial product, manufactured and marketed by integrated professional apparatuses of image and commerce (Turner 2004). TV shows such as *American Idol* and *X Factor* build their annual narratives around making visible this process of manufacture and marketing, inviting the voting audience to join in the process of designing the commodity that will be sold to them, after the season ends, as the winner's CD or the top ten finalists' concert tour.

Blogs such as Gawker or Perez Hilton emphasize the visibility of celebrities' backstage personae. They are entertainment media built upon the capacity of the many to watch the few. Ubiquitous surveillance itself has become a ubiquitous theme in popular culture. It animates the plots of films (*The Bourne Ultimatum, Enemy of the State, Hidden, Red Road*), of TV shows (*24, Spooks*) and the mechanics of videogames such as the *Metal Gear Solid* series. Each of these uses surveillance as a narrative device. But each explores the implications of communications media making the many visible to the few. Reality TV, however, like other celebrity media, exploits the possibilities of making the few visible to the many – the inmates of the *Big Brother* house, the castaways of *Survivor*, the hopefuls on *X Factor*. Different entertainment industries produce celebrity in different ways – the film industry emphasizing the individualism of the star, rock music trading in authenticity (Marshall 1997). With reality TV, ordinary people aspire to become extraordinary through submitting their very ordinariness to visibility. To appear on a reality show is to be given access to the 'media centre' that many perceive to be the place that counts today (Couldry 2003). Reality TV shows produce and largely discard an annual crop of fresh celebrities, whose fame derives from their mediated visibility and which tends to evaporate once they are uncoupled from the engine of the show, in what Turner calls 'the destructive cycle of discovery, exploitation and disposal' (2004: 84).

To talk of such programmes in such terms as exploitation and marketing is not necessarily to fall into moralizing about them – the authors enjoy them as much as anyone else – but rather to maintain a focus on the underlying truth that celebrities are intended to sell things. And one provocative analysis of reality TV is that its annual cast of characters are intended to sell surveillance to the viewer, to normalize and even glamorize a life lived under constant scrutiny (Andrejevic 2002, 2004).

Reality TV rose to prominence in the same period that saw the rise of Web 2.0, and shares with it an emphasis on the demotic and the ordinary (Turner 2010). Reality shows are also convergent media events, in which the viewer is required to participate – by phone, text or email – and in which the show extends beyond its broadcast slot into a 24/7 online presence (Turner and Tay 2009; Kavka 2011). Andrejevic argues that a show such as *Big Brother* should be understood as 'playing an important role in training viewers and consumers for their role in an "interactive" economy' (2002: 251). Such programming inculcates a world-view 'which equates submission to comprehensive surveillance with self-expression and self-knowledge' (2002: 253). There is a parallel, Andrejevic argues, between the *Big Brother* housemates and the monitored consumer: both are employed in 'the work of being watched' (2004: 97). His argument identifies the growing economic importance of customization, through which consumers can be charged a premium for a product designed around their own preferences – so you can order your computer built to your own specs, or get the U2 special-edition iPod, but not, as revealed in the famous correspondence between the manufacturer and Jonah Peretti, get Nike shoes emblazoned with the word 'sweatshop' (Peretti 2001). Such customization legitimizes consumer surveillance, as corporations gather information about users on the basis that it will enable them to better meet their customers' needs – a transaction that requires the customer to submit to intensive visibility (consider the closely targeted ads that appear above Gmail messages, keyed to the vocabulary in the emails exchanged). Reality TV, for Andrejevic, becomes a strategy for promoting the desirability of being watched, selling this as a form of empowerment: 'equating self-disclosure with freedom and authenticity' (2002: 268). Andrejevic (2007) emphasizes the uses of networked digital media for monitoring. As he argues, we can also use them to monitor each other, in an any-to-any visibility distinctive to the convergent environment – 'the democratization of voyeurism on a global scale' (Virilio 2002: 109) – as people perform and display themselves through networked digital media.

On 1 March 2011 for example, Charlie Sheen, the highest-paid actor on US television, signed up for Twitter, introducing his new catch-phrase 'winning' in his first tweet. In a little over 24 hours, he had a million followers, and his other signature lines became top trending topics on Twitter (#tigerblood). It was hard to move for Charlie Sheen at that time. Videos of erratic interviews in which he acted out a public conflict with his employers at the TV show *Two And A Half Men* were all over YouTube and Facebook, and his battles with Warner Bros and apparent breakdown made headlines even in countries like the UK, where his show was not widely watched. Sheen and his catchphrases were the meme of the month, remixed into multiple new contexts, video mash-ups, opinion columns, Twitter topics and the inevitable lolcats delivering quotes from his TV interviews such as 'I'm a Vatican assassin warlock.' Reports of Sheen's troubled history with rehab, divorces and arrests, and of his firing by Warner Bros the week after his arrival on Twitter, swirled through the media alongside reports that his Twitter account was a money-making venture through sponsored advertising, and corrosive reviews of his spoken-word theatre tour of the US. Most breakdowns are private affairs, visible only to family, friends and colleagues. Charlie Sheen appeared to perform a breakdown for millions on Twitter and YouTube, from where it leaked across a wider spectrum of popular culture. Whether he was experiencing a real breakdown or whether it was all an elaborate stunt, it offers an extreme example of how convergent media allow people to use networked digital technologies to display and perform for others.

Consider the camgirls who display themselves and perform for anonymous audiences (Snyder 2000; White 2003; Turner 2004) – they may find opportunities for self-expression and empowerment or they may find themselves unknowingly aggregated in contexts which could undercut that self-expression or empowerment, such as the user-generated porn site YouPorn.com. Consider the thousands of home-performance music videos on YouTube from which Kutiman could construct his mash-ups, discussed in Chapter 4. Consider *Life in a Day*, the Ridley Scott-produced feature film composed from thousands of uploaded YouTube videos all shot on 24 July 2010. Consider the randomized video-chat sensation Chatroulette, which allows point-to-point video connections between unknown and unknowable users, many of whom have not yet bothered to get dressed for the day. Consider Blippy, the social media tool that allows its users to post details of every credit-card purchase they make – 'more interesting than going through old receipts', observed US satirist Stephen Colbert in 2010, 'it's going through *new* receipts'. Consider the Big Sister brothel in Prague, which offers customers free sexual services in exchange for their consent to video of these being distributed online and by DVD. Consider Post Secret, the popular blog which shares postcards with secrets sent in by strangers. And consider location-based social media tools such as Foursquare. Foursquare allows us to display our location and, if we check in to a particular location often enough, to become the 'mayor' of that spot – the Betty Ford Clinic, Riker's Island prison, and the Forest Lawn cemetery all have Foursquare mayors, but the last word on Foursquare display goes to NASA astronaut Doug Wheelock, who checked in from outer space in October 2010. Across the convergent media environment, enhanced forms of visibility are not only implicated in surveillance imposed upon us from without, but also in dimensions of performance and display with which we choose to engage. As Andrew Keen (2011) observes, 'We are becoming WikiLeakers of our own lives.'

Together in electric dreams

Marcus Westbury is a writer from the post-industrial city of Newcastle in New South Wales, Australia. He has started a number of cultural festivals and writers' events, presented a TV series about contemporary art, and been a cultural commentator for the *Age* newspaper in Melbourne. In 2008, he set up a project called Renew Newcastle in response to the decline of the city centre. Westbury established that there were around 150 empty buildings in the city centre, as well as lots of artists of all descriptions in need of affordable space to work. So the Renew Newcastle project created a non-profit company which borrows the properties from their owners on a short-term basis and makes them available for free to the creative types who need space to develop their work. Within less than a year, Renew Newcastle had enabled 36 projects, cleaning up two dozen otherwise vacant, boarded-up or derelict buildings in the process. Its website <http://renewnewcastle.org> records dozens of examples of completed projects – exhibitions, fashion shows, kids' festivals, installations, workshops.

Renew Newcastle was launched and developed through social media, because there was no money for any other option. Westbury was unable to get any interest from local or national funding bodies in supporting the idea, and failed to sell it as a TV documentary project. 'Indeed', he writes, 'it's amazing just how unsuccessful everything other than social media was at incubating this project' (2010). He started a Facebook group for the project in late 2008, which very rapidly grew to its current size of around 3500 people:

> Every day I woke up it seemed someone new, in most cases someone I'd never met, was joining the group. Many were emailing me directly

> to tell me that they believed in the project and they wanted me to do it. While the powers that be could see little interest or value in it, the people of Newcastle certainly could. How can you say no to that? Like word of mouth – or gossip – social media like Facebook in this case can become a self-perpetuating brushfire. (Westbury 2010)

Westbury had certain advantages in using social media to drive this initiative. He had had more than a decade's experience in setting up arts festivals and so had a contacts list with thousands of likely supporters. Social media enabled Westbury to make that contacts list visible, rather than locked away in his mobile phone. His Friends and contacts quickly signed up, and as this appeared in their news feeds, some of their Friends and contacts in turn joined the group. The Facebook group made these people visible to each other and in turn made their support for the idea visible to others. Renew Newcastle is an example of how mediated visibility can enable people to establish connections with others who are now visible to them in new ways and to whom they are now visible in turn. Convergent media can enable groups to form from individuals who might otherwise not have known of each other's existence or shared interests. It is *the visibility of the few to the few* – what used to be discussed as virtual communities (Rheingold 1993, 2000; Smith and Kollock 1999; Willson 2007).

Renew Newcastle is grounded in an actual community – in a small city, with networks of inhabitants who know each other away from Facebook, as well as networks of people on Facebook who can contribute ideas and enthusiasm, who can make connections and introductions. The project speaks, as Westbury argues, to a participatory culture of people who are making and sharing their own media, in all the ways we discussed in the previous chapter, which made the concept a natural fit with what its future participants were already doing. Howard Rheingold has argued that 'The greatest value of virtual community remains in its self-organizational aspects' (2000: 173); the greatest impact of convergent media, he suggests, will come from 'the new forms of culture that will emerge from virtual communities' (2000: 173). 'Virtual community' as a term has rather fallen out of fashion, but self-organizing groups are an undeniable element of the convergent media environment. Renew Newcastle is an example of an attempt to develop a long-term project through a self-organizing group. But some of the most potent examples are of shifting coalitions, of ad hoc groups, coming together on a temporary and contingent basis, for whom 'community' may not be the best term – such coalitions are not about creating a movement, but about creating a moment.

When Julian Assange of WikiLeaks was arrested in London in December 2010, such a contingent movement briefly swelled in his support. Using the collective label 'Anonymous', thousands of people around the world took part in Operation Payback, joining an online swarm launching denial-of-service attacks against the websites of organizations which had cut off their services to WikiLeaks – Amazon, Mastercard, Visa and PayPal among them. Anonymous used various versions of an application called LOIC (Low Orbit Ion Cannon) to bombard the target website with multiple repeated attempts to reload the page, with the aim of overloading the targeted server and preventing the site from operating.

The ways in which the convergent media environment has been used by those trying to effect some kind of cultural, political or social change have drawn a lot of research attention (Meikle 2002; McCaughey and Ayers 2003; Atton 2004; Van de Donk *et al.* 2004; De Jong *et al.* 2005; Boler 2008; Shirky 2008; Lievrouw 2011). Meikle (2010) grounds Internet activism within Berners-Lee's concept of intercreativity (see Chapter 5), through which the crucial element is collaborative online creativity – from this perspective, convergent media activism is about people not only interacting, but creating together. He identifies four dimensions of Net activism – intercreative texts (the reworking and reimagining of existing media texts and images, creating new texts or hybrid subversions of existing texts); intercreative tactics (approaches which develop new variations on established tactics and protest gestures); intercreative strategies (activism which draws upon the traditions of alternative media to create an open, participant-centred media space that represents a strategic alternative to the established media); and intercreative networks (new media network models, including those which link open source software to experimental online publishing practices). A denial-of-service attack, as practised by Anonymous, is in this schema an example of an intercreative tactic, a digital analogue of a mass sit-in blocking a public place.

Political uses of denial-of-service attacks have been made in the past under the banner of 'electronic civil disobedience' (ECD). The practice of ECD has been established since the mid-1990s (Critical Art Ensemble 1994, 1995) and certain key characteristics have emerged – actions are publicized in advance in order to draw as many participants as possible; actions do not cause damage to the targeted site, but merely simulate a sit-in; and participants are open about their goals and identities (Jordan and Taylor 2004; Jordan 2007; Meikle 2002, 2008b). This last point, however, about openness and visibility, is one which provokes disagreement. The early important theorists of ECD, Critical Art Ensemble argued for a clandestine approach to ECD actions, proposing electronic civil disobedience as 'an underground activity that should be kept out of the public/popular sphere (as in the hacker tradition) and the eye of the media' (2001: 14). But in subsequent developments of this position by the Electronic Disturbance Theater and others (Wray 1998), ECD becomes instead a media event, a pseudo-event (Boorstin 1992 [1961]), an attempt to draw attention to an issue. The more people visibly join in, the more legitimacy can be claimed for the tactic. So the visibility of the participants and the visibility of the action itself are crucial. It has antecedents in the civil disobedience strategies of Gandhi or the US Civil Rights movement, but is in other ways native to the convergent media environment, as military academics Arquilla and Ronfeldt note:

> The [information] revolution is favoring and strengthening network forms of organization, often giving them an advantage over hierarchical forms. The rise of networks means that power is migrating to nonstate actors, because they are able to organize into sprawling multiorganizational networks [...] more readily than can traditional, hierarchical, state actors. This means that conflicts may increasingly be waged by "networks," perhaps more than by "hierarchies". It also means that whoever masters the network form stands to gain the advantage. (Arquilla and Ronfeldt 2001: 1)

A key metaphor for explaining practices such as Operation Payback is *swarming*: 'a seemingly amorphous, but deliberately structured, co-ordinated, strategic way to strike from all directions at a particular point or points' (Arquilla and Ronfeldt 2001: 12). This is the principle underlying the tactic of Operation Payback. An analogous concept is Howard Rheingold's 'smart mobs'. Smart mobs, writes Rheingold, 'consist of people who are able to act in concert even if they don't know each other' (2002: xii).

But Operation Payback, in contrast to an electronic civil disobedience campaign for media attention, was an underground activity in which participants sought to avoid visibility. The tensions between visibility and secrecy were central to the event. Participants banded together under the collective pseudonym 'Anonymous', but as one study found at the time (Pras *et al.* 2010), the LOIC application they used to swarm their targeted websites did nothing to disguise their identities. It revealed the IP addresses through which their computers were connected to the network, and this information was recorded by the targeted servers. The process was analogous, wrote Pras *et al.* to 'overwhelming someone with letters, but putting your real home address at the back of the envelope' (2010: 9) – as five UK participants learned the hard way in January 2011, when they were arrested for taking part in the denial-of-service attacks (BBC News, 27 January). As Morozov (2011) argues, convergent media make activists visible to the authorities as well as to each other – mediated visibility is, again, 'a double-edged sword' (Thompson 2005: 41).

The Anonymous movement emerged from the website 4chan.org (Coleman 2011), founded by Christopher 'moot' Poole in 2003 as a space for sharing and discussing Japanese popular culture, such as *anime* and *manga*. It was created by copying and translating the freely available source code of a Japanese 'image board' called Futaba (Krotoski 2010). 4chan is divided into dozens of separate boards for users to post on different topics (cosplay, pokemon, weapons) including /b/, the 'random' board, from which many of the most popular memes emerge (rickrolling, for example, through which a link purporting to be about something else leads to the YouTube video of Rick Astley singing 'Never Gonna Give You Up'). Lolcats emerged from the 4chan practice of observing 'Caturday' by posting pictures of cats on Saturdays, with the iconic picture of the grey cat asking 'I can has cheezburger?' becoming the starting-point for the blog of that name (Grossman 2008).

Speaking to the TED conference in 2010, Poole claimed the site was receiving 700,000 posts a day, and had seven million unique users. He argued that a crucial element of the site's success was that it was anonymous – that it required no registration, and that it maintained no archive, so material would not persist to be searchable or drive its makers further towards Zittrain's 'reputation bankruptcy':

> what I think is really intriguing about a community like 4chan is just that it's this open place [...] it's raw, it's unfiltered. And sites like it are kind of going the way of the dinosaur right now. They're endangered because we're moving towards social networking. We're moving towards persistent identity. We're moving towards, you know, a lack of privacy, really. We're sacrificing a lot of that, and I think in doing so, moving towards those things, we're losing something valuable. (Poole 2010)

Anonymity on 4chan is not just a technical feature, but a political choice. The site advocates online anonymity as a principle to be protected in a media environment of increasing visibility. It also, more questionably, advocates anonymity as a vehicle for collective action as participants, made visible to each other and so able to connect, attempt to act in concert while remaining invisible to others. There are precedents for collective pseudonyms used in art and activism – Karen Eliot, Luther Blissett – but 'Anonymous' rejects this disguise. Anonymity, in this position, becomes an expression of collective identity and purpose:

> Because you didn't need to register on 4chan, people started to appreciate it, and realise how radically different it was. We began to see anonymity not just as an aspect or feature, but as a thing, as a principle, as an idea that we are one, we are a collective, we are Anonymous. People then came to the site who not only saw Anonymous as a principle, but started to exploit anonymity as a new platform where they could be rebellious and no one knew who they were. [...] Services where you have a persistent, registered identity such as Twitter and Facebook – in many cases it's your real identity – limit what users want to say and read [...] The world still needs a Google, and Facebook. But it also needs the anonymous, ephemeral, open 4chan. (interviewed in Krotoski 2010: 9)

Rushkoff (2009) describes spending time researching 4chan, and being cautious of upsetting anyone while he was on the site. It felt to him like a 'bad neighbourhood – one where if you break some custom you're unaware of, you could get hurt'. But his attempts to retain professional distance were curtailed:

> I scrolled by something I had never seen in all my 20-some-odd years online: genuine child porn. Someone had posted the unmistakably clear image of two pubescent boys engaged in oral sex. Not fake Russian teenagers or young-looking models, but kids. It hit me harder and deeper than I thought it would. Not just the image, which set off its own chain of emotions in me as a parent, but the fact that this contraband was now in my cache, on my hard drive somewhere. I had visions of Pete Townshend getting carted off by the cops for "researching" child porn. So I was infected, after all. Not just by an indecent, illegal image, but by indecency and illegality itself. (Rushkoff 2009)

Rushkoff's experience and anxiety illustrate yet again Thompson's observation that mediated visibility is a double-edged sword. He had not just seen something that he wished had not been visible – more than that, his own viewing was itself also visible, recorded in traces across the net, retrievable by others with the right tools and motivations;

persistent, replicable, searchable, scalable, to recall boyd's (2011) points from Chapter 3.

Conclusion

In January 2010, Paul Chambers from Yorkshire was preparing for a trip to Northern Ireland to meet a new friend he'd made on Twitter. A weather forecast reported that bad weather had forced the temporary closure of the airport in Doncaster from where he was scheduled to fly. 'Crap! Robin Hood Airport is closed', he posted on Twitter to his more than 600 followers, 'You've got a week and a bit to get your shit together otherwise I'm blowing the airport sky high!' He was, we shouldn't need to point out, joking. But we do need to point it out, because a surprising number of people took Chambers at his word, despite the well-established principle that airport bombers do not generally announce their plans in writing to hundreds of strangers in advance. A team of detectives arrested Paul Chambers under anti-terrorist legislation, and he was convicted of sending a 'menacing message', which gave him a criminal conviction, and cost him not only his job but also the next job he was to find afterwards (Chambers 2010; Cohen 2010). Thousands of supporters came together on Twitter to retweet Chambers's original message with the hashtag #IAmSpartacus (a reference to the pivotal scene of solidarity in Kubrick's film *Spartacus*).

Networked digital media bring with them new kinds of visibility, new opportunities and requirements to monitor and be monitored, to perform and display, and to connect with others who are newly visible to us and to whom we are ourselves in turn made visible. As Paul Chambers can attest, this visibility can sometimes bring us to the notice of invisible audiences who we had never imagined, with consequences for our lives and reputations that cannot always be anticipated. This was crystallized when the rise of location-based social media inspired a website called Please Rob Me, which streamed feeds of people announcing to the world that they were far from home. Individuals struggle to find the appropriate balance between privacy and multiple competing interests. We disclose our location data in order to entertain ourselves and others when we check in to public spaces; we trade off our viewing history in exchange for better recommendations when watching streaming videos; we let a third party such as Google store our personal data in the cloud so that we still have it when our computers suffer their inevitable hard-drive failure. And we open ourselves up to ever-wider visibility and potential scrutiny on a range of social networks.

The examples in this chapter illustrate how the convergent media environment has shifted the parameters of our visibility. Combining the connected capability of a global computer network with the cultural sensibilities of the media has reshaped the ways we can see each other – and who gets to see whom. The intrusion of the media has long raised questions over privacy and the 'right to be let alone' (Warren and Brandeis 1890). But the idea of absolute privacy is challenged by developments in media technologies. At the same time, changing social values have allowed – even celebrated – its commodification. Indeed, society has submitted to visibility in the structure of many of our institutions; surveillance is an accepted part of modern managerial – and media – cultures. As Foucault observes: 'We are neither in the amphitheatre, nor on the stage, but in the panoptic machine, invested by its effects of power, which we bring to ourselves since we are part of its mechanism' (1977: 217).

Surveillance isn't new, nor is the public scrutiny of celebrity figures. What have emerged with the new technologies are questions of control over the dimensions of our mediated visibility. On the one hand, we are at the mercy of corporations such as Google or Facebook, whose motivations can ignore the complexity of personal privacy and identity. On the other hand, the Internet has given us greater control over other aspects of being seen. We now have the tools to voluntarily make ourselves visible for reasons of social or commercial gain and those same tools provide us with the ability to connect to others who have chosen to make themselves visible to us – or people like us.

Time, Space and Convergent Media

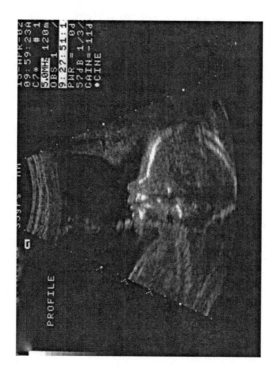

7

The image is an ultrasound scan of one of the authors' daughters. It was taken *in utero* more than four months before she was born. Such scans are a routine feature of pregnancy – a technician passes an ultrasound probe over the mother's body, generating the image on a standard portable TV monitor (and so, as someone who studies the media, the author is naturally thrilled to report that the first time he saw his daughter was on television). Images of this sort, extraordinary though they are, are now routine. Expectant parents set them as the wallpaper on their phones and share them on Facebook. The ultrasound technician might add a caption reading 'your next grandchild' and print off a hard copy that can be sent to the grandparents. All of this is now taken for granted – second nature.

And yet those things which are second nature are very often those that we ought to stop and think about. As John Fiske once suggested, 'Communication is too often taken for granted when it should be taken to pieces' (1990: xiv). So what are some of the taken-for-granted elements of the ultrasound image? First, think about how the image is framed – it is presented as a profile portrait, a way of framing the world that is not natural but was rather learned from the development of linear perspective (Berger 1972; Bolter and Grusin 1999; Mirzoeff 2009). Perspective is a particular strategy of representing the world that, as Mirzoeff argues, 'allows us to order and control what we see' (2009: 29). It constructs a separation between the world of the observer and the world of the picture, opening up a one-way window between both. There are many other ways the image could have represented the unborn baby – in 3D, as an animation, as a set of graphs – but the framed window of this profile portrait is the one that we have most come to take for granted as the way the world is represented.

If this image deploys a particular way of mediating space, it also uses a particular way of mediating time – note the date and time stamped at the top-left of the image. The image is encoded with standardized calendrical and clock time. This is one of the structuring principles of modernity: standardized global time; a uniform system of time, taking Greenwich Mean Time as its base (Carey 1989: 223–7; Giddens 1990: 17–21; Robertson 1992: 59). Standardized time is itself a product of communications media, made possible by the widespread adoption of the telegraph in the second half of the nineteenth century (Carey 1989).

In its taken-for-granted framing as a portrait and its taken-for-granted implication in standardized time, the image is an example of how media technologies make possible particular experiences of space and time. But there are also other aspects of these in the ultrasound image. First, it expresses another experience of space that is in no way natural and should not yet be taken for granted. The ultrasound breaches the boundaries of the body, reaches inside the womb, in order to produce an image. We are now visible to others even *in utero*. And once created, that image has circulated from printed copy to scanned jpeg, passing from the author's laptop to phone to disk, and now to this printed page, from where its further circulation can only be guessed. The image speaks to ways in which we can use communication technologies to challenge spatial boundaries, breach barriers, break down walls keeping the personal and the public separate.

This image also speaks to particular ways of using technologies to shape our experience of time, beyond its use of the clock. It is an image of a child, but one taken 20 weeks before birth. It makes possible an acceleration of this most fundamental personal relationship, as parents proudly show off pictures of the child before it is even born. It speaks to ways in which we can use communication technologies to manage time as a resource – to speed it up, slow it down, customize our experience of time – rather than as a constraint to which we are subject (Castells 2000). It illustrates what Castells calls 'timeless time':

> *Timeless time* refers to the desequencing of social action, either by the compression of time or by the random ordering of the moments of the sequence; for instance, in the blurring of the lifecycle under the conditions of flexible working patterns and increased reproductive choice. (Castells *et al.* 2007: 171)

The image is used to here to illustrate the point that all developments in communication technology make possible changes in the experience of space and time. And this is just one example of the kind of second-nature way in which we may take media forms for granted.

Media, time and space

One starting point for thinking about the relationships between space, time and media is the work of Canadian economist Harold Innis (1999 [1951], 2007 [1950]). Innis distinguished between 'space-binding' and 'time-binding' media, arguing that the physical properties of different media forms made each particularly suited either towards portability across space or durability through time. For example, a complex piece of architecture, covered in hieroglyphics, can be used to communicate messages through time, down through the ages, but, on the other hand, it is not very portable. Time-binding media, according to Innis, tend to create hierarchical 'monopolies of knowledge' (2007: 62) through which information tends to be concentrated in the hands of a priestly caste or other elite. Space-binding media, in contrast, Innis argues, tend to democratize access to knowledge, and access to the tools of its creation, distribution and reception.

Innis takes ancient Egypt as an example. He argues that as the civilization changed from an absolute monarchy to one that he characterizes as more democratic, this coincided with a changed emphasis on communications medium. The ancient Egyptians moved from stone as a medium to papyrus, which was lighter and so could be widely transported and circulated. It was easier to write on, and writing could be done more quickly. As Innis put it, 'thought gained lightness' (2007: 36). It was *possible* to write more, so people did; moreover, they began to write about increasingly secular things, as daily circumstances provoked thoughts that seemed worth recording. Literacy began to be a valued skill and one route to professional prestige as a scribe. There were changes in religious practice and these flowed through to changes in the power-structure of the empire. The point of Innis's argument is that a change in the primary means of communication made possible changes in the wider social organization of the empire. An important consequence of this argument is that different media forms enable different kinds of control over access and production of knowledge and information, as well as enabling particular experiences of space and time.

The *printing press*, for example, made it possible for information to spread far beyond the local area (Febvre and Martin 1976; Postman 1992; Eisenstein 1993). It was, in Innis's terms, a space-binding medium, one whose intrinsic properties made it suitable for effective communication across distance. It also made possible developments in the formation of national consciousness, adding a new status to the local vernacular language, and with the development of the daily newspaper, creating a new daily ritual for the maintenance of the imagined community (Anderson 1991).

A telling example of the influence of print is that of Christopher Columbus. Columbus reached land in the Caribbean on 12 October 1492, but it's now commonly accepted that he was *not* the first European to reach the Americas. He wasn't even close. Vikings had reached the continent several centuries earlier and had left artefacts and material evidence in Newfoundland (Levinson 1997: 25). What was different about Columbus was that he was the first European to reach the Americas after the invention of the printing press. The eight-page pamphlet reporting his achievement was the late fifteenth-century equivalent of a best-seller (Levinson 1997: 27; Stephens 2007: 71–4). Levinson records that in 1493 it was printed not only in Latin, but also in French, in Italian, German and Spanish. The use of vernacular languages here was a significant shift:

> news of Columbus' voyage was in no sense a rendition of an ancient, sacred work; it was a hot-off-the-press first edition in every sense. That it was rendered not only in the retro-formation of Latin but the new languages of the day made perfect sense. (Levinson 1997: 27)

Printing made people living in a territory visible to each other in new ways, by enabling the development of the newspaper and the novel, and by fostering literate uses of vernacular languages, which allowed populations to share in stories about 'people like us', spurring the development of new kinds of national consciousness (Anderson 1991).

The *telegraph* made it possible for information to travel much faster than someone on a horse could carry it. Communication became separated from transportation (Carey 1989). Telegraphy enabled a new emphasis on speed in communication, particularly in relation to news (Schudson 1978; Blondheim 1994; Standage 1998). The movement of information about events began to have a real-time impact on the events themselves. Consider the September 11 attacks on New York and Washington, in which the fourth plane, United Airlines Flight 93, did not reach its intended destination, as passengers found out about what had happened on the other planes via mobile phones and intervened. In this instance, the real-time circulation of information about the event changed the way the event itself unfolded, a phenomenon that became increasingly common with the rise of live TV news in the post-CNN era (Friedland 1992; Wark 1994; Bourdon 2000; Marriott 2007).

The *photograph* made possible new kinds of relationship with the past, again changing our experience of time. Each of us now maintains a sense of continuity with the past which is different from those which were possible before the assemblage of collections of family photographs. Each of us can maintain a family record of visual images of parents, grandparents and friends who are no longer with us. And we can share and memorialize these through Flickr, Facebook or personal sites. This makes possible an entirely different sense of personal historical time than was possible before photography (Barthes 1981).

The *phonograph* introduced the recording of sound for the first time. 'Sound', as Peters notes, 'is fundamentally an event' (1999: 164). To arrest the ephemeral flow of sound is, he argues, 'a more shocking emblem of modernity than the photograph' (p. 160). Images could be fixed as far back as cave paintings, but fixing sound, freezing a sonic moment, is a radically different form of intervention in our experience of time. Individual musical performances and improvisations, which before recording were always once-in-a-lifetime events, could now be captured and saved, studied and imitated, reworked and reimagined. With recording and then with broadcasting, as Jordan points out, 'sound was separated from its source and began to exist independently' (2008: 254). Music and voices could now travel and circulate further than ever, seeding new kinds of influence and combination, new forms of hybrid and collaboration, and laying the cultural groundwork throughout the twentieth century for the rise of sample and remix culture.

Broadcasting introduced the phenomenon of centralized transmission to dispersed individual households adding up to the largest audiences in human history – and not just dispersed audiences, but simultaneous ones (Kern 1983). Broadcasting brought the public world into the private spatial domain of the home, and it took the private out into the public domain (Meyrowitz 1985). Public conversations – and the public, and conversation – changed. Radio enabled a new kind of general public on a new scale, with new kinds of shared national events (Scannell and Cardiff 1991). And it brought the words of political leaders into the homes of their citizens in a new form of political intimacy – when Japanese Emperor Hirohito addressed his nation on 15 August 1945 to announce its surrender with the words 'the war situation has developed not necessarily to Japan's advantage', it was the first time his people had ever heard an emperor's voice (Emperor Hirohito 1993 [1945]: 155).

Broadcasting is still premised on an industrial schedule, an inflexible timetable, broken up into daily segments (breakfast radio, prime-time TV) and organized around the flow of individual programmes (Williams 1974). But a significant aspect of the convergent media environment has been the amplification of the potential that was first offered by the VCR to customize that schedule (Kompare 2006). Digital video recorders with huge hard disks, broadband, DVD box-sets, BitTorrent, podcasts, YouTube, and catch-up services such as the BBC iPlayer all enable users to time-shift our experience of broadcasting, in an everyday illustration of Castells's 'timeless time'.

Videogames, as an indigenous form of computer media (into which all other forms of media are, of course, converging), also enable a distinct experience of space. Games as apparently diverse as the various instalments of the *Guitar Hero, Mario, Halo* and *Grand Theft Auto* series all represent space and challenge the player to control it. Videogames create an illusion of navigable space, of territory and place, that the gameplay invites or commands us to negotiate, navigate and master (Manovich 2001). This is true of the earliest influential games, *Spacewar!, Pong* and *Adventure;* true of *Mario* and *Zelda*, of *Myst* and *Doom;* true of the *Grand Theft Auto, Halo* and *Modern Warfare* series; true of phone games such as *Angry Birds* and Facebook games such as *Farmville*. This is not just an incidental observation, but is rather at the core of what games are. Indeed, videogames, writes James Newman, 'can be *defined* as a form by the emphasis they place on spatial exploration, navigation and mastery' (2004: 122, emphasis added).

Mobile phones enact a breaking open of public and private spaces, breaking down spaces, as Wark (2000) observes, as a sampler breaks down music. The ways in which users adopt and adapt mobile devices means that the private can always intrude into any social environment now. There is no social space that can't be privatized with a phone. Levinson goes so far as to point to the prison metaphor implicit in the term 'cell phone'. The price we pay for being able to contact anyone, anywhere, anytime, is that anyone else can contact us – anywhere, anytime. The pressure to be always available, always in touch, Levinson observes, 'can imprison us in a cell of omni-accessibility' (2004: xiii). From a less anxious perspective, the mobile allows us to rethink the context in which we do things. Everyday social activities – working, studying, travelling, waiting – all offer new contexts for communication and connection. As Rheingold observes:

> As more people on city streets and on public transportation spend more time speaking to other people who are not physically co-present, the nature of public spaces and other aspects of social geography are changing before our eyes and ears; some of these changes will benefit the public good and others will erode it. (2002: xxii)

We can eliminate space and distance, and we've been doing that for centuries now, through increasing processes of time-space compression: 'processes that so revolutionize the objective qualities of space and time that are we are forced to alter, sometimes in quite radical ways, how we represent the world to ourselves' (Harvey 1989: 240). But we can't eliminate place. Rather, place gets *customized*. It gets reimagined on the terms of the mobile, communicating individual (Castells *et al.* 2007: 250–1).

In none of these examples are we suggesting that a particular technological innovation *determined* the changes in which we see it implicated. As discussed in Chapter 1, the relationships between technology and culture are more complex than that. Rather, we are suggesting that the ways in which those innovations are adopted and adapted make possible altered approaches to mediating our experiences of time and space. The following four sections discuss different ways in which convergent media are implicated in changes to our experiences of mediated space and time. First, how TV viewers can now customize the broadcast schedule, moving TV viewing away from an industrial model of simultaneous reception and towards an on-demand database that users navigate, search and consult. Second, how videogames construct a sense of space and place that users, again, navigate and search, exploring the spatial environment in order to understand its rules. Third, how convergent media illustrate the acceleration of culture, as in Google Instant – search results that are returned before you have finished typing the query. This is part of a wider spectrum of what Hartley has termed 'frequencies of public writing' (2008: 36–60). And finally, how media texts, images, and users' responses to these now circulate and flow across global networks.

Catching up with TV

Is there anything on? There's last night's episode of *Eastenders*, there's *Never Mind the Buzzcocks* from two nights ago, or there's the last two weeks of the *Human Planet* series. There are repeats of *Doctor Who* and *Silent Witness*, the whole series of *So You Think You Can Dance?*, a documentary on the making of *Screamadelica* by Primal Scream, and a vintage Bruce Springsteen concert. Or we could watch the news live, or listen to any of nine BBC radio stations. And that's just some of what's available at this exact moment, on the train, on the BBC iPlayer – on the phone.

The BBC iPlayer was launched in December 2007. Users can watch or listen to BBC TV and radio programmes from the past seven days from their web browser or download them to watch in the next 30 days. In some cases programmes can be streamed live, in others the service allows users to catch up with shows they may have missed, including some entire runs of series. As well as on computers, the iPlayer works on many phones and on the games consoles Nintendo Wii and Sony PlayStation 3. The use of online catch-up services like the iPlayer is growing rapidly, with 41 per cent of UK households using such services (Ofcom 2011: 93). The BBC iPlayer alone is accessed by 15 per cent of UK Internet users (Ofcom 2011: 106).

Audiences now have many more ways of accessing this content on their own schedule. We can use an online catch-up service such as the iPlayer or 4oD or the US Hulu or Australian iView. Some major broadcasters, including Channel 4, now offer archival content through YouTube, allowing them some control over their advertising. Catch-up TV is often also available through the websites of specific programmes (the CBS *Survivor* site in the US or the *MasterChef* site in Australia, for instance) or broadcast networks, not just through dedicated portals and applications like the iPlayer (Marshall 2009). We can also time-shift our viewing through digital video recorders with large hard disks, saving an entire series to watch later. Forty-six per cent of UK homes have a digital video recorder, and those households time-shift 14 per cent of their TV viewing (Ofcom 2011: 103). Movie channels and those with imported programming are among the most recorded for later viewing; news and live sports channels, not surprisingly, are among the least. Taking digital video recorders and broadband into account, UK adults watch over four hours of time-shifted or 'non-linear' material each week (Ofcom 2010: 100–7). Then there are further options – we can wait for the DVD box set (plus extras) to binge on our favourite dramas over an entire weekend. DVD box sets refocus TV around a publishing model, turning the text from an ephemeral moment to a collectable item (Kompare 2006; Hills 2007; Bennett and Brown 2008). Or we can download the latest episode of our favourite overseas show using BitTorrent, hours after it has aired elsewhere and perhaps years before it will be screened on free-to-air TV where we live (Leaver 2008). 'We no longer watch films or TV', suggests Geert Lovink, 'we watch databases' (2008: 9).

The iPlayer and the other examples above illustrate a profound shift away from the logic of the broadcast paradigm. It's important to see the convergent media environment as one which adds new elements to existing systems, and in which, as a result, both old and new persist and are changed (Bolter and Grusin 1999). New media do not necessarily replace existing forms – but they do *displace* them. For example, the imagined end of television has been a consistent theme in academic debates, its uncertain futures hailed in titles such as *Turning Off The Television* (Given 2003), *Life After Television* (Gilder 1992) or *Television After TV* (Spigel and Olsson 2004). This is only to be expected – as new media technologies develop, claims about the end of an era inevitably emerge. Yet television, of course, is not dead, and the broadcast model still generates robust audiences in many parts of the world. But, while not dead, TV is being reshaped, reimagined and reinvented in unpredictable ways. Broadcasting has become only one of a set of options for the distribution of TV content, alongside cable, DVDs, Internet downloads, and online video streams. Simultaneously, audiences have embraced new modes of engagement with audio-visual products, with many seamlessly shifting from the role of consumer to that of producer.

In terms of time, the two defining characteristics of the broadcast model are *regularity* (shows are programmed in regular slots and on regular days) and *simultaneity* (the audience are assembled at the same time in many dispersed places). Many of the most famous broadcasting events of the TV era are notable not just for their content or cultural resonances, but as instances of the most enormous simultaneous audiences:

> Television's emblematic moments – the shooting of J. R. Ewing in *Dallas* or J. F. Kennedy in Dallas; the moon landings; the twin towers; Princess Diana's wedding and funeral; the Olympics and football World Cup finals – the cliffhangers, weddings, departures and finales gathered populations from across all demographic and hierarchical boundaries into fleetingly attained but nevertheless real moments of "we-dom", a simultaneous commonalty of attention that could sometimes aggregate to the billions. (Hartley 2009b: 23)

Broadcasting still draws enormous simultaneous audiences, particularly for scheduled major events (the Super Bowl, the Olympics, the season finales of *American Idol* or *X Factor*) or for unexpected ones (the September 11 attacks). But as Lotz points out: 'Although television can still function as a mass medium, in most cases it does so by aggregating a collection of niche audiences' (2007: 28). Moreover, the biggest scheduled TV events of the convergent media era are not confined to broadcast television, but are rather those which take place across a range of media forms:

> The major ratings successes of the twenty-first century have been multi-platform, multimedia events. One significant example is *Big Brother*, with its websites, chat-rooms, live video streaming, and its key narrative moments – the evictions, for instance – turned into public events by being performed before a live audience. (Turner and Tay 2009: 7)

A series of developments, spanning several decades, have given audiences progressively more control over their TV viewing schedules. Uricchio (2004) discusses Williams's (1974) concept of flow, situating it within the network era in which the viewer was limited to a handful of channels. Uricchio argues that the first significant technological development that allowed the viewer to intervene in this strategy of broadcast flow was earlier even than the VCR. It was the remote control, which allowed the viewer to move from a programming-centred conception of flow to a more viewer-centred one. It was 'a "subversive technology" that demonstrated from its start that viewers had the ability to disrupt program flow and thus the economic flow so central to commercial television' (Uricchio 2004: 171).

Lotz (2007) distinguishes between the network era of TV broadcasting, characterized by the dominance of a small number of providers operating to an industrial schedule; what she calls the 'multi-channel transition' era, from the mid 1980s to around 2005, in which the user's experience of television changed through the introduction of many new channels and services, such as the VCR and cable; and the ongoing emergence of the 'post-network era', characterized by, among other things, multiple devices, an expanded range of funding and financing models and a rise in amateur production (YouTube), and the availability of TV content anywhere, any time. We should note that Lotz is describing the US experience, and there is much global variation in this as well (Turner and Tay 2009), but the broad contours of her argument are widely applicable in other developed countries. Lotz argues that the multi-channel transitional period introduced audiences to increased choice and control over how and when they watched TV content, while the post-network era introduces greater convenience, customization and community (taken together, she describes these as 'the five Cs of the post-network era' (Lotz 2007: 245).

The rise of non-linear TV has implications, including for audience measurement, an activity which Ang (1991) dubbed 'desperately seeking the audience', and for the capacity of commercial networks to deliver mass audiences to advertisers (Curtin 2009; Turner and Tay 2009). David Simon, co-creator of *The Wire,* one of the most critically acclaimed TV shows of its era, as well as of *Treme* and *Generation Kill,* explained to one interviewer in 2008 how non-linear viewing fits into his understanding of TV:

> I no longer take seriously our Sunday-night Nielsen [ratings] numbers. Like for *Generation Kill,* the Iraq mini series which is on in America now, it's drawing 1.3 million on Sunday night. I don't care. I know from experience now that a certain percentage of the audience is waiting for the box-set. A certain percentage is going to catch it on illegal downloads, off BitTorrent and that stuff. A certain percentage is going to wait until they're all available on HBO on demand and then watch them in succession. And a certain number of people are TiVOing it. The whole notion of appointment television is dead now in America. We've reached the point of measuring when people watch any show at a given time is irrelevant. Television is now more of a lending library; you watch it when you want to watch it on your own terms. (interviewed in Hepworth 2008)

Simon is describing a shift in TV viewing, away from the broadcast schedule and towards a model in which users *consult* distributed databases of TV content to their own timetable. If consultation (Bordewijk and Kaam 1986) is now an important mode of interaction with TV, customizing the temporal schedule, there is also a spatial dimension to this, discussed in our next section.

CTRL + Space

You are in a maze of twisty little passages, all alike. Welcome to Farmville – harvest your crops. In the vast, deep forest of Hyrule. ... Thank you Mario, but our princess is in another castle. There she is ... Liberty City. These quotes from videogames as diverse as *Farmville* and *Grand Theft Auto IV* underscore the construction and exploration of virtual space as a core characteristic of the form (Manovich 2001; Murray 2003; Newman 2004). They speak to the game as a space – a cave, a farm, a forest, a fantasy kingdom, an entire contemporary city – that the player explores and navigates. The prefix *cyber* in the words cyberspace and cyberculture, after all, denotes *navigation*. But the player does more than just navigate. To play a videogame is to learn the rules that govern its environment, and to learn how to apply and exploit them. To complete a game is to fully understand and apply its rules and to control and master the space it offers. 'All your base are belong to us', indeed.

While some approach videogames as particular kinds of interactive narrative (Aarseth 1997; Murray 1997), this perspective fails to capture the experience of actually playing a game – think of *Tetris* or *Rock Band*, for instance, even though some have tried to cast even *Tetris* as a narrative about winning or losing, with the player as the hero battling against the environment of the game (Murray 2004: 2). Juul (2001) has identified some of the key limitations of this view, highlighting the differences between the reader or viewer of a story and the player of a game, and between the experience of a past-tense narration and the present-tense exploration of a game. Instead, games are better seen within what Manovich has identified as the cultural logic of the database – as a digital environment which users 'view, navigate, search' (Manovich 2001: 219). As Mark Deuze has it: 'The core content of a computer game – like news for a newspaper – is the various maps and scenarios within which players can roam free' (2007b: 253). 'Roaming free' is part of the appeal of a game like *Grand Theft Auto IV* or *Legend of Zelda: Twilight Princess,* but in other cases (such as *Guitar Hero*) the experience is better described as accommodating oneself to the constraints demanded by the space. But in all of these cases, exploring computer-generated space and mastering the on-screen environment, is fundamental. Janet Murray traces the phenomenon of computer-space to two intrinsic features of human-computer interaction: processing (computers not only record instructions but *execute* them) and participation (users can input and manipulate information):

> The creation of the illusion of space within the machine, which can be achieved with only a text-based display, is the result of its capacity for accepting navigational commands from us and then responding according to its programming in a consistent manner that reinforces our notion of space. That is, we can program the responses of the computer to simulate any space we can imagine, displaying 'north' and 'south' or 'left' and 'right' appropriately so that the participating user will form a reliable mental map of the symbolically represented territory. [...] It is not accidental that we refer to information in digital networks as existing in 'cyberspace,' or that the first computer game to be massively distributed by network was a text-based exploration of a virtual cave. (Murray 2003: 6)

Consider an example of gameplay from the best-selling *Guitar Hero* franchise. *Guitar Hero 5* (2009) features a level built around 'Smells Like Teen Spirit' by Nirvana. The level opens with a simulated performance video of a CGI version of Nirvana taking the stage before a cheering crowd. While this continues to play, a guitar neck and fretboard appears superimposed over the band, projecting forwards into the centre of the on-screen space. Six different-coloured lines represent the guitar strings, while correspondingly coloured dots representing individual notes and chord combinations travel towards the player, who must capture each as it reaches a certain point on screen by clicking on their controller at the precise moment. To play the game is to build a representation of the song as an experience in space. 'Sound', as Peters observes, 'is fundamentally an event' (1999: 164), an ephemeral flow of vibrations, but *Guitar Hero* instead takes recorded sound and represents this as a spatial environment that the player has to master by learning and applying its rules.

Why does this matter? If videogames are spatial simulations of rule-based systems, then the form can be used for purposes other than entertainment. Bogost (2007) offers many examples of games being used in politics, education and marketing. And in *Newsgames* (2010), Bogost,

Ferrari and Schweizer analyse a range of ways in which the seemingly incommensurable systems of videogames and news are converging (see also Trippenbach 2009). They find 'editorial' games, often short and simple animations, analogous to op-ed commentaries or newspaper cartoons. They find infographics and documentary videogames, puzzles and quizzes, and they find emerging uses of games as platforms for players to add and manipulate their own content, all used to explore current affairs issues and to extend these beyond the familiar news genres.

Videogames and the news each have a very different cultural status. Games are often seen as both trivial and threatening – on the one hand a waste of time, and on the other, a risky source of malign influences on impressionable minds. Although the average age of gamers, and the cultural penetration of games, continue to rise, and although family-friendly consoles such as Nintendo's Wii and the rise of casual and social gaming on smartphones and social network media have all taken games far beyond their stereotypical demographics, they are still often analysed from what we might call a protective perspective (for example Byron 2008).

The news, on the other hand, is high-status. The news trades in the authorized pronouncements of the powerful. It is a system of texts and processes of cultural negotiation, social debate and political authority. The news is the main public forum for social discussion (how we organize ourselves and each other) and cultural discussion (how we feel about that). The news, as we discussed in Chapter 2, is the industrial production of non-fiction drama, and makes a claim to define the basis of social reality by stating what count as the 'top stories' on any given day.

How can these two cultural systems converge? What they share is a representation of rules. The news is a representation of social authority – who gets to speak and what they get to speak about. A videogame is a simulation of a rule-based system (Frasca 2004). It challenges the player to work out how an environment is organized and to understand its rules:

> Games display text, images, sounds, and video, but they also do much more: *games simulate how things work* by constructing models that people can interact with [...] a type of experience irreducible to any other, earlier medium. (Bogost, Ferrari and Schweizer 2010: 6, original emphasis)

As Galloway suggests, there are ever-more examples of 'games that reflect critically on the minutia of everyday life, replete as it is with struggle, personal drama and injustice' (2004; see also Moe 2008).

Here we can compare two examples. In October 2007 the UK *Guardian* and *Observer* newspapers launched a three-year project to promote development in the Ugandan village of Katine. Over the lifetime of the project, working with established charities and corporate partners – Barclays bank pledged to match donations from readers – the Katine project contributed to the healthcare, educational and water facilities of the village – new books and desks in schools, new boreholes, more than 7000 mosquito nets, health workers and onsite medical testing, and a range of other interventions. The project was extensively documented on the news organization's website <http://www.guardian.co.uk/katine>, which built up into a considerable archive of reports, commentaries, videos, galleries and other multimedia resources.

Shortly after the end of the Katine project, in late 2010, an iPhone game called *Raise the Village* was published by an organization called New Charity Era. *Raise the Village* creates a virtual version of the Kapir Atiira village, also in Uganda. The village, population roughly 1400, is remote and impoverished, with HIV/AIDS, underdevelopment, and low levels of health and literacy, all major issues. The game invites the player to construct their own version of Kapir Atiira on their mobile device, learning about the basics of village life as they go. To make progress, the player needs to purchase some of the in-game currency, florins, which they can then use to buy supplies. What's distinctive about *Raise the Village* is that the charity behind the app uses the money paid by players for florins to buy the same items for the villagers themselves. So if you buy a mosquito net to equip your hut within the game, the money you spend goes towards buying an actual mosquito net in Uganda. And as an added incentive, the app will send photos to your phone of the actual mosquito net being delivered when it arrives in the actual village. The app also offers text message updates and blogs written by aid workers connected to Kapir Atiira.

Raise the Village is an intriguing illustration of the issues-focused videogame, built around exploring a simulation of a specific place. It extends the familiar model of *Farmville* or *Sim City* into a tangible offline outcome. Compared to the resources mobilized by *The Guardian*'s Katine project, however, it is a tiny intervention; moreover, some may find something distasteful or colonialist about the representation of the problems of a real place as a game – there is something a bit jarring about using a very expensive handheld device to simulate the purchase of beans in Africa, with photos of those actual beans being delivered offered as incentive to complete the level. But this is an emerging area, and the convergence of news and videogames, and the potential for their wider and deeper use, provides a striking response to Herbert Gans's contention that journalists 'will have to learn how complicated events can be described and explained in a more easily understandable fashion; and how connections between events and their contexts can be made intelligibly' (2009: 23). 'There is nothing medium-specific about journalism,' as Bogost *et al.* point out, 'no reason that its output must take the familiar form of text, image, or video' (Bogost, Ferrari and Schweizer 2010: 180). This dimension of convergence offers new possibilities for users of both games and the news to engage with these representations of rules and of authority, in order to understand them – and potentially then to challenge them.

Faster, Pussycat! Kill! Kill!

Google is pretty fast. Even here in this café, with only a so-so wi-fi connection, a search for 'Charles de Gaulle Airport' comes back with this underneath the search box: 'About 3,440,000 results (0.16 seconds)'. That's not bad. But Google thinks things should be faster. In September 2010 it introduced Google Instant, which returns search results before you've finished typing them. In the same example search, Google has already suggested 'Charles de Gaulle Airport' at the point where the user has only typed 'Charles de'. Its website explains the rationale for Google Instant like this: 'people type slowly, but read quickly, typically taking 300 milliseconds between keystrokes, but only 30 milliseconds (a tenth of the time!) to glance at another part of the page. This means that you can scan a results page while you type.' Perhaps our uncertainty about French spelling slowed us down – Google reports that the average search term takes nine seconds to type, which Google Instant can speed up by from two to five seconds. 'If everyone uses Google Instant globally,' the site suggests, 'we estimate this will save more than 3.5 billion seconds a day. That's 11 hours saved every second.'

Faster! Eleven hours saved every second! Convergent media tend towards acceleration, as network capacity and processor speeds improve. But what might we miss as we pick up speed? Paul Virilio, whose concern with speed has animated much of his writing, has warned that networked digital technologies bring with them the risk of new kinds of accident. In Virilio's analysis, every technological development introduces a distinct kind of accident – so the invention of the train, he argues, was also the invention of the train crash (1983). 'One of the major problems now facing political as well as military strategists',

Virilio argues, 'is the phenomenon of immediacy, of instantaneity. For "real time" now takes precedence over real space, now dominates the planet' (2007: 106).

Google Instant by default urges the user to accept the recommended search result, rather than selecting from the range returned. In this, it is a vivid reminder that search engines are not neutral (Meikle 2002: 109–11; Hargittai 2007; Nightingale 2007, 2011; Jensen 2010: 92–4). For example, hacker journal *2600* has compiled a 'blacklist' of words excluded from Google Instant suggestions – 'vodka' elicits suggestions from the search engine before you've finished typing it, but 'cocaine' does not (http://www.2600.com/googleblacklist). More important than this, Google Instant may be faster, but it's also a search result in which the user has conceded a certain amount of independent judgment. Google Instant is but one example of what John Tomlinson terms 'the condition of immediacy' (2007: 72) that now pervades our social and cultural lives. Tomlinson observes this condition of immediacy in phenomena as diverse as home-working, speed dating, 24-hour shopping, mobile phone use and search engines. His use of the term 'immediacy' draws upon three related aspects – rapid delivery, physical or cultural proximity, and the central location of 'media' within the word itself. Communication, space and time are all linked in this analysis. Instantaneity and ubiquity – which as Virilio notes are 'attributes of the divine now applied to the human' (1997: 70) – become part of the daily fabric of our lives. *'What's happening?'* asks Twitter. *'What's on your mind?'* asks Facebook. Communication moves from sharing what has happened to sharing what is happening now, and indeed, what has not quite happened yet.

Richard Grusin identifies a strategy of 'premediation', which he argues is a political and communicative strategy to prevent the US public ever again experiencing the kind of traumatic surprise they encountered on 11 September 2001 (2010: 4). The horror of liveness, as mediated that day, gives way, Grusin argues, to communication strategies designed to ensure that no such event will be experienced 'live' again – rather, they will be fully mediated in advance. His strongest example is his analysis of the build-up to the invasion of Iraq in March 2003:

> It was premediated as a war in which the United States and Britain would go it almost alone and as a war in which they would go in with the support of the United Nations. It was premediated as a war with a northern and a southern front, or one that would be waged primarily from the south. It was premediated as an overwhelming

aerial assault leading to the immediate surrender of the Iraqi people, who would welcome the American liberators with open arms. It was premediated as a war that would lead quickly to a military coup, or to the capture, murder, or exile of Saddam Hussein and his immediate circle [...] While each of these scenarios had its own level of plausibility and its own set of motivations, one thing was consistent among them all – the way in which they participated in a logic of premediation in which the mediation of war and its aftermath always preceded the events themselves, in which such real events as war and its aftermath occurred only after they had also been premediated by networked media, by government spokesmen, and by the culture at large. (Grusin 2010: 44–5)

'Time in communicative life', argues John Hartley in a wide-ranging essay about media and time, 'can be understood not merely as sequence but also in terms of *frequency*' (2008: 36). In particular, the different frequencies at which media texts circulate are fundamental to their cultural status, their uses and the meanings they help to generate. Very low-frequency public writing, such as public monuments, have a different cultural status from the very-high frequency, or up-to-the-second, circulation of breaking news updates on Twitter. Journalism, Hartley observes, has consistently moved to higher frequencies throughout its history, from the weekly to the daily paper, from the nightly news to rolling news, and with the liveness of satellite TV now competing with Bloomberg terminals and Twitter for the fastest possible circulation of updates and information (McNair 2006). Live rolling news has been criticized as news that 'almost wants to be wrong' (Katz 1992: 9), relying as it does on the imminent update – 'each bit (as it were) self-destructing in order to make room for the next' (Doane 1990: 224). But, live news delivery is now superseded and pre-empted by news coverage that *precedes* the event, with much professional news management now relying on strategies of leaks, briefing, image management and spin (Gaber 2000), as the rebuttal of one's opponents' points is pre-empted by prebuttal of points they have not yet made.

Calling out around the world

50 Cent is a busy guy. The rapper (real name Curtis Jackson) is a recording artist, a performer, an actor. He provides voiceovers for videogames, has co-authored a novel and produces a reality TV show. He's also an

entrepreneur, who markets products as diverse as sports shoes, bottled water, scents and condoms. But, above all, 50 Cent tweets. He tweets a lot. As of September 2011, he has made more than 5200 tweets to his more than 4,900,000 followers, all of whom have received an unusual degree of insight and many of whom have shared Jackson's tweets by re-tweeting them: 'I think I'm confused now I want a black girl who can do anal like its nothing. I'm sorry I was just watching porn', for example, posted by 50 Cent on 28 August 2010, was re-tweeted by hundreds of people, as well as being satirized in YouTube reply videos, such as one featuring a sweet elderly lady reading the tweet aloud beside a Christmas tree. A UK comedian posting as @English50cent offered a simultaneous translation service on Twitter, rephrasing the rapper's tweets into standard English – so 50 Cent's original 'I'm a take my belt off and beat one of you little motherfuckers were your mama and daddy at anyway bad ass kids' becomes 'I am going to remove my trousers and attack some children'. When Twitter users re-tweet one of the rapper's pronouncements, when these are in turn re-tweeted by others, when a YouTube video is responded to in the creation of another video (Burgess and Green 2009), this illustrates one of the cultural logics of convergent media – circulation. Media texts and images are not only broadcast from the few to the many, but are circulated through networks, often with innumerable points of origin and recirculation, creating new and dispersed experiences of mediated space.

'Each of the modern media', writes James Carey, 'has increased the capacity for controlling space' (1989: 136). Carey identifies two important ways in which communication could be viewed – a transmission view and a ritual one. These were not different kinds of message or modes of communicating, but rather two broad perspectives from which communication itself could be understood – as the sending of messages across space for purposes of organization and control (transmission) or as the maintenance of community through time (ritual). From the transmission perspective, communication is 'a process whereby messages are transmitted and distributed in space for the control of distance and people' (Carey 1989: 15). This way of thinking about communication, Carey argues, is the most common and is bound up in the kinds of key words we use in talking about messages – send, receive, transmit, broadcast, even 'giving information to others' (Carey 1989: 15). The transmission view of communication grew out of a metaphor of transportation. Before the development of the electric telegraph in the mid-nineteenth century, 'communication' and 'transportation' were synonyms – the movement of meanings and thoughts were seen as no different from the movement of people or goods:

> The center of this idea of communication is the transmission of signals or messages over distance for the purpose of control. It is a view of communication that derives from one of the most ancient of human dreams: the desire to increase the speed and effect of messages as they travel in space. (Carey 1989: 15)

Much of what goes on in the study of media is rooted in the transmission perspective – analysis of persuasion, power, influence and choice. This transmission perspective, argues Carey, views communication not in all its messy diversity, but as a process by which people 'alternatively pursue power or flee anxiety' (1989: 32).

In contrast, the ritual view of communication, Carey writes, 'is directed not toward the extension of messages in space but toward the maintenance of society in time; not the act of imparting information but the representation of shared beliefs' (Carey 1989: 18). The ritual perspective links 'communication' with connected terms such as 'community', 'communion' and 'common'. Rather than sending messages across space for the purposes of control, Carey argues that to think of communication from a ritual point of view is to see it as a ceremony that draws the community together. It is to see communication as 'not the act of imparting information or influence but the creation, representation, and celebration of shared even if illusory beliefs' (Carey 1989: 43).

In the convergent media environment, Carey's two perspectives are joined by a third perspective on communication – circulation (Sumiala 2008). This perspective draws on Castells's analysis of the network society (2000) and on Latour's development of actor-network theory (2005), to identify the ways in which individuals now circulate ideas, information, meanings (and noise) through networks. Rather than the one-way transmission of messages or the shared maintenance of a community, mediated circulation is

> a number of *encounters* with different actors: new and old media, images, texts, viewers, subjects, venues, consumers, vendors, markets, experts, journalists, producers. In short, circulation in today's world is acted out in cultural and social *networks*. (Sumiala 2008: 44, original emphasis)

Sumiala analyses the circulation of images of torture captured at the Abu Ghraib prison in Baghdad in 2004. As digital photographs these were intrinsically open to copying, reproduction, manipulation; they appeared and reappeared across websites, print and broadcast media, each cross-referencing others, and were reworked into different contexts and commentaries (including as graffiti images parodying the style of Apple's then-current iPod ads). As the Abu Ghraib images pass through these cultural networks, each 'encounter' opens up different kinds of association, different possibilities for meaning, different vectors for further circulation. 'The process of circulation', Sumiala writes, 'can be described as an endless chain of associations and relationships developed in those encounters' (2008: 55). Each encounter establishes new relations between the viewing individuals and the subjects of the photos, separated from the specific spatial location of the prison, the invisible made visible. 'The communicative logic of the new media technology', Sumiala argues, 'makes it possible for us to get invited to such a media spectacle as the [Abu Ghraib] image scandal on a scale unlikely or even unimaginable for earlier generations' (2008: 54).

Media images are not the only things that flow through networks. So too do finance, technologies, ideas and people (Appadurai 1996). There are flows of money and capital, passing through the always-on global casinos of networked financial markets. There are flows of technology, including those technologies that characterize the convergent media environment, but also other consumer electronics, agricultural innovations, industrial plants, medicines, transportation. There are flows of ideas and ideologies – discourses of liberal democracy and the free market, multiple variants of environmental consciousness, ideas of sexual politics and identities, religious doctrines (Castells 2004); as Andrew Ross observes, the rapid and varied deployment of creative industries policies (discussed in Chapter 8) around the world is evidence of 'the ready globalization of ideas about governance' (2007: 38). And there are flows of people – businesspeople, tourists, students, migrants and refugees among them, on a scale unprecedented in human history. To give just one example, Urry notes that at any given moment 360,000 air travellers are in flight above the United States alone (2007: 3).

To return from Abu Ghraib to 50 Cent's Twitter feed might seem like bathos, but one reason for beginning this section with the rapper is that the development of rap music itself illustrates the complex networks of encounters between the global flows identified by Appadurai. Rap music is, on the one hand, a style that is deeply implicated in specific places (Rose 1994; Forman 2000) and on the other hand a genre that has flowed across cultural borders, being reinvented in each new territory (Mitchell 2001) in what Lipsitz has described as a 'diasporic conversation' (1994: 27). The music itself was made possible by the adoption and adaptation of a range of technologies (Rose 1994) – drum machines, samplers, synthesizers, cassettes as DIY record labels, and the reinvention of the turntable as a tool of production rather than reproduction (Shapiro 2002). The vocal delivery (itself referred to as 'flow') can be traced back to West Africa, which was the origin of the call-and-response chants, and boasting games, which had been a feature of Afro-American culture for a long time before hip-hop records appeared (Toop 1984), or to Jamaican DJs improvising rhymes over extended dub mixes of current hits to play at sound system parties (Letts 1996; Werner 1998). An early hip-hop hit like 'Planet Rock' by Afrika Bambaataa in 1982 was influenced as much by German electronic group Kraftwerk as by anything happening in the South Bronx. Flows of capital were pivotal too – the eventual commercialization of rap was given impetus by MTV, which initially did not play clips by any black artists at all, but capitulated to an ultimatum by Michael Jackson's record company CBS; by 1999 rap music had become the biggest-selling musical genre in the US. As people, money, technologies, images and ideas flow through networks the form has continually been reinvented. French rappers acknowledge African and Arabic influences, specific to France's cultural mix and history (George 1998: 202). Japanese DJ Krush played a key role in developing an abstract, instrumental strain of hip-hop. German youth from Turkish and Moroccan minority backgrounds appropriate elements of rap culture to explore questions of cultural identity and racism (Bennett 1999). Birmingham's Mike Skinner (The Streets) can create a distinctively British take on the form through his accent, word-choice and lyrical concerns ('I bashed my head hard earlier due to the brew').

In his book *A Change Is Gonna Come*, Craig Werner examines racial politics in America through the vehicle of the history of black popular music forms. According to Werner, at the heart of both popular music and popular struggles (like the sixties' Civil Rights movement), is the principle of *call-and-response*:

> An individual voice, frequently a preacher or singer, calls out in a way that asks for a response. The response can be verbal, musical, physical – anything that communicates with the leader or the rest of the group. The response can affirm, argue, redirect the dialogue, raise a new question. Any response that gains attention and elicits a response of its own becomes a new call. (Werner 1998: 11)

Culture is an ongoing public conversation, where we negotiate and piece together what Raymond Williams (1965) called the 'structure of feeling'. Werner's call-and-response metaphor gestures towards the complexity of the process in its acknowledgment that responses can come from anywhere and take things off in any direction, much as Afrika Bambaataa responded to both reggae and German electronic music. In the convergent media environment, culture circulates further and faster than before, through digital networks of connected individuals.

Conclusion

At 11.35 p.m. on 1 May 2011, US President Barack Obama delivered a live national address, broadcast simultaneously across the major US TV networks and online, announcing that US Navy Seals had killed Al-Qaida leader Osama bin Laden in a raid on his compound in Pakistan. The next day, a photograph appeared on the official Flickr stream of the White House. The image shows Obama, Hillary Clinton and eleven other senior staff. Obama looks uncharacteristically tense; Clinton clasps her hand over her mouth in anxiety. They are not looking at the camera, but at an unseen screen off to its left, where they are watching video updates of the bin Laden operation as it happens, sent from a helmet-mounted camera worn by a Navy Seal, from which video passed to a portable router on the site to the Black Hawk helicopter to satellite and on to the White House. Osama bin Laden's secret compound itself had aroused CIA suspicions because, among other reasons, it was conspicuously absent from the convergent media environment, with no phone line and no Internet connection – although, as it turned out later, the compound was on Google Maps.

As the Navy Seals were attacking the compound, and at the same moment captured in the White House photo of the Situation Room, a Pakistani software consultant called Sohaib Athar was tweeting about the unusual Sunday night in his neighbourhood: 'Helicopter hovering above Abbottabad at 1am (is a rare event)'; 'Go away helicopter – before I take out my giant swatter :-/'; and then 'A huge window shaking bang here [...] I hope its not the start of something nasty :-S.' Sohaib Athar, the world learned the next day, had inadvertently covered the raid in real time on Twitter, demonstrating that convergent media can make visible even a covert assault by US special forces on Osama bin Laden. The next day, as the world's news media descended on his Twitter feed, Athar put the novelty into perspective with another tweet from rural

Pakistan: 'I am JUST a tweeter, awake at the time of the crash. Not many twitter users in Abbottabad, these guys are more into facebook.'

In these mediated facets of this single event are illustrations of multiple ways in which convergent media make possible different experiences of mediated time – from the simultaneity of a broadcast address by a national leader to the consultation of databases; from the real-time video updates watched in the White House situation room to the customized communication flows of Twitter. Global, national and hyperlocal flows of information, meanwhile, converge in the spatial dimensions of the event, as places never intended to converge are brought together by the circulation of images through public and private, official and domestic, covert and broadcast spaces – we look at the online photograph of Barack Obama, watching his unseen screen, and we see his reaction to unknowable images made possible by a US Navy Seal establishing a wireless connection in Pakistan that relayed images through networks of military hardware and satellite, not only to the White House situation room, but further on to whichever convergent device that we ourselves use to look at the photo.

The history of communications media is a history of changing relationships with time and space. Such changes, of course, provoke a range of tensions – central to those tensions are questions of control over information flows, and with them our temporal and spatial experiences. The capacity of audiences to engage with media in the time and space of their own choosing opens up significant shifts in their relationships with much of the established media. In response to that perceived shift, those industries seek to maintain control over their media products. Such struggles of control over time and space exemplify regulatory debates in the convergent media environment, to which we turn in Chapter 8.

Regulation, Policy and Convergent Media

8

On 27 January 2011, Egypt left the Internet. In an attempt to reduce the organizational power of protesters against the Mubarak regime, the Egyptian Government ordered the country's Internet service providers to shut down all international connections to the Net. The Egyptian action was a response to an uprising in Tunisia earlier that month, which had been dubbed by some as the Twitter revolution (Zuckerman 2011), as had the events surrounding the Iranian election in 2009 (Morozov 2011). It confirmed two things – first, that governments are wary of the potential of media and communications tools; and second, and despite rhetoric to the contrary, that governments do have an ability to exercise control over the Internet (Goldsmith and Wu 2006). Even in the convergent media world, government policy does matter. However, the contrast with how governments manage longer-established media forms was stark – while the Egyptian authorities policed television by restricting the content broadcast on national TV networks, it appeared they believed their best available mechanism to control the messages circulating on the Internet was to shut the whole thing down.

Governments have always intervened in the media environment, shaping both the industries and content through a variety of policy mechanisms. As the media have converged around the Internet – a global, distributed computer network – a dramatically different regulatory environment has emerged, which provokes both threats and opportunities for those charged with ensuring the stability of their nation-states. This chapter contextualizes these policy challenges and examines some key examples. Media policy exists at the junctures of industries and cultures (Hesmondhalgh 2007). The outcomes of media policy debates affect, constrain and enable what's possible for media producers – and audiences. These debates are about writing the rules by which media audiences and media professionals can operate. Policy influences the shape of our society, our economy, our culture; it is where winners and losers are often decided; an arena where priorities are defined and articulated. Media policy is nothing less than a battle over how societies and cultures are able to engage with ideas – over who has access to the tools, who has permission to speak, and what they are allowed to say. It provides the framework for our engagement with ideas and determines the parameters of competition, discussion and debate, marking the boundaries that delimit our social and cultural possibilities. For example, countries have often used media and communications policy as cultural policy – 'to promote and sustain a symbolic notion of nationhood' (Raboy 2002: 6). And because so much of our time is taken up by our media engagement, and because our identities are so much defined through that engagement – and because there is so much money to be made in the creative industries – media policy can be a particularly bloody battleground.

The use of tools such as licensing powers, ownership restrictions and content rules suggest that media policy is 'the development in government-initiated fora of formal mechanisms for structuring media systems' (Freedman 2008: 11). But this is a limited view of media policy, which as Freedman then argues, involves a more diverse range of actors and processes. In order to develop effective media policy, governments must juggle relationships with media industries for economic outcomes – for example, nurturing the sector's viability, thus providing jobs – against a desire for particular cultural outcomes, including responsibilities to citizens who come together in various ways as media audiences. So national governments face the challenges of addressing the concerns of both media industries and audiences in a networked digital environment which now operates on a global scale and in real time. The challenge – not always met – is to speak to cultural and philosophical ideas, as well as economic ones. Media policy is, in Pearce's words, 'a site of struggle' (2000: 353).

One reason for this is that government policy is only one part of the regulatory environment. Lawrence Lessig identifies four mechanisms of constraint: 'laws, social norms, markets and "nature" (or the "architecture" of real space)' (2006: 247). For Lessig, regulation in the form of law or policy has traditionally been the domain of the nation state. But outside of government there are also unspecified social norms that may run counter to the law but are considered acceptable social behaviour. Then there is the marketplace, which defines the boundaries for socio-economic activity, and 'nature', by which Lessig refers to constraints in the form of physical limits that either exist in the natural world or are defined in a man-made one. In the context of the Internet, Lessig understands 'nature' as 'code' or technological architecture in the form of constraints designed into particular implementations of computer and communications hardware and software (see our example of the shaping of the DVD in Chapter 1).

These four realms do not exist in isolation. Each mode of regulation imposes restrictions on the others. The law constrains the allowable activities in the marketplace; nature defines the possibilities of the law; and social norms can bring about both marketplace and policy failure. Moreover, individuals are capable of conforming to a self-generated set of moral and ethical guidelines that may actually be 'anti-social' or 'anti-market' as well as 'anti-law'. To that end, the privilege of individual choice is often codified into the law as rights that citizens have in order to protect them from the unnecessary intrusions of the state, their neighbours or the marketplace. So the regulatory space is complex and intertwined, with government policy merely one part of the equation. The convergent media environment has further complicated the regulatory challenge – the 'site of struggle' is a web of overlapping sites, each contested by a number of actors on stages with developing regulatory possibilities. Where older media paradigms enabled law or markets to be dominant influences, the networked nature of the convergent media environment allows users the new capability to develop contrary social norms.

In this chapter, we consider three related ways in which policy debates are implicated in the convergent media environment. We take as our starting point a taxonomy of different types of Internet politics, proposed by David Resnick. Surveying the Internet at the end of the twentieth century, Resnick identified three broad forms of relevant politics – 'politics within the Net, politics which impacts the Net, and political uses of the Net' (1998: 55). We adapt Resnick's three distinctions to develop an analogous taxonomy of policy approaches to convergent media and distinguish between three ways of thinking about policy in the convergent media environment. The first is policy *within* the network – how activities within particular convergent media environments might be regulated or self-regulated. The second is policy *which impacts on* the network – how the technical infrastructure and social context of the network might be shaped, and how policy might enable or constrain its development. Our key example here is the 'Net neutrality' debate. And the third is policy *using* the network, which explores how the creative and communicative uses of convergent media technologies have been mobilized in policy debates. Here we consider policy discourses which focus on the inputs of media industries, as in the creative industries discourse, and on the outputs, as in shifting regimes of intellectual property. Media policy has always been a contested domain – this chapter explores how media convergence has added significant new dimensions to that contest.

Policy within the network

The early Internet provided a space that users were quick to claim as a regulation-free zone, uncontrolled by external institutions. Claiming a so-called cyberspace as their own, many rejected any role for governments or nation states. Instead, they championed a digital libertarianism that privileged individual choice and an organic and evolutionary social normalization. For example, in the 1990s, four key Internet futurists staked their claim for a libertarian future with their 'Magna Carta for the Knowledge Age'. The Internet, they wrote:

> spells the death of the central institutional paradigm of modern life, the bureaucratic organization. (Governments, including the American government, are the last great redoubt of bureaucratic power on the face of the planet, and for them the coming change will be profound and probably traumatic). (Dyson *et al.* 1994)

John Perry Barlow's early and much-cited 'Declaration of the Independence of Cyberspace', similarly, celebrated a new era of apparent liberty:

> Governments of the Industrial World, you weary giants of flesh and steel, I come from Cyberspace, the new home of Mind. On behalf of the future, I ask you of the past to leave us alone. You are not welcome among us. You have no sovereignty where we gather. (Barlow 1996)

This conception of the Internet was as a virtual community (Rheingold 1993; Turkle 1995) where groups of people with similar interests used computer bulletin boards, MUDs and MOOs, and participated in relatively small online groups that could be self-managed by internal oversight. In such spaces, a controllable quantity and quality of conversation occurred, and conflict could be mediated to reasonable outcomes. The most famous example was a virtual rape in the online community of

LambdaMOO, described in Julian Dibbell's (1993) article 'A Rape in Cyberspace', in which the perpetrator was brought to justice by members of the community itself. The contemporary incarnations of such spaces are social networks with hundreds of millions of users, such as Facebook and Myspace, but it's clear that the scale of those spaces is entirely different from the types of virtual community explored by Howard Rheingold (1993). In many ways, the network's growth and development parallels historical change in wider society. Writing in 1887, Frederic Tönnies understood a shift from *gemeinschaft* to *gesellschaft*, from community to society. He explained a change in social organization driven by the rise of the industrialized marketplace and the commercialization and commodification of the production process (Tönnies 1963: 223–31).

A similar shift might be observed in the convergent media environment as small, self-governing spaces like LambdaMoo have been joined by vast corporate enterprises like Facebook, with similar struggles for both voice and market power as have raged in other periods of historical change. As virtual spaces have become commercialized and commodified, the need for policy intervention *within* the Internet is hotly debated. Some argue that the marketplace is the best regulatory tool and that if, for example, privacy issues emerge on a social network, then users will simply move elsewhere. In a similar vein, others argue that such spaces should be self-policed, and even though the architecture of a social network might be shaped by technology providers, individuals can determine their own privacy settings, and debate standards within their own communities, pushing back or shifting providers should the services they require fail to live up to expectations. The counter-view to this suggests that the dominance of particular actors on the scale of the leading Web 2.0 firms, for instance, requires regulatory intervention.

A key example of this debate is Facebook and the vast amounts of personal information that people place on their Facebook pages. How is this information managed? Is government intervention required to rein in the possibilities of abuse? On more than one occasion, pushback from users over default privacy settings has resulted in a change in Facebook policies (boyd 2008; Grimmelmann 2010). Time and again, firms like Google (with Buzz) or Facebook (with Beacon) implement changes and then backtrack in the face of user antipathy. danah boyd of Microsoft summarizes, describing an anti-government, anti-regulation libertarian approach:

> The problem is that we in the tech industry don't like regulation. Not because we're evil but because we know that regulation tends to make

a mess of things. We like the threat of regulation and we hope that it will keep things at bay without actually requiring stupidity. So somehow, the social norm has been to push as far as possible and then pull back quickly when regulatory threats emerge. (boyd 2010b)

If we acknowledge some capacity for those in virtual spaces to self-regulate, the logical next step is that outside intervention in the form of government regulation is unnecessary. But the convergent media are now much more than just a space 'within the network'. As virtual communities have morphed into social networks, the Internet is clearly not separate from the rest of the world, but is rather an intrinsic part of everyday life, with complicated relationships to other parts of society and culture. Contemporary virtual communities do not exist in isolation. The networks are too large and diverse, and the speed at which information flows is too rapid to maintain a discrete, isolated space. In that context, the anti-regulation manifestos of the 1990s exhibit a striking naivety. Indeed, we would argue that the idea of constraining activity 'within the network' is no longer possible and the romantic notions of the Internet as an ungovernable frontier can't be sustained as the convergent media environment implicates the network in all of our information activities – which means in just about everything.

Policies which impact on the network

Because the network is clearly central, policies *about* the network – with respect to access or broadband speeds, for example – will shape the affordances of the convergent media environment. For example, there is continuing debate about how the technical networks which carry our information should be built and regulated, with clear parallels to policy debates in the broadcast environment over spectrum allocations which shape analogue network usage. In each case, governments must take into account a range of contending perspectives, including those of established media and communications industries, newer technology companies, and users. For example, the Australian Government sees the building of such networks as key economic infrastructure development and is directly funding the construction of a national broadband network, a policy approach that remains contested.

Where such networks are owned and controlled by private corporations, the policy contests shift to how those networks can be used – a key example is the idea of Net neutrality. This is the principle that Internet service providers should treat all data in the same way and should not be permitted to privilege particular content with faster transfer speeds. For example, Net neutrality would be undermined should a service provider allow a video file sent by Disney to move more quickly through the network than a video file sent from your house.

Former Google CEO Eric Schmidt describes the issue as follows:

> Today the Internet is an information highway where anybody – no matter how large or small, how traditional or unconventional – has equal access. But the phone and cable monopolies, who control almost all Internet access, want the power to choose who gets access to high-speed lanes and whose content gets seen first and fastest. They want to build a two-tiered system and block the on-ramps for those who can't pay. (Schmidt 2006)

Or as Tim Wu puts it, 'net neutrality is what prevents the telephone and cable industry from killing Google, Amazon, Wikipedia, blogs, or anything else that might incur their displeasure' (2010: 286). Concerns over Net neutrality reflect the shift from broadcast to broadband. With spectrum scarcity no longer a factor in limiting information flows, the debate has moved to how bandwidth should best be managed. Tim Berners-Lee argues that there are real threats to the World Wide Web as it has been understood until now:

> The Web as we know it, however, is being threatened in different ways. Some of its most successful inhabitants have begun to chip away at its principles. Large social-networking sites are walling off information posted by their users from the rest of the Web. Wireless Internet providers are being tempted to slow traffic to sites with which they have not made deals. (Berners-Lee 2010)

Some argue that mandating Net neutrality would hamper Internet service providers' abilities to ease congestion, and maximize profits, leading to fewer investment incentives (Yoo 2006; Davidson and Swanson 2010). But others (Lemley and Lessig 2004; Herman 2009) claim that Net neutrality provides a stable and predictable platform for innovation, not subject to the whims of individual providers.

Tim Wu argues that Net neutrality principles are at 'the core of the Internet's design' (Wu 2010: 267) and contends that the desires of large media corporations to tame the Internet have consistently butted against the reality that the architecture of the network privileges user choice over provider control. 'In the same spirit as the end-to-end principle', he writes, 'the neutrality principle holds that the big decisions concerning how to use the medium are best left to the "ends" of the network, not the carriers of information' (Wu 2010: 202).

Wu cites the failed 2000 Time Warner/AOL merger as an example of corporate America misunderstanding the workings of the Internet, and underestimating the difficulty of corralling audiences towards particular content. However, he also concedes that overturning Net neutrality can succeed and uses the example of mainland China 'when it drove an exasperated Google out of its sovereign territory by demanding exclusive control over what Google let users find' (2010: 267). The clear implication is that while Net neutrality might originally have been a result of network architecture, its continuation requires appropriate government policy. Indeed, some governments have proposed taking action to ensure that Net neutrality remains. In the USA, the Federal Communications Commission signified its intent to codify Net neutrality (Genachowski 2009), and at the time of writing was in the process of negotiating a regulatory stance that would prohibit service providers from discriminating against particular content (Tessler 2010).

Again, the role of government is contested. Many technical standards have developed, not through national government mandate, but through a combination of market forces and collaboration through larger technical bodies such as the Moving Picture Experts Group or non-governmental organizations such as the International Telecommunications Union. The usefulness of this regulatory approach is mixed. Indeed, Lawrence Lessig suggests that the development of technology is implicitly in the hands of the market and shaped by corporations where the engineers and scientists that develop hardware and software work. So the profit motive is central to technological development. Lessig goes on to argue that letting technology be the determining regulating factor is allowing, by default, corporations to determine the shape of the network:

> We are entering a very different world where code is written within companies; where standards are the product of competition; where standards tied to a dominant standard have advantages. We are entering a world where code is corporate in a commercial sense, and leaving a world where code was corporate in a very different sense. (Lessig 2000: 207)

Just as the modern shopping centre and the private toll-road represent the privatization of traditionally public spaces, so does the proprietary code of operating systems, networking protocols and online environments. In these realms, whether built in bricks and mortar, asphalt or in computer code, the power of citizens is reduced to consumer choice, and regulation becomes the sole domain of capital at the expense of democratic institutions. The ongoing Net neutrality debate exemplifies this tension.

Policies for using the network

In this section, we turn to policies that align closely with traditional media and cultural policy, although focused on the different affordances of convergent media technology. Because of their perceived influence, governments have always intervened in the electronic media. Historically, the shape of national broadcasting, both radio and television, was largely determined by policy choices. So television in the UK, for example, was built around the BBC for decades, a strong public service broadcaster exemplifying a policy concern for public good and a model of social responsibility. Conversely, the US television industry was largely built on a policy of allowing the market to determine appropriate outcomes, with government intervention only in place to address market failure. In both cases, policy implementation was relatively straightforward because government licences are required to access the limited allocation of electromagnetic spectrum essential for terrestrial broadcasting. In the early electronic media environment, governments imposed strict restrictions on broadcast licence conditions and relatively onerous content censorship. For example, in Australia 'it was determined that broadcasters be fit and proper persons. Particularly, they were not to favour one political view over others and were to provide equitable access to all political parties' (Albon and Papandrea 1998: 4).

The 1980s saw the emergence of a wider range of media outlets, as cable and satellite systems challenged terrestrial broadcasting, and the costs of print production decreased dramatically with the introduction of digital computers. This marked shift away from scarcity saw governments turn to the marketplace with a move towards industry self-regulation. Coinciding with a broader political shift towards less government intervention (Castells 2004), media policies were largely determined in the context of a media marketplace inhabited by media proprietors. Policy frameworks developed to allow media industries to largely self-regulate, subject to a code of practice overseen by an industry regulator. In Australia, the Broadcasting Services Act of 1992 exemplified this approach (Hawke 1995: 44), while in the UK context, some have argued that the 2003 establishment of Ofcom – the Office of Communications, a statutory body with responsibility for convergent media, overseeing broadcasting and telecommunications – represented a move away from the public service function of allocating broadcast spectrum towards a regime controlled by market power (Smith 2006). As well as Ofcom's emphasis on discourses of 'market' and 'competition', Doyle and Vick (2005) point to its introduction of the awkward term 'citizen-consumers' to define those in whose interests it operates – a phrase which also occurs in Hartley's important 2005 definition of 'creative industries', discussed in more detail below.

The policy demands of the current convergent media environment mark the latest phase in the evolution of policy approaches and reflect the realities of further decentralization of both media production and consumption (Cunningham and Turner 2010: 4). Established institutions remain a significant part of the environment, but the number of players has increased. At the same time, scarcity is no longer a constraint and the convergence of media around the global network of the Internet has switched the policy focus to that network of networks. Stuart Cunningham observes that government interventions distinguish between *input* (production subsidy) and *output* (regulation) (Cunningham 1992: 25). The idea of *inputs* can be extended to include those broader concerns over the shape and nature of the media industries – with questions of ownership, access and of the dimensions of a public media sector. Such policy might be considered *indirect*, working on the assumption that by structuring media industries appropriately, government policy can influence the shape of media content and shift the national culture in a particular direction. Regulation of *outputs* is *content* policy that speaks more directly to cultural concerns. For example, national classification laws in many parts of the world require films and videogames to be classified and restrict their distribution according to that classification. The converged media environment is vastly different from Cunningham's portrait of 1992, but while the targets of input and output regulation may differ – and have broadened to include a more diverse range of actors – the general approaches remain. In policy terms, governments still seek to exercise control over the usage of the network by either creating the incentives for particular inputs, or seeking to control specific media outputs.

Controlling inputs

The most direct way to seek control over inputs is to provide state funding for particular projects, and the media sector has a long history of public service broadcasting, designed to ensure that public-good values were maintained in an expensive and highly specialized media market-place. In the 1920s, two key types of media institution developed in the US and the UK: commercial networks in the US, and public service broadcasting (PSB) in the UK. Both offered centralized transmission to individual households: in the US model by advertising-funded commercial stations and networks; in the British model by state-funded networks with a public service brief to, as the BBC's charter put it, 'inform, educate and entertain'. These became the templates for the development of radio, and then television, broadcasting in other contexts, including the ABC in Australia.

In a broadcast environment characterized by few-to-many communication, the importance of a public service model is easy to argue. The costs of producing and distributing media through broadcasting require significant investment, and the imagined power of the broadcast media was immense. The easiest way for governments to ensure that there remains a public service element to this media industry is to facilitate its funding – as in the licence fee in the UK or through direct public funding as in Australia – and to then ensure that the publicly funded network is transparently held accountable to a charter, which provides a mechanism to counter the market's failure to provide a diverse and inclusive range of universally accessible media products.

But the convergent media environment has provoked new questions about the roles of public service broadcasters. 'Increasing numbers now buy broadcast entertainment and mobile telephony as a matter of course', points out Philip Schlesinger, 'making unquestioned future public support for the [BBC] licence fee more and more doubtful' (2008: 46–7). The UK Communications Act of 2003 and its establishment of Ofcom places the PSB ethos of public service firmly within market discourses of demand and competition. Seen from within this perspective, in which a public service like the BBC is viewed in terms of market competition, some, such as News Corporation's James Murdoch, claim that taxpayer subsidy gives the BBC an unfair advantage:

> The all-media world offers great opportunities for our society. We could take the approach of trust and freedom and apply it through the whole of the media, broadcasting included. But we are doing the opposite. We are using the interconnectedness of the media as a way of opening the door to the expansion of control. This is already happening. There is a land-grab, pure and simple, going on – and in the interests of a free society it should be sternly resisted. The land grab

is spear-headed by the BBC. The scale and scope of its current activities and future ambitions is chilling. (Murdoch 2009)

Others suggest that while public service media is no longer required to fill gaps unaddressed by commercial operators, it still has a role to play; for example in innovation (Cunningham 2009). Terry Flew argues that:

> The basis for supporting public service media is not simply that of market failure in a limited channel environment, but the capacity to promote innovative, engaging and inclusive Australian information and entertainment content in a world of seemingly limitless media choice. (Flew 2009)

The innovation demonstrated by examples such as the BBC's iPlayer software, and its use of user-generated content as discussed in Chapter 2, suggests some basis for Flew's argument, but that same innovation also supports Murdoch's accusations. However, the government funding of public service media does ensure that innovation is not the sole domain of corporate interests, and that the development of new media technologies and forms retains a public good dimension.

As well as controlling inputs by direct funding, governments have long sought restrictions on media ownership. This key media policy has revolved around ensuring that the scarce resources of broadcasting and print were fairly distributed, and that no single entity controlled too much of what many considered an omnipotent media. One approach to limiting that perceived power has been to restrict the number and type of media outlets that a single corporation should own. However, as discussed in Chapter 2, with the bulk of global media outlets still controlled by a handful of corporate entities, that approach to regulating media ownership has largely failed (Bagdikian 2004; Castells 2009). Australia represents an exceptional case here, with News Corporation owning more than two-thirds of newspapers, as well as having significant stakes in broadcasting and other media.

Media ownership is as important as ever in the convergent media environment. The key global communication firms are both more concentrated (in their range of owners) and more extended (in their global reach) than ever before. And while the Internet may provide access to a much greater range of media providers, many users still obtain their media from a handful of sources. One 2010 Pew report found that, for American users: 'One in five online news users (21%) say they routinely rely on just one website for their news and information, and another

57% rely on between two and five websites' (Project for Excellence in Journalism 2010). Hindman (2009) has shown the extent to which the blogosphere is dominated by a small number of high-profile bloggers. What's more, a small number of aggregators have emerged which threaten to dominate web access. August 2010 figures from comScore show that in the US, people spent 9.9 per cent of their web time using Facebook, another 9.6 per cent on Google sites, and 9.1 per cent on Yahoo! sites (MSNBC 2010). And research by Hewlett Packard's Social Computing Research Group has found that 72 per cent of re-tweets on Twitter come from a small number of mainstream media outlets like @cnnbrk or @nytimes (Asur *et al.* 2011).

It's apparent that encouraging users to engage with a diverse range of media sources remains a challenge, but unclear whether government intervention in media ownership is the most useful tool to ensure diversity. To date, government responses suggest that ownership still matters, and regulators have been amending ownership policies to better suit the new environment. For example, US Federal Communications Commission (FCC) reviews of cross-media ownership in the USA resulted in the development of a Diversity Index, which 'measures the availability of various media outlets and assigns a weight to each based on its relative use by consumers as a source of news and information. It investigated the contribution of cable television, magazines, the Internet and other sources as well as outlets already covered by cross-media restrictions' (Given 2008: 264).

Another approach has focused on shaping the environment within the broader realm within which information products, including the media, are created. Since the mid-1990s, questions of creativity and intellectual property have become increasingly central to questions of public policy. Such questions converge in the 'creative industries' policy discourse that attempts to articulate the role of media and related industries in an increasingly global and digital context (Hartley 2005; Flew and Cunningham 2010). While this discourse has its pre-histories, like everything else in this book, most commentators take its basic starting point to be the definition offered by the UK government Department for Culture, Media and Sport (DCMS) in two 'mapping documents' published in 1998 and 2001. The idea of creative industries has since developed rapidly and in different ways in different parts of the world (Ross 2007; Hartley 2009). Flew and Cunningham (2010) identify adoptions and adaptations of the concept in China, Singapore, Hong Kong, Taiwan, Korea, the US and Australia, as well as at the supra-national level by both the European Union and UNESCO.

In the DCMS definition, the creative industries are: 'those industries which have their origin in individual creativity, skill and talent and which have a potential for wealth and job creation through the generation and exploitation of intellectual property' (DCMS 2001: 5). Those industries are then listed as: advertising, architecture, the art and antiques market, crafts, design, designer fashion, film and video, interactive leisure software, music, the performing arts, publishing, software and computer services, television and radio.

Such list-based definitions can often appear a bit *ad hoc*, and there are a number of other sectors which could be included. Why not academic research, for example? As Lovink and Rossiter point out, publicly funded research is increasingly capitalized by multinational publishers to whom academics assign their copyrights:

> The creative industries meme dominates research funding calls in the humanities, after all. But don't expect to read the results too easily – they come at a cost as well, with the vast majority of academics happily transferring their results of state-funded research into commercial publishing houses that charge crazy fees for access to their journals. (2007: 15)

But the significance of the discourse is not in the listing of relevant industries, but rather in the attempt to re-think existing industries as well as emerging ones, in a rapidly changing context, in which the various forms of media convergence discussed throughout this book are crucial.

Much of the considerable controversy surrounding the concept derives from the tensions between the seemingly incommensurable terms 'creative' and 'industries'. Notice how the DCMS definition is in two parts. The first part emphasizes creativity, art and artisanship. The second part emphasizes economic returns – wealth creation, job creation – and highlights the exploitation of intellectual property for economic reasons. In this, it marked a clear move away from the idea that the state should support sectors such as film production or broadcasting for cultural reasons. It's also worth noting that this definition defines those creative industries in terms of their input – creativity. This is distinct from the labelling of other industries, which is more often in terms of their outputs – the car industry, for instance, produces cars. The creative industries, in contrast, produce something else – they produce intellectual property.

What *is* creativity anyway? Richard Florida observes that creativity is not necessarily the same thing as intelligence, that it can be understood as being able to synthesize, and that it involves taking risks. This means it can be, as Florida puts it, 'downright *subversive*, since it disrupts existing patterns of thought and life' (2002: 31). But not all approaches see a subversive outcome. David Gauntlett suggests that the key elements of creativity can be defined like this:

> Everyday creativity refers to a process that brings together at least one active human mind, and the material or digital world, in the activity of making something which is novel in that context, and is a process which evokes a feeling of joy. (2011: 76)

Gauntlett's emphasis here – *'evokes a feeling of joy'* – is on how a piece of creativity is experienced by its maker as well as by anyone else with whom it is shared. It's an approach to creativity as something we experience or feel as much as something we recognize when we see it on the walls of an art gallery. John Howkins argues that for an idea to count as "creative" it must be personal, original, meaningful and useful (2005: 118–19). None of those things alone necessarily has any economic value – that gets added later. Howkins's definition includes the affective dimension of Gauntlett's (*personal, meaningful*) but makes the link towards the commercialization of creativity (*useful*). Creative industries, says Howkins, are those where the main kind of work that takes place is brain work, and where the outcome is intellectual property.

John Hartley offers a distinct approach to 'creative industries' which focuses on processes of convergence:

> The idea of the creative industries seeks to describe the conceptual and practical *convergence* of (1) the creative arts (individual talent) with (2) Cultural Industries (mass scale), in the context of (3) new media technologies (ICTs) within (4) a new knowledge economy, for the use of (5) newly-interactive citizen-consumers. (2005: 5, emphasis and numbering added)

A key example of how Hartley's five-part definition of "creative industries" works in practice is Charles Leadbeater's discussion of Delia Smith's cookery books and chocolate-cake recipes. These combine (1) the packaging of individual creativity (her recipes) by (2) cultural industries (both book publishers and TV broadcasters, in this example), to be (3 and 4) distributed and marketed globally by major commercial operations, using sophisticated media campaigns (including her TV programmes, which can be seen as advertisements for the books). And then finally (5) the viewers and readers of these books and TV programmes, whose creative participation is required to turn the cake recipe into an actual cake (Leadbeater 1999; Hartley 2005: 110–11).

But this linkage of creativity and property is the key reason why the idea of creative industries has proved controversial. The very term, as Lovink and Rossiter observe, 'provokes an interesting range of human responses, from curiosity to outrage and disgust' (2007: 11). For some critics, the concept of creative industries leads to 'the reduction of creativity to the formal indifference of the market' (Neilson and Rossiter 2005). If intellectual property is the output of those industries based on creativity, then does this lead us towards a view in which only those ideas which can be commodified as intellectual property will count as creative? Critics often connect creative industries discourses with the equally broad and contested discourse of neoliberalism (Freedman 2008; Couldry 2010a). Hesmondhalgh has argued that it reframes policy away from conceptions of public service or the public good and instead 'helps to legitimate the expanding role of the corporate cultural industries in the symbolic life of modern societies' (2005: 105).

As well, the creative industries discourse could concede too much to increasingly harsh copyright regimes, thus disadvantaging creative workers whose job security is increasingly precarious (Terranova 2004; Neilson and Rossiter 2005; Deuze 2007a; Ross 2007). Similarly, given that in practice, it often relies upon the participation of creative audiences – including 'pro-ams' (Leadbeater and Miller 2004) – a major question is the extent to which their creations are to be accommodated within regimes of intellectual property (Lessig 2004; Wark 2004; Deuze 2007b).

Controlling outputs

In April 2009, Hollywood's upcoming summer blockbuster *X-Men Origins: Wolverine* was leaked online. The film was due for release the following month, but several different unfinished versions of the movie were shared online through BitTorrent. Fox, the studio behind the film, were to claim there had been 4.5 million illicit downloads of the work-in-progress within a month of the leak (*Variety*, 6 May 2009). The *Wolverine* example is just one of many where users have bypassed traditional distribution channels to obtain media products through online sharing. Production companies are largely as one in condemning the practice and have managed to convince regulatory bodies that these acts of 'piracy' must be stamped out – the main argument being that they threaten the viability of the media industry in question. But for users, the situation is more nuanced. Beginning with digital music and Napster in the late 1990s, users have demonstrated a desire to download television shows, movies and books, as well as music. Motivations vary. Often BitTorrent is used to bypass geographical limitations imposed by content corporations; other times the lure of the free might prove to be too strong. In the *Wolverine* case, the leaked movie was not even finished. Viewers of these working prints watched entire scenes composed of unrendered wireframe computer graphics, often with missing audio. It may be that some fans were motivated to download such prints by a desire to see the work-in-progress, to peek behind the finished product and witness the secrets of its construction. But each of these motivations complicates the regulatory environment and exemplifies new policy tensions.

The world's first copyright legislation, the Statute of Anne 1710, was devised to balance the competing interests of authors and the wider desires of society. The law secured literary property to authors in order to provide an incentive to create works that would inform and advance society – hence the statute's title, 'An Act For The Encouragement of Learning'. Since then, copyright has been massaged by various interests, shaped by technological change and extended in both scope and duration (Lessig 2004; McLeod 2005). As with previous technological developments, the digitization of material adds new dimensions to the copyright debate and further alters the balance of rights between intellectual property owners and users. Whereas the difficulty of copying materials has traditionally provided a measure of protection for copyright owners, digital technologies have not only made it easy to duplicate material, they have allowed this duplication to occur without degradation. Moreover, the network allows unprecedented distribution of material, legitimately copied or otherwise.

For some (Kelly 2008; Anderson 2009), this has fundamentally altered the marketplace for traditional media products. In the late twentieth century, their value was linked to their relative scarcity. This scarcity was in some cases due to the need to produce a physical object like a book, a vinyl record or a videotape, or in other cases because distribution mechanisms were limited, as in the case of radio spectrum for broadcasting. Scarcity is not a natural part of the convergent media environment, but must be manufactured artificially to preserve its value. In this new 'nature', many users have become accustomed to taking advantage of the possible, as opposed to the legal. They have displayed contempt for heavy-handed attempts to enforce notions of intellectual property rights that are perceived as unnatural, and in this altered context, the gap between legally required behaviour and actual practice has widened considerably.

Governments, for the most part, have responded on behalf of copyright owners by altering copyright laws to support existing industries whose profitability has depended on scarcity. For example, the UK Digital Economy Act 2010, the American Digital Millennium Copyright Act 1998 and the Australian Copyright Amendment (Digital Agenda) Act 2000 have all represented coordinated responses to the copyright challenges allowed by digitization. But governments have also acknowledged the realities of changes in usage, for example, by allowing a modicum of time- and format-shifting for personal use, enshrining in law some types of practices in common use. The scale of illegal downloading activity illustrates the complexity of regulating behaviour. But overt downloading of copyright material is only one consequence of the new nature – file sharing is merely the most visible example of a cultural shift from centralized distribution overseen by gatekeepers to networked distribution driven by creative audiences.

The kinds of remixed convergent texts discussed in Chapters 4 and 5, and their subsequent distribution through networks such as YouTube and Vimeo, demonstrate how much the new nature has allowed a reformation of the media landscape. Such repurposing of copyright material falls foul of the copyright acts of many countries, but, since 1740 the law has recognized exceptions to copyright that permit copying under certain circumstances. In the USA, much of this usage would normally fall under the Fair Use Act (Kaplan 1967; Samuels 2000; Aufderheide 2011). However, not all countries have Fair Use doctrines. For example, Australia, like other common law countries such as Great Britain and Canada, provides statutory exceptions to claims of copyright infringement by virtue of a fair dealing defence. The provisions for fair dealing are extremely precise and apply only in situations where the use is for research or study, criticism or review, or reporting news. The idea of Fair Use exemplifies the contradiction between the new nature and both legal and market-based regulation. The Internet is a global distribution mechanism, essentially allowing the free movement of bits wherever there is a network connection. But the law remains stubbornly national, and varies from country to country. What's more, markets are also based within particular regions, and the sale of copyright material is still dependent on geographical restrictions.

Indeed, geography has long been a key mechanism for exploiting the scarce commodity value of media products. Dividing the world into sales territories is common practice in media industries. The most visible example in recent times has been the DVD marketplace, where the planet is cut up into geographical regions, somewhat arbitrarily for sales and marketing purposes. For example, Australia, a predominantly English-speaking country, shares Region 4 with predominantly Spanish and Portuguese-speaking South and Central America. Another example is book publishing, which has territories divided around language commonalities. In the English-speaking world, the most powerful publishing industries, in the US and the UK respectively, have divided the book market between them. US and UK publishers seek exclusive territories from which the other's competing editions of the same book are excluded. So for example, in this cosy arrangement, the US publishers of Dan Brown's latest novel cannot sell their edition into the UK market, and vice versa. Traditionally, the UK market has covered the old Commonwealth, Ireland and South Africa, while the US market is essentially the USA. As a result, there is a lucrative trade in territorial rights as publishers in different territories compete for the right to sell titles.

Governments have not always warmed to these trade arrangements, and over the latter half of the twentieth century, several countries legislated against such restrictions. India became an open market for publishing in the late 1960s, Singapore in the mid-1980s and New Zealand in 1998. In 1996, Australia required local publication within 30 days of first publication, or else booksellers were free to sell overseas editions. Mainland Europe is a single open market, and the 1992 EC single market principle is in continual conflict with the practice in which the UK is an exclusive territory and the rest of Europe an open market (Clark and Phillips 2008: 62). Of course, the Internet has shifted the debate over such territorial rights. For example, the online purchase of physical books through Amazon and its competitors has theoretically meant the end of territorial restrictions for book lovers, with buyers taking a global sweep of the Net in search of both the best price and availability. A further intrusion is the potential of ebooks – a physical title might take a week or so to arrive, but a digital book can be downloaded instantly. The same is true for music, television and video material – there are any number of international sources from which a consumer can, in principle, source their media.

But territorial rights are still strongly maintained and supported. Indeed, rather than being weakened, territory has become enshrined in the new technologies, and enforcing territorial rights is easier with electronic editions than physical products. Rather than relying on legislative restrictions, the shift from objects to digital files has fundamentally shifted the mechanism for regulation. It is now embedded into the new digital objects, which makes enforcement far more rigid. Apple's iTunes music store is a perfect example. Before digital downloads, territorial markets in the recorded music space were becoming less rigid – CDs bought over the Internet could be shipped globally with little fear that territorial copyright restrictions would be enforced, as most countries do not have sufficient customs resources to police individual purchases. But an entirely new regime emerged with digital downloads. iTunes stores are territorial and encumbered with mechanisms that prevent the actual purchase of music from outside the territorial zones. By restricting access to credit card holders with addresses in the appropriate territory, the digital version of the music and video store now has territorial rights *embedded* in the technology of purchase and distribution. Other services exercise similar restrictions, with some – including Hulu, the BBC iPlayer, the ABC iView, and many websites of particular US TV programmes or networks, such as those on Comedy Central – checking that the IP address of the computer attempting to access the material is in the appropriate territory before downloading or streaming is permitted. If all versions of these media stores were identical, then there would be fewer issues. However, the uneven distribution of territorial rights results in each country's stores having different content available at any particular time – made all the more frustrating because users can often visit alternative stores, where they can browse but not buy.

There are, of course, ways to bypass those restrictions, and some people will always be able to subvert such mechanisms – but existing laws suggest that such actions are not legal since they contravene the rights of local publishers, whereas the analogous purchase of a physical good like a CD or book from an overseas retailer does not. These inconsistencies suggest that copyright laws have some way to develop to address the obvious tensions that the convergent media environment provokes.

The Great Firewall

On 20 December 2010, Fang Binxing opened a Sina microblogging account. Within hours, his first few postings had attracted thousands of abusive comments and the response was such that it wasn't long before all of his original posts and comments had been taken down (*China Digital Times*, 21 December 2010). As well as being the President of Beijing University of Posts and Telecommunications, Fang was known as the 'father of the Great Firewall', the Chinese Government's attempt to censor the Internet. His online hounding exemplifies the contested nature of content regulation in the new media environment. Regulating output also involves government control over material for reasons of culture or politics, rather than economics. Whether censorship is in place to protect vulnerable members of society from potentially distressing material, or to restrict political speech, it has been a mainstay of media policy.

Early Internet advocates were convinced that the technical nature of the Internet prevented government interference, and that any attempt to restrict access to particular material was doomed to failure. But the Great Firewall of China demonstrates that effective censorship of the Net, denying access to the majority of users, is a distinct possibility. The Chinese system deploys an assemblage of technical approaches to filtering Internet access within China (Wang and Faris 2008), including the blocking of specific IP addresses with Domain Name System (DNS) tampering, and disconnection triggered by a list of banned keywords. IP address blocking simply blocks particular content from particular Internet addresses – YouTube, for example has been banned in China since March 2009, and Facebook is also inaccessible at the time of writing. The current status of websites is easily tested. Typing a URL into the search box at <http://www.greatfirewallofchina.org> routes the request through Chinese proxy servers and provides instant notification of blocking. DNS tampering is more subtle and redirects website requests to another location. For example, google.com has at times been redirected to google.cn. And finally, when a router in the system detects a banned keyword, the Great Firewall can send a reset instruction which simply breaks the connection, resulting in a 'server unexpectedly dropped the connection' error message.

The Great Firewall is just one part of the Chinese effort to regulate the Internet. All Internet service and content providers fall under the jurisdiction of the Ministry of Information Industry, a super-ministry which covers all aspects of computer-based communications. Some of the regulatory impositions include the requirement for ISPs and Internet cafés to keep records of user identities and session logs for up to 60 days. As well, ISPs are held responsible for the content they host, so they often deploy their own filters – both technical and human – to ensure compliance. (Wang and Faris 2008: 107). Moreover, all domestic websites must be registered, and there is constant monitoring of chat rooms, often with active participants who direct discussion as per government instruction (Zhou 2008).

Google's forays into the Chinese search engine marketplace are illustrative. Google launched Google.cn in 2006, with search results subject to government censorship. In response to criticism that it was doing the bidding of an oppressive regime, Google argued that it would be

more damaging to have no presence in China – and made the commitment that, just as with other localized Google pages, the Google.
cn page would have a link to the uncensored Google.com. Steven Levy
describes the process:

> A demand would come from a government ministry to take down
> TEN items; Google would typically take down seven and hope that
> the compromise resolved the matter. Sometimes after a few days or
> weeks Google would quietly restore links it had censored. Every five
> months Google's policy review committee in China would meet to
> make sure it was filtering the minimum it could possibly get away
> with. It was, as Google China engineering director Jun Liu put it,
> "trench warfare," but he believed that Google's continuing prob-
> lems were proof that it was indeed moving the democracy needle in
> China. (Levy 2011: 303)

However, as the Chinese Government's censorship demands increased,
Google found itself increasingly conflicted. The turning point came when
the company discovered that a number of Gmail accounts had been
hacked – not only accounts used by its engineers, but also those used
by Chinese activists – and the evidence suggested that the attacks were
linked to the Chinese Government. In January 2010, Google ended its
China censorship experiment.

Of course, Chinese Government control over the Internet is far from
absolute – individual users have found ways to subvert the Great Firewall
(Xia 2008) and the government itself appears to be softening its stance
in certain instances. For example, the burgeoning Chinese middle class
is taking to bloggers like Han-Han (Jacobs 2010) and engaging with
websites such as Qidian, a DIY literary space that encourages creativity.
As Duncan Hewitt writes:

> in October 2009 a group of intellectuals released an open letter call-
> ing for greater protection of freedom of speech online. A commen-
> tary in the official China Daily also argued that "oppression of online
> opinions brings about nothing but humiliation to government . . .
> The conventional and arbitrary way of handling online information
> and public opinion does not work [any more]". (Hewitt 2009)

Attempts to censor the network are not solely the domain of totali-
tarian regimes, or of governments on the edge of collapse. In 1999,
the Australian Government introduced a complaints-based system for

regulating online content – censorship in the name of child protection. Using the existing guidelines for regulating film and video, the policy empowered the Australian Broadcasting Authority (since reconstituted as the Australian Communications and Media Authority or ACMA) to issue takedown notices for material deemed prohibited. In 2007, the Federal Government proposed an expansion of this scheme and introduced legislation that would mandate ISP-level filtering of all Internet content. Opposition to the filter – which, at the time of writing, was still the subject of robust debate – is based on a range of arguments from the technical (it will slow down the Internet) to the cultural (Electronic Frontiers Australia 2006). The Federal Government has maintained that the Internet must be regulated like any other media form, while its opponents have argued that such an approach restricts its potential uses.

Conclusion

New technologies have always been demonized as causes of social disruption (Standage 2006), but they are better thought of as amplifiers of existing social and cultural concerns. New media do not create new issues, but rather exacerbate and accelerate existing ones. In creating different social spaces with reconfigured notions of time, speed, space and access, convergent media make the invisible visible. Previously unseen, and often marginal, cultural activity can now be easily found. So debates over Internet censorship are debates over censorship more generally – they are arguments about who has the right to determine what is accessible in the media, and what is not. This is reflected in arguments over film, television and phone sex lines (for example, Coleman 2000; Mills 2001; Vnuk 2003) but is also apparent in the idea that cultural policy debates are, of course, political. These debates are located in contests over control, and the powerful often use the tools of restriction to rein in cultural manifestations which threaten existing hierarchies (Coleman 2000: 15). Outside of those political contests and despite obvious limitations, the Great Firewall of China, the proposed Australian Internet filter, and the Egyptian solution of just switching the whole thing off, all debunk the myth that the Internet is an uncontrollable frontier. Notwithstanding the extent to which policy approaches generally fail to take into account the complexity of media usage, governments *can* exercise control over the network and in many instances it can result in effective censorship – most Chinese Internet users, for example, see only what their government permits.

Media policy has always been a complicated and disputed realm, as governments have struggled to balance competing demands in a complex regulatory space. Convergent media technologies have exacerbated that complexity, and debates over the contested roles of policy, social norms, markets and technological architecture are a key part of current regulatory tensions. Here too, there is a prehistory:

> History shows a typical progression of information technologies: from somebody's hobby to somebody's industry; from jury-rigged contraption to slick production marvel; from a freely accessible channel to one strictly controlled by a single corporation or cartel – from open to closed system. (Wu 2010: 6; see also Meikle 2002 on 'Version 1.0 and Version 2.0' of the Internet)

In the contemporary convergent environment, an unprecedented number of actors are staking claims for the legitimacy of one regulatory mechanism over another. Whereas older media forms allowed more substantive government intervention over both inputs and outputs, policy approaches in the convergent media environment need to acknowledge a wider range of stakeholders and a developing role for policy relative to other regulatory mechanisms.

Conclusion

In January 2011, the Australian state of Queensland experienced catastrophic flooding – hundreds of millimetres of rain, overflowing catchments, rising rivers, flash flooding and, tragically, injury and death. The disaster was widespread, with floodwaters covering an area larger than France and Germany combined, but the nation's attention was focused first on a torrential flash flood in Toowoomba, and then on the state's capital, Brisbane, being consumed by its river. Floods happen only too often in Australia, and the 2011 floods were constantly compared to the last 'big one' in Brisbane in 1974. The two floods may have had comparable physical impacts, but the media coverage of each was very different. In the intervening 37 years, the media environment had been transformed.

In 1974, colour television had not yet arrived in Australia, and both broadcast and press coverage were constrained by limited communications – newspaper reports, tied to print production schedules, were well behind events, while broadcast journalists had to cope without lightweight video cameras, satellite uplinks or mobile phones. Transmitting images and text was slow, cumbersome and expensive – email was not yet available, and even fax machines were not yet in common use. For audiences, there was no subscription television service, whether cable or satellite, there were fewer radio and television channels, and many areas relied entirely on the ABC, the nation's public service broadcaster, for any coverage at all.

The 2011 floods took place in a very different media environment. The ABC's 24-hour news channel and its competitor Sky News were able to provide constant rolling updates and hourly media briefings from emergency coordinators and local politicians. Other major broadcasting networks replaced regular programming with continuing updates, and fundraising appeals for flood victims. Rather than being constrained by print publishing schedules or network news cycles, the convergent environment allowed media organizations to publish material as it became available – critical in situations that change as rapidly as natural disasters. Creative audiences were also able to provide much broader coverage – local and national news websites featured gallery after gallery of photos and video that captured local flood occurrences, and this material also made up much of the footage broadcast on both terrestrial and cable networks. Many of the most indelible images – such as dramatic video of cars being washed away on Toowoomba streets – were captured by non-professionals with convergent media devices. The ABC produced a Flood Crisis Map that drew together crowdsourced emergency information, mashing up user reports with a Google map of Queensland.

The websites of established news organizations provided a particular framing for user-generated content, but such material was also being uploaded to Twitter, Facebook, Flickr, YouTube and Vimeo. One Brisbanite created a live video stream of the view from his balcony, allowing people to watch the inexorable rise of the river in real time. One YouTube user's video of Toowoomba in flood received over five million views. Others drew on material accessed from the National Library or local archives to create animated simulations of the effects on Brisbane of a predicted 5.5m water level or to publish comparative maps of the 1974 flood, with these again being picked up by the established media. On Twitter, the hashtag '#qldfloods' was used to draw together updates on tide levels and road closures, calls for donations and offers of help, and links to the latest coverage and commentary. Local authorities used Twitter to communicate emergency information – the Brisbane Council and the Queensland Police and Emergency services regularly tweeted updates and instructions. Facebook was also a source of emergency information from authorities, and other users created Facebook pages for specific neighbourhoods to get answers to particular questions of access and impact. And, of course, there was a 'Queensland Floods 2011' iPhone app, which brought together news updates, Twitter feeds, emergency contact information and fund-raising appeals.

The 2011 floods, in short, took place within a convergent media environment, their coverage exemplifying all of the continuities and transformations that we have discussed in this book. The very presence of the Internet was the most obvious of the changes in the mediascape, but it did not replace newspapers, radio or television. Rather, it allowed new possibilities that both complemented older media forms (allowing emergency services to communicate up-to-date information via Twitter as well as radio) and displaced them (websites allowing more up-to-date information than print newspapers). Forms of media texts that were quite distinct at the time of the 1974 floods converged into multimedia presentations combining words, pictures, audio, video and animation. As images and reports, video and comments, moved across the convergent media landscape, they were remixed and recombined in ways that their original authors might not always have envisaged, their narrative elements scattered across multiple platforms and geographical locations. Flood media messages circulated through complex possibilities of mediated time – from the simultaneity of broadcast flow to on-demand database consultation, ever faster in every case – and space – as hyper-local, metropolitan, regional, national and global flows of information intersected.

The invention of the digital computer, the development of the global network of the Internet, and its emergence as an end-to-end media network increasingly accessed on mobile and wireless devices have all enabled a range of possibilities for media. The possibilities offered by the Internet are contested – what some value as a genuinely innovative open communications tool, others would prefer to constrain and control, and in the media realm, this often occurs for commercial reasons. One clear dimension of the contest is apparent in how the Internet has disrupted traditional media business models. The newspaper industry has watched its revenue stream from classified ads flow online to searchable listings, and is experimenting with a range of online delivery options in order to sustain its business. The Internet's low barriers to entry have empowered new content providers, but it is crucial to avoid the temptation to dismiss established media industries as nearly-extinct dinosaurs. Large media corporations still possess the capacity to exercise enormous resources of symbolic, economic and political power. They retain much of their ability to shape the convergent media environment through influencing both content and context, and can still command huge audiences. The most influential are now those who manifest a convergence between the old and the new. Some of these – Google, Apple, Microsoft – were originally computer software and hardware companies. Others – News Corporation, Time Warner, Disney – were originally media companies. Together with public service broadcasters – the BBC, the ABC – reinventing themselves for the convergent era, they shape the contours of industrial convergence – contours which will influence much of what happens in the media landscape, including in other media that set out to directly counter, oppose or supplant the bigger players.

The vital uses of social network media such as Twitter in the flood events point to the complexity of the convergent environment, with its multiple hybrids of personal and public communication – hybrids which are already taking on a seriousness and a pervasiveness that move them beyond visions of social media as 'hanging out, messing around, and geeking out' (Ito *et al.* 2010), however much so many of us may also enjoy doing all of those things. The persistence and accessibility of the data shared on Facebook, Twitter and other social media platforms challenge what had seemed to be settled social conventions – private messages take on public elements, and users find themselves negotiating new terrain between public personae and private lives. As users of convergent media we access and organize, we manipulate and create, we collaborate upon and share media meanings and media texts. Our interpretations, our experiences, the senses we make of our lives and our cultures are now made visible in new ways. Our identities and experiences become digitized, networked, and visible, passing through databases of surveillance and permission, of access and record, and we learn to work out ways of living with the persistence of our digital traces. Regulatory frameworks predicated on being able to control scarce resources struggle for relevance in a digital environment where scarcity is often artificially enforced, and controlling information flows is fraught with difficulty.

In the convergent environment, the established platforms of radio, television, newspapers, magazines and recorded music have all been displaced by a range of networked digital media products with new affordances of engagement and interactivity. Whenever such change occurs, enticing possibilities of shifts in power also emerge – a consistent, if sometimes utopian, discourse since the emergence of the Internet has been one which relocates power away from hierarchical institutions towards networks of users and citizens. The reality is, of course, more complex. Some actors retain a disproportionate amount of symbolic power, and despite the rhetoric, emerging players such as Facebook or Google are as likely to act for reasons of capital as those with longer histories in the sector.

In our introduction we highlighted processes of both continuity and contestation. Changes in media reflect both consistency (the cultural roles of news or sport, for example) and change (from broadcast television to online video on demand, for example). Transformation is a struggle; each shift within the converged media environment is a contested one; each step towards a particular outcome is invariably met by a push back from an alternative. So where some commentators (Jenkins 2008; Shirky 2008) see collaborative user-generated content on the World Wide Web as the next logical transformation in media production, others (Keen 2007; Carr 2010) dismiss it as having limited value. And such contests don't just play out in rhetorical debates, but also in practice as institutions like the BBC and News Corporation experiment with the various flavours of UGC.

The idea of convergence is itself, of course, contested, particularly in the realm of technical implementation. For some, the idea of convergence can suggest that there is a certain inevitability about how media technology is evolving. In this view, because the Internet is the key enabler of so much new media activity, it's tempting to imagine a media environment where all media are built on Internet protocols – where digital networks replace terrestrial ones, and where multi-purpose, networked screens are omnipresent and replace paper and what we currently call television. Such visions don't appear too far-fetched when we look at experiments such as *The Daily* on the iPad instead of *The Times*, or iPlayer on the iPhone instead of BBC1. But technical possibility is in no way the only requirement for change. There are also social, political, industrial and cultural factors that come into play, and the shape of our media environment at any given moment reflects the outcome of contests across any number of those realms – contending technological solutions, contests between business models and practices, struggles over who is authorized to speak in the converged media environment, cultural habits and expectations, and policy battles over ownership and control, censorship and standards, access and literacy, privacy and visibility.

The outcomes of such contests will determine the shape of our future convergent media environment. Whether change occurs at a technical level or involves institutional decisions, the consequences are real. Whether change is driven by established media firms or by grassroots audience behaviour, these developments matter. The convergent media environment is making possible a redistribution of symbolic power – the capacity to speak, to create, to argue and persuade. And by understanding the contested nature of convergent media, each of us may just make a difference.

References

Aarseth, Espen (1997) *Cybertext: Experiments in Ergodic Literature*, Baltimore: Johns Hopkins University Press.

Abbate, Janet (2000) *Inventing the Internet*, Cambridge, MA: MIT Press.

Adorno, Theodor W. and Horkheimer, Max (1995) [1972] 'The Culture Industry: Enlightenment as Mass Deception' in Oliver Boyd-Barrett and Chris Newbold (eds) *Approaches to Media*, London: Arnold, pp. 77–80.

Albon, Robert and Papandrea, Franco (1998) *Media Regulation in Australia and the Public Interest*, Melbourne: Institute of Public Affairs.

Allan, Stuart (2009) 'Histories of Citizen Journalism' in Stuart Allan and Einar Thorsen (eds) *Citizen Journalism: Global Perspectives*, New York: Peter Lang, pp. 17–31.

—— and Thorsen, Einar (eds) (2009) *Citizen Journalism: Global Perspectives*, New York: Peter Lang.

—— and Thorsen, Einar (2011) 'Journalism, Public Service and BBC News Online' in Graham Meikle and Guy Redden (eds) *News Online*, Basingstoke: Palgrave Macmillan, pp. 20–37.

Anderson, Benedict (1991) *Imagined Communities* (revised edition) London: Verso.

Anderson, Chris (2004) 'The Long Tail' *Wired*, 12.10, <http://www.wired.com/wired/archive/12.10/tail.html>, accessed 24 April 2010.

—— (2007) *The Long Tail: How Endless Choice is Creating Unlimited Demand*, London: Random House Business Books.

—— (2009) *Free: The Future of a Radical Price*, New York: Hyperion.

Andrejevic, Mark (2002) 'The Kinder, Gentler Gaze of Big Brother: Reality TV in the Era of Digital Capitalism', *New Media & Society*, vol. 4, no. 2, pp. 251–70.

—— (2004) *Reality TV: The Work of Being Watched*, Lanham, MD: Rowman & Littlefield.

—— (2007) *iSpy: Surveillance and Power in the Interactive Era*, Lawrence, KS: University of Kansas Press.

—— (2009) 'Critical Media Studies 2.0: An Interactive Upgrade?', *Interactions*, vol. 1, no. 1, pp. 35–51.

—— (2011) 'Social Network Exploitation' in Zizi Papacharissi (ed.) *A Networked Self: Identity, Community, and Culture on Social Network Sites*, London: Routledge, pp. 82–101.

Ang, Ien (1985) *Watching Dallas: Soap Opera and the Melodramatic Imagination*, London: Methuen.

—— (1991) *Desperately Seeking the Audience*, London: Routledge.

—— (1996) *Living Room Wars*, London: Routledge.

Appadurai, Arjun (1996) *Modernity At Large: Cultural Dimensions of Globalization*, Minneapolis: University of Minnesota Press.

Arquilla, John and Ronfeldt, David (2001) 'The Advent of Netwar (Revisited)' in John Arquilla and David Ronfeldt (eds) *Networks and Netwars: The Future of Terror, Crime, and Militancy*, Santa Monica, CA: RAND Corporation, pp. 1–25, <http://www.rand.org/pubs/monograph_reports/MR1382>, accessed 12 February 2011.

Arvidsson, Adam (2006) '"Quality Singles": Internet Dating and the Work of Fantasy', *New Media & Society*, vol. 8, no. 4, pp. 671–90.

Assange, Julian (2010a) 'Why the World Needs WikiLeaks', *TED*, July, <http://www.ted.com/talks/julian_assange_why_the_world_needs_wikileaks.html>, accessed 5 November 2010.

—— (2010b) 'Don't Shoot Messenger for Revealing Uncomfortable Truths', *The Australian*, 7 December, <http://www.theaustralian.com.au/in-depth/wikileaks/dont-shoot-messenger-for-revealing-uncomfortable-truths/story-fn775xjq-1225967241332>, accessed 7 December 2010.

Asur, Sitaram, Huberman, Bernarado A., Szabo, Gabor and Wang, Chunyan (2011) *Trends in Social Media: Persistence and Decay*, Social Computing Lab, Palo Alto: HP Labs, <http://www.scribd.com/doc/48665388/Trends-in-Social-Media-Persistence-and-Decay>, accessed 16 February 2011.

Atton, Chris (2004) *An Alternative Internet*, Edinburgh: Edinburgh University Press.

Aufderheide, Patricia (2011) 'Copyright, Fair Use, and Social Networks' in Zizi Papacharissi (ed.) *A Networked Self: Identity, Community, and Culture on Social Network Sites*, London: Routledge, pp. 274–90.

Australian Government (1994) *Creative Nation: Commonwealth Cultural Policy*, October, <http://www.nla.gov.au/creative.nation/creative.html>, accessed 16 February 2011.

Ayers, Michael D. (2006) 'The Cyberactivism of a Dangermouse' in Michael D. Ayers (ed.) *Cybersounds: Essays on Virtual Music Culture*, New York: Peter Lang, pp. 127–36.

Bacon-Smith, Camille (1992) *Enterprising Women*, Philadelphia: University of Pennsylvania Press.

Bagdikian, Ben H. (2004) *The New Media Monopoly*, Boston: Beacon Press.

Baldwin, Craig (director) (1995) *Sonic Outlaws*, documentary film, San Francisco.

Ball, Kirstie and Murakami Wood, David (eds) (2006) *A Report on the Surveillance Society*, Information Commissioner's Office [UK], 2 November, <http://www.ico.gov.uk/upload/documents/library/data_protection/practical_application/surveillance_society_summary_06.pdf>, accessed 9 August 2010.

Ballard, J. G. (1974) 'Introduction to the French edition of *Crash*' in *Crash*, London: Panther.

Barker, Martin (2001) 'The Newson Report: a Case Study in Common Sense' in Martin Barker and Julian Petley (eds) *Ill Effects: the Media/Violence Debate* (second edition) London: Routledge, pp. 27–46.

Barlow, John Perry (1996) 'A Cyberspace Independence Declaration', *Electronic Frontier Foundation* <https://projects.eff.org/~barlow/Declaration-Final.html>, accessed 16 February 2011.

Barr, Trevor (2000) *newmedia.com.au: The Changing Face of Australia's Media and Communications*, Sydney: Allen & Unwin.

Barthes, Roland (1981) *Camera Lucida: Reflections on Photography*, London: Vintage.

Battelle, John (2005) *The Search*, New York: Penguin.

Baym, Nancy K. (2000) *Tune In, Log On: Soaps, Fandom and Online Community*, Thousand Oaks, CA: Sage.

—— (2010) *Personal Connections in the Digital Age*, Cambridge: Polity.

BBC (2010) *Annual Report and Accounts 2009/10*, <http://www.bbc.co.uk/annual report>, accessed 17 February 2011.

Beckett, Charlie (2008) *SuperMedia: Saving Journalism So It Can Save The World*, Oxford: Blackwell.

Beniger, James (1986) *The Control Revolution*, Cambridge, MA: Harvard University Press.

Benkler, Yochai (2006) *The Wealth of Networks*, New Haven: Yale University Press.

Bennett, Andy (1999) 'Hip Hop am Maim: The Localization of Rap Music and Hip Hop Culture', *Media, Culture & Society*, vol. 21, no. 1, pp. 77–91.

Bennett, James and Brown, Tom (2008) 'Introduction: Past the Boundaries of "New" and "Old" Media: Film and Television *After* DVD' in James Bennett and Tom Brown (eds) *Film and Television After DVD*, London: Routledge, pp. 1–18.

Bennett, James and Strange, Niki (2008) 'The BBC's Second-Shift Aesthetics: Interactive Television, Multi-Platform Projects and Public Service Content for a Digital Era', *Media International Australia*, no. 126, pp. 106–19.

Berger, John (1972) *Ways of Seeing*, London: BBC and Penguin.

Berners-Lee, Tim (1999) *Weaving the Web*, London: Orion Business Books.

—— (2010) 'Long Live the Web: A Call for Continued Open Standards and Neutrality', *Scientific American*, 22 November, <http://www.scientificamerican. com/article.cfm?id=long-live-the-web>, accessed 23 November 2010.

Bird, S. Elizabeth (2009) 'The Future of Journalism in the Digital Environment', *Journalism: Theory, Practice and Criticism*, vol. 10, no. 3, pp. 293–5.

—— (2010) 'News Practices in Everyday Life: Beyond Audience Response' in Stuart Allan (ed.) *The Routledge Companion to News and Journalism*, London: Routledge, pp. 417–27.

—— and Dardenne, Robert W. (1997) [1988] 'Myth, Chronicle and Story: Exploring the Narrative Qualities of News', in Dan Berkowitz (ed.), *Social Meanings of News*, Thousand Oaks: Sage, pp. 333–50.

Blondheim, Menahem (1994) *News Over The Wires: The Telegraph and the Flow of Public Information in America, 1844–1897*, Cambridge, MA: Harvard University Press.

Bogost, Ian (2007) *Persuasive Games*, Cambridge, MA: MIT Press.

—— and Ferrari, Simon and Schweizer, Bobby (2010) *Newsgames*, Cambridge, MA: MIT Press.

Boler, Megan (ed.) (2008) *Digital Media and Democracy*, Cambridge, MA: MIT Press.

Bolter, Jay David and Grusin, Richard (1999) *Remediation: Understanding New Media*, Cambridge, MA: MIT Press.

Boorstin, Daniel (1992) [1961] *The Image*, New York: Vintage.

Bordewijk, Jan L. and van Kaam, Ben (1986) 'Towards a New Classification of Tele-Information Services', *Intermedia*, vol. 14, no. 1, pp. 16–21.

Bordwell, David (2009) 'Now Leaving from Platform 1', *Observations on Film Art*, 19 August, <http://www.davidbordwell.net/blog/2009/08/19/now-leaving-from-platform-1>, accessed 6 May 2011.

Born, Georgina (2004) *Uncertain Vision: Birt, Dyke and the Reinvention of the BBC*, London: Secker & Warburg.

Bourdieu, Pierre (1991) *Language and Symbolic Power*, Cambridge: Polity.

Bourdon, Jérôme (2000) 'Live Television Is Still Alive: On Television As An Unfulfilled Promise', *Media, Culture and Society*, vol. 22, no. 5, pp. 531–56.

Boyce, George (1978) 'The Fourth Estate: the Reappraisal of a Concept' in George Boyce, James Curran and Pauline Wingate (eds) *Newspaper History: From the Seventeenth Century to the Present Day*, London: Constable, pp. 19–40.

boyd, danah (2006) 'Friends, Friendsters, and MySpace Top 8: Writing Community Into Being on Social Network Sites', *First Monday*, vol. 11, no. 12, <http://firstmonday.org/htbin/cgiwrap/bin/ojs/index.php/fm/article/view/1418/1336>, accessed 1 October 2010.

—— (2007) 'Why Youth ♥ Social Network Sites: The Role of Networked Publics in Teenage Social Life' in David Buckingham (ed.) *Youth, Identity, and Digital Media*, Cambridge, MA: MIT Press, pp. 119–42.

—— (2008) 'Facebook's Privacy Trainwreck: Exposure, Invasion and Social Convergence', *Convergence*, vol. 14, no. 1, pp. 13–20.

—— (2010a) 'Facebook and "Radical Transparency" (a rant)', *Apophenia*, 14 May, <http://www.zephoria.org/thoughts/archives/2010/05/14/facebook-and-radical-transparency-a-rant.html>, accessed 20 August 2010.

—— (2010b) 'Facebook is a Utility; Utilities Get Regulated', *Apophenia*, 15 May, <http://www.zephoria.org/thoughts/archives/2010/05/15/facebook-is-a-utility-utilities-get-regulated.html>, accessed 16 February 2011.

—— (2011) 'Social Network Sites as Networked Publics: Affordances, Dynamics, and Implications' in Zizi Papacharissi (ed.) *A Networked Self: Identity, Community, and Culture on Social Network Sites*, London: Routledge, pp. 39–58.

—— and Ellison, Nicole B. (2007) 'Social Network Sites: Definition, History and Scholarship', *Journal of Computer-Mediated Communication*, vol. 13, no. 11, <http://jcmc.indiana.edu/vol13/issue1/boyd.ellison.html>, accessed 17 December 2007.

—— and Hargittai, Eszter (2010) 'Facebook Privacy Settings: Who Cares?', *First Monday*, vol. 15, no. 8, <http://firstmonday.org/htbin/cgiwrap/bin/ojs/index.php/fm/article/view/3086/2589>, accessed 4 February 2011.

Brand, Stewart (1988) *The Media Lab*, New York: Penguin.

Brecht, Bertolt (1993) [1932] 'The Radio as an Apparatus of Communication', in Neil Strauss (ed.) *Radiotext(e)*, New York: Semiotext(e), pp. 15–17.

Briggs, Asa and Burke, Peter (2005) *A Social History of the Media: from Gutenberg to the Internet* (second edition), Cambridge: Polity.

Brooker, Will and Jermyn, Deborah (eds) (2003) *The Audience Studies Reader*, London: Routledge.

Brookey, Robert Alan (2007) 'The Format Wars: Drawing the Battle Lines for the Next DVD', *Convergence*, vol. 13, no. 2, pp. 199–211.

Bruns, Axel (2005) *Gatewatching: Collaborative Online News Production*, New York: Peter Lang.

—— (2008a) *Blogs, Wikipedia, Second Life, and Beyond: From Production To Produsage*, New York: Peter Lang.

—— (2008b) 'The Active Audience: Transforming Journalism from Gatekeeping to Gatewatching' in Chris Paterson and David Domingo (eds) *Making Online News: The Ethnography of New Media Production*, New York: Peter Lang, pp. 171–84.

—— (2011) 'News Produsage in a Pro-Am Mediasphere: Why Citizen Journalism Matters' in Graham Meikle and Guy Redden (eds) *News Online*, Basingstoke: Palgrave Macmillan, pp. 132–47.

—— and Jacobs, Joanne (eds) (2006) *Uses of Blogs*, New York: Peter Lang.

Burgess, Jean and Green, Joshua (2009) *YouTube*, Cambridge: Polity.

Burnett, Robert and Marshall, P. David (2003) *Web Theory: An Introduction*, London: Routledge.

Burroughs, William (1982) 'Interview with William S. Burroughs' in John Calder (ed.) *A William Burroughs Reader*, London: Picador, pp. 262–7.

Bush, Vannevar (1945) 'As We May Think', *Atlantic Monthly*, July, <http://www.theatlantic.com/past/docs/unbound/flashbks/computer/bushf.htm>, accessed 4 October 2010.

Byron, Tanya (2008) *Safer Children in a Digital World*, London: Department for Children, Schools and Families [UK], <http://www.dcsf.gov.uk/byronreview>, accessed 25 January 2011.

Campbell, Mel (2009) 'YouCan'tTube', *The Enthusiast*, 24 January, <http://www.theenthusiast.com.au/archives/2009/youcanttube>, accessed 10 January 2011.

Cane, Mike (2010) 'The iPad is the World's First Transmedia Device', *Mike Cane's iPad Test*, 2 March, <http://ipadtest.wordpress.com/2010/03/02/the-ipad-is-the-worlds-first-transmedia-device>, accessed 16 February 2011.

Carey, James (1989) *Communication as Culture*, New York: Routledge.

—— (1997) 'Afterword: the Culture in Question' in Eve Stryker Munson and Catherine A. Warren (eds) *James Carey: A Critical Reader*, Minneapolis: University of Minnesota Press, pp. 308–39.

Carr, Nicolas (2010) *The Shallows: What the Internet is Doing to Our Brains*, New York: W.W. Norton.

Castells, Manuel (1998) *End of Millennium*, Oxford: Blackwell.

—— (2000) *The Rise of the Network Society* (second edition), Oxford: Blackwell.

—— (2001) *The Internet Galaxy*, Oxford: Oxford University Press.

—— (2004) *The Power of Identity* (second edition), Oxford: Blackwell.

—— (2009) *Communication Power*, Oxford: Oxford University Press.

—— and Fernandez-Ardevol, Mireia, Linchuan Qiu, Jack, and Sey, Araba (2007) *Mobile Communication and Society: A Global Perspective*, Cambridge, MA: MIT Press.

Chambers, Paul (2010) 'My Tweet Was Silly, But the Police Reaction Was Absurd', *Guardian*, 11 May, http://www.guardian.co.uk/commentisfree/libertycentral/2010/may/11/tweet-joke-criminal-record-airport>, accessed 11 February 2011.

Chandler, Annemarie and Neumark, Norie (eds) (2005) *At A Distance: Precursors to Art and Activism on the Internet*, Cambridge, MA: MIT Press.

Chenoweth, Neil (2001) *Virtual Murdoch*, London: Secker & Warburg.

Cheung, Charles (2007) 'Identity Construction and Self-Presentation on Personal Homepages: Emancipatory Potentials and Reality Constraints' in David Bell and Barbara M. Kennedy (eds) *The Cybercultures Reader* (second edition), London: Routledge, pp. 273–85.

Clark, Giles and Phillips, Angus (2008) *Inside Book Publishing*, London: Routledge

Clinton, Hillary (2010) 'Internet Freedom', *Foreign Policy*, 21 January, <http://www.foreignpolicy.com/articles/2010/01/21/internet_freedom>, accessed 7 December 2010.

Cohen, Bernard (1963) *The Press and Foreign Policy*, Princeton: Princeton University Press.

Cohen, Nick (2010) 'Twitter and Terrifying Tale of Modern Britain', *Observer*, 19 September <http://www.guardian.co.uk/commentisfree/2010/sep/19/nick-cohen-terrorism-twitter>, accessed 11 February 2011.

Coleman, E. Gabriella (2011) 'Anonymous: From the Lulz to Collective Action', *The New Everyday*, 6 April, <http://mediacommons.futureofthebook.org/tne/pieces/anonymous-lulz-collective-action>, accessed 11 May 2011.

Coleman, Peter (2000) *Obscenity, Blasphemy, Sedition*, Sydney: Duffy & Snellgrove.

Collins, Richard (2004) '"Ises" And "Oughts": Public Service Broadcasting in Europe' in Robert C. Allen and Annette Hill (eds) *The Television Studies Reader*, London: Routledge, pp. 33–51.

Consalvo, Mia (2003) '*Zelda 64* and Video Game Fans', *Television & New Media*, vol. 4, no. 3, pp. 321–34.

Couldry, Nick (2003) *Media Rituals*, London: Routledge.

—— (2010a) *Why Voice Matters*, London: Sage.

—— (2010b) 'New Online News Sources and Writer-Gatherers' in Natalie Fenton (ed.) *New Media, Old News: Journalism & Democracy in the Digital Age*, London: Sage, pp. 138–52.

—— (2011) 'More Sociology, More Culture, More Politics: Or, a Modest Proposal for "Convergence" Studies', *Cultural Studies*, vol. 25, nos. 4–5, pp. 487–501.

Crawford, Kate (2011) 'News to Me: Twitter and the Personal Networking of News' in Graham Meikle and Guy Redden (eds) *News Online*, Basingstoke: Palgrave Macmillan, pp. 115–31.

Critical Art Ensemble (1994) *The Electronic Disturbance*, New York: Autonomedia.

—— (1995) *Electronic Civil Disobedience and Other Unpopular Ideas*, New York: Autonomedia.

—— (2001) *Digital Resistance: Explorations in Tactical Media*, New York: Autonomedia.

Cunningham, Stuart (1992) *Framing Culture – Criticism and Policy in Australia*, St Leonards: Allen & Unwin.

—— (2009) 'Reinventing Television: The Work of the "Innovation" Unit' in Graeme Turner and Jinna Tay (eds) *Television Studies After TV: Understanding Television in the Post-Broadcast Era*, London: Routledge, pp. 83–92.

—— and Turner, Graeme (2010) (eds) *The Media and Communications in Australia* (third edition), Crows Nest: Allen & Unwin.

Curran, James and Seaton, Jean (2010) *Power Without Responsibility: The Press, Broadcasting, and New Media in Britain* (seventh edition), London: Routledge.

Curtin, Michael (2009) 'Matrix Media', in Graeme Turner and Jinna Tay (eds) *Television Studies After TV: Understanding Television in the Post-Broadcast Era*, London: Routledge, pp. 9–19.

David, Matthew (2010) *Peer to Peer and the Music Industry: The Criminalisation of Sharing*, London: Sage.

Davidson, Charles M. and Swanson, Bret T. (2010) 'Net Neutrality, Investment & Jobs: Assessing the Potential Impacts of the FCC's Proposed Net Neutrality Rules on the Broadband Ecosystem', *Advanced Communications Law & Policy Institute*, New York Law School, June 2010, <http://www.nyls.edu/user_files/1/3/4/30/83/Davidson%20&%20Swanson%20-%20NN%20Economic%20Impact%20Paper%20-%20FINAL.pdf>, accessed 21 December 2010.

Dean, Jodi (2010) *Blog Theory*, Cambridge: Polity.

Dean, Peter (2007) 'DVDs: Add-Ons or Bygones?' *Convergence*, vol. 13, no. 2, pp. 119–28.

Debord, Guy (1987) [1967] *The Society of the Spectacle*, Exeter: Rebel Press.

—— and Wolman, Gil (1981) [1956] 'Methods of Detournement', in Ken Knabb (ed.), *Situationist International Anthology*, Berkeley: Bureau of Public Secrets, pp. 8–14.

De Certeau, Michel (1984) *The Practice of Everyday Life*, Berkeley: University of California Press.

De Jong, Wilma, Shaw, Martin and Stammers, Neil (eds) (2005) *Global Activism, Global Media*, London: Pluto.

Deleuze, Gilles (1992) 'Postscript on the Societies of Control', *October*, no. 59, pp. 3–7.

Dena, Christy (2008) 'Emerging Participatory Culture Practices: Player-Created Tiers in Alternate Reality Games', *Convergence*, vol. 14, no. 1, pp. 41–57.

Department for Culture, Media and Sport [UK] (2001) *Creative Industries: Mapping Document 2001*, London: Department for Culture, Media and Sport.

Dery, Mark (1993) *Culture Jamming: Hacking, Slashing and Sniping in the Empire of Signs*, Westfield, NJ: Open Magazine Pamphlet Series no. 25.

Deuze, Mark (2007a) *Media Work*, Cambridge: Polity.

—— (2007b) 'Convergence Culture in the Creative Industries', *International Journal of Cultural Studies*, vol. 10, no. 2, pp. 243–63.

—— (2009a) 'The Future of Citizen Journalism' in Stuart Allan and Einar Thorsen (eds) *Citizen Journalism: Global Perspectives*, New York: Peter Lang, pp. 255–64.

—— (2009b) 'Technology and the Individual Journalist: Agency Beyond Imitation and Change' in Barbie Zelizer (ed.) *The Changing Faces of Journalism: Tabloidization, Technology and Truthiness*, New York: Routledge, pp. 82–97.

—— (2010) 'Journalism and Convergence Culture' in Stuart Allan (ed.) *The Routledge Companion to News and Journalism*, London: Routledge, pp. 267–76.

—— and Fortunati, Leopoldina (2011) 'Journalism Without Journalists: On the Power Shift From Journalists to Employers and Audiences' in Graham Meikle and Guy Redden (eds) *News Online*, Basingstoke: Palgrave Macmillan, pp. 164–77.

Dibbell, Julian (1993) 'A Rape in Cyberspace', *Julian Dibbell*, <http://www.juliandibbell.com/articles/a-rape-in-cyberspace>, accessed 16 February 2011.

Dinehart, Stephen E. (2009) 'Creators of Transmedia Stories: Jeff Gomez', *The Narrative Design Explorer*, 15 September, <http://narrativedesign.org/2009/09/creators-of-transmedia-stories-3-jeff-gomez>, accessed 16 February 2011.

Doane, Mary Ann (1990) 'Information, Crisis, Catastrophe' in Patricia Mellencamp (ed.) *Logics of Television*, Bloomington: Indiana University Press, pp. 222–39.

Doctorow, Cory (2006) 'Disney Exec: Piracy is Just a Business Model', *Boing Boing*, 10 October, <http://www.boingboing.net/2006/10/10/disney-exec-piracy-i.html>, accessed 8 December 2009.

—— (2008) 'Foreword' in Paul D. Miller (ed.) *Sound Unbound: Sampling Digital Music and Culture*, Cambridge, MA: MIT Press, pp. ix–xi.

Dovey, Jonathan and Lister, Martin (2009) 'Straw Men or Cyborgs?' *Interactions*, vol. 1, no. 1, pp. 129–45.

Doyle, Gillian (2002) *Understanding Media Economics*, London: Sage.

—— and Vick, Douglas W. (2005) 'The Communications Act 2003: A New Regulatory Framework in the UK', *Convergence*, vol. 11, no. 3, pp. 75–94.

Drew, Jesse (2005) 'From the Gulf War to the Battle of Seattle: Building an International Alternative Media Network' in Annmarie Chandler and Norie Neumark (eds) *At A Distance: Precursors to Art and Activism on the Internet*, Cambridge, MA: MIT Press, pp. 210–24.

Driscoll, Catherine and Gregg, Melissa (2011) 'Convergence Culture and the Legacy of Feminist Cultural Studies', *Cultural Studies*, vol. 25, nos. 4–5, pp. 566–84.

Duncombe, Stephen (1997) *Notes From Underground: Zines and the Politics of Alternative Culture*, London: Verso.

Dwyer, Tim (2010) *Media Convergence*, Maidenhead: Open University Press.

Dyson, Esther, Toffler, Alvin, Gilder, George and Keyworth, George (1994) 'Cyberspace and the American Dream: a Magna Carta for the Knowledge Age', *Progress and Freedom Foundation*, <http://www.pff.org/issues-pubs/future insights/fi1.2magnacarta.html>, accessed 16 February 2011.

Eco, Umberto (2010) 'Not Such Wicked Leaks', *Presseurop*, 2 December, <http://www.presseurop.eu/en/content/article/414871-not-such-wicked-leaks>, accessed 13 February 2011.

Eglash, Ron, Croissant, Jennifer, Di Chiro, Giovanna and Fouche, Rayvon (eds) (2004) *Appropriating Technology*, Minneapolis: University of Minnesota Press.

Eisenstein, Elizabeth (1993) *The Printing Revolution in Early Modern Europe*, Cambridge: Cambridge University Press.

Electronic Frontiers Australia (2006) 'Labor's Mandatory ISP Internet Blocking Plan', *Electronic Frontiers Australia*, 29 March, <http://www.efa.org.au/censorship/mandatory-isp-blocking>, accessed 16 February 2011.

Ellison, Nicole B., Heino, Rebecca and Gibbs, Jennifer (2006) 'Managing Impressions Online: Self-Presentation Processes in the Online Dating Environment', *Journal of Computer-Mediated Communication*, vol. 11, no. 2, <http://jcmc.indiana.edu/vol11/issue2/ellison.html>, accessed 4 February 2011.

Ellison, Nicole B., Steinfield, Charles and Lampe, Cliff (2007) 'The Benefits of Facebook "Friends": Social Capital and College Students' Use of Online Social Network Sites', *Journal of Computer-Mediated Communication*, vol. 12, no. 4, <http://jcmc.indiana.edu/vol12/issue4/ellison.html>, accessed 12 May 2011.

Eltringham, Matthew (2009) 'The Audience and the News' in Charles Miller (ed.) *The Future of Journalism: Papers from a Conference Organised by the BBC College of Journalism*, <http://www.bbc.co.uk/blogs/theeditors/future_of_journalism.pdf>, pp. 50–5, accessed 6 August 2009.

Emperor Hirohito (1993) [1945] 'Imperial Surrender Broadcast' in Neil Strauss (ed.) *Radiotext(e)*, New York: Semiotext(e), pp. 155–6.

Engelbart, Douglas (2003) [1962] 'From *Augmenting Human Intellect: A Conceptual Framework*' in Noah Wardrip-Fruin and Nick Montfort (eds) *The New Media Reader*, Cambridge, MA: MIT Press, pp. 93–108.

Ericson, Richard V., Baranek, Patricia M. and Chan, Janet B. L. (1989) *Negotiating Control: A Study of News Sources*, Milton Keynes: Open University Press.

Eshun, Kodwo (1998) *More Brilliant Than the Sun*, London: Quartet Books.

Evans, Elizabeth (2011) *Transmedia Television: Audiences, New Media and Daily Life*, London: Routledge.

Febvre, Lucien and Martin, Henri-Jean (1976) *The Coming of the Book: The Impact of Printing 1450–1800*, London: NLB.

Fischer, Claude S. (1992) *America Calling: A Social History of the Telephone to 1940*, Berkeley: University of California Press.

Fishman, Mark (1980) *Manufacturing The News*, Austin: University of Texas Press.

Fiske, John (1989) *Understanding Popular Culture*, London: Routledge.

—— (1990) *Introduction to Communication Studies* (second edition), London: Routledge.

Flew, Terry (1995) 'Images of a Nation: Economic and Cultural Aspects of Australian Content Regulations for Commercial Television' in Jennifer Craik, Julie James Bailey and Albert Moran (eds), *Public Voices, Private Interests*, St Leonards: Allen and Unwin, pp. 73–85.

—— (2008) *New Media: An Introduction* (third edition), Melbourne: Oxford University Press.

—— (2009) 'The ABC – and SBS – of Social Innovation', *Terry Flew*, 25 January, <http://terryflew.blogspot.com/2009/01/abc-and-sbs-of-social-innovation.html>, accessed 16 February 2011.

—— and Cunningham, Stuart (2010) 'Creative Industries After the First Decade of Debate', *The Information Society*, vol. 26, no. 2, pp. 113–23.

Florida, Richard (2002) *The Rise of the Creative Class*, New York: Basic Books.

Forman, Murray (2000) '"Represent": Race, Space and Place in Rap Music', *Popular Music*, vol. 19, no. 1, pp. 65–90.

Foucault, Michel (1977) *Discipline and Punish*, Harmondsworth: Penguin.

—— (1980) 'The Eye of Power' in Colin Gordon (ed.) *Power/Knowledge: Selected Interviews and Other Writings 1972–1977*, Brighton: Harvester Press, pp. 146–65.

Frasca, Gonzalo (2004) 'Videogames of the Oppressed: Critical Thinking, Education, Tolerance, and Other Trivial Issues' in Pat Harrigan and Noah Wardrip-Fruin (eds) *First Person: New Media as Story, Performance, and Game*, Cambridge, MA: MIT Press, pp. 85–94.

Freedman, Des (2008) *The Politics of Media Policy*, Cambridge: Polity.

—— (2010) 'The Political Economy of the "New" News Environment' in Natalie Fenton (ed.) *New Media, Old News: Journalism & Democracy in the Digital Age*, London: Sage, pp. 35–50.

Friedland, Lewis A. (1992) *Covering the World: International Television News Services*, New York: Twentieth Century Fund.

Gaber, Ivor (2000) 'Government By Spin: An Analysis of the Process', *Media, Culture & Society*, vol. 22, no. 4, pp. 507–18.

Galloway, Alexander R. (2004) 'Social Realism in Gaming', *Game Studies*, vol. 4, no. 1, <http://www.gamestudies.org/0401/galloway>, accessed 13 February 2006.

Galloway, Alexander R. (2004) *Protocol: How Control Exists After Decentralization*, Cambridge, MA: MIT Press.

Galtung, Johan and Ruge, Mari Holmboe (1965) 'The Structure of Foreign News', *Journal of Peace Research*, vol. 2, no. 1, pp. 64–91.

Gane, Nicholas and Beer, David (2008) *New Media*, Oxford: Berg.

Gans, Herbert J. (1979) *Deciding What's News*, New York: Pantheon.

—— (2009) 'Can Popularization Help the News Media?' in Barbie Zelizer (ed.) *The Changing Faces of Journalism: Tabloidization, Technology and Truthiness*, New York: Routledge, pp. 17–28.

Garnham, Nicholas (2003) 'A Response to Elizabeth Jacka's "Democracy as Defeat"', *Television & New Media*, vol. 4, no. 2, pp. 193–200.

Gauntlett, David (1998) 'Ten Things Wrong With the "Effects" Model' in Roger Dickinson, Ramaswami Harindranath and Olga Linné (eds) *Approaches To Audiences: A Reader*, London: Arnold, pp. 120–30.

—— (2007) 'Media Studies 2.0', *Theory.org.uk: Media/Identity/Resources and Projects*, <http://www.theory.org.uk/mediastudies2.htm>, accessed 28 January 2008.

—— (2008) 'Case Study: Wikipedia' in Glen Creeber and Royston Martin (eds) *Digital Cultures*, Maidenhead: Open University Press, pp. 39–45.

—— (2009) 'Media Studies 2.0: A Response', *Interactions*, vol. 1, no. 1, pp. 147–57.

—— (2011) *Making is Connecting*, Cambridge: Polity.

Genachowski, Julius (2009) 'Preserving a Free and Open Internet: A Platform for Innovation, Opportunity, and Prosperity', *The Brookings Institution*, 19 September,

<http://hraunfoss.fcc.gov/edocs_public/attachmatch/DOC-293568A1.pdf>, accessed 16 February 2011.

George, Nelson (1998) *Hip Hop America*, Harmondsworth: Penguin.

Gibson, William (1986) 'Burning Chrome', collected in (1995) *Burning Chrome and Other Stories*, London: HarperCollins.

—— (2001) 'Foreword' in Randall Packer and Ken Jordan (eds) *Multimedia: From Wagner to Virtual Reality*, New York: W. W. Norton, pp. ix–xii.

—— (2010) 'Google's Earth', *New York Times*, 31 August, <http://www.nytimes.com/2010/09/01/opinion/01gibson.html>, accessed 11 May 2011.

Giddens, Anthony (1990) *The Consequences of Modernity*, Stanford: Polity.

Giddings, Seth and Lister, Martin (eds) (2011) *The New Media and Technocultures Reader*, London: Routledge.

Gilder, George (1992) *Life After Television*, New York: W. W. Norton.

Gillespie, Marie (1995) *Television, Ethnicity and Cultural Change*, London: Routledge.

Gillmor, Dan (2004) *We The Media: Grassroots Journalism by the People, for the People*, Sebastopol, CA: O'Reilly.

Gitelman, Lisa and Pingree, Geoffrey B. (eds) (2003) *New Media, 1740–1915*, Cambridge, MA: MIT Press.

Gitlin, Todd (1983) *Inside Prime Time*, New York: Pantheon.

Given, Jock (2003) *Turning Off The Television*, Sydney: UNSW Press.

—— (2008) 'Cross-Media Ownership Laws: Refinement of Rejection', *UNSW Law Journal*, vol. 30, no. 1, pp. 258–68.

Glaser, Mark (2010) 'Citizen Journalism: Widening World Views, Extending Democracy' in Stuart Allan (ed.) *The Routledge Companion to News and Journalism*, London: Routledge, pp. 578–90.

Goffman, Erving (1959) *The Presentation of Self in Everyday Life*, London: Penguin.

Goggin, Gerard (2006) *Cell Phone Culture*, London: Routledge.

—— (2011) *Global Mobile Media*, New York: Routledge.

Goldacre, Ben (2011) 'Nerd Saves Entire BBC Archive for $3.99, You Can Help For Free', *Ben Goldacre – Secondary Blog*, 10 February, <http://bengoldacre.posterous.com/nerd-saves-entire-bbc-archive-for-399-you-can>, accessed 31 August 2011.

Goldsmith, Jack and Wu, Tim (2006) *Who Controls The Internet?* New York: Oxford University Press.

Goldstein, Richard (1995) [1967] '1966: A Quiet Evening at the Balloon Farm' in Hanif Kureishi and Jon Savage (eds) *The Faber Book of Pop*, London: Faber, pp. 273–7.

Gould, Emily (2007) 'Coordinates of the Rich and Famous', *New York Times*, 4 May, <http://www.nytimes.com/2007/05/04/opinion/04gould.html>, accessed 23 August 2010.

Gray, Christopher (1988) *Leaving the Twentieth Century*, London: Rebel Press.

Gray, Jonathan, Sandvoss, Cornel and Harrington, C. Lee (eds) (2007) *Fandom: Identities and Communities in a Mediated World*, New York: New York University Press.

Green, Joshua and Jenkins, Henry (2011) 'Spreadable Media: How Audiences Create Value and Meaning in a Networked Economy' in Virginia Nightingale (ed.) *The Handbook of Media Audiences*, Malden, MA: Blackwell, pp. 109–27.

Green, Lelia (2002) *Communication, Technology and Society*, London: Sage.

Green, Nicola and Haddon, Leslie (2009) *Mobile Communications*, Oxford: Berg.

Greenberg, Andy (2010) 'An Interview With WikiLeaks' Julian Assange', *Forbes*, 29 November, <http://blogs.forbes.com/andygreenberg/2010/11/29/an-interview-with-wikileaks-julian-assange>, accessed 10 December 2010.

Greenwald, Robert (director) (2004) *Outfoxed: Rupert Murdoch's War on Journalism*, documentary film, Culver City, California.

Grimmelmann, James (2010) 'Privacy as Product Safety', *Widener Law Journal*, vol. 19, pp. 793–827.

Gripsrud, Jostein (2004) 'Broadcast Television: The Chances of Its Survival in a Digital Age' in Lynn Spigel and Jan Olsson (eds) *Television After TV: Essays on a Medium in Transition*, Durham: Duke University Press, pp. 210–23.

Grossman, Lev (2006) 'Time's Person of the Year: You', *Time*, 13 December, <http://www.time.com/time/magazine/article/0,9171,1569514,00.html>, accessed 4 October 2010.

—— (2008) 'The Master of Memes', *Time*, 9 July, <http://www.time.com/time/business/article/0,8599,1821435,00.html>, accessed 11 February 2011.

Grusin, Richard (2010) *Premediation: Affect and Mediality After 9/11*, Basingstoke: Palgrave Macmillan.

Habermas, Jürgen (1974) 'The Public Sphere: an Encyclopedia Article', *New German Critique*, vol. 1, no. 3, pp. 49–55.

—— (1989) *The Structural Transformation of the Public Sphere*, Cambridge, MA: MIT Press.

Hafner, Katie and Lyon, Matthew (1998) *Where Wizards Stay Up Late: the Origins of the Internet*, New York: Touchstone.

Halavais, Alexander (2009) *Search Engine Society*, Cambridge: Polity.

Hall, Stuart (1981) 'The Determinations of News Photographs', in Stanley Cohen and Jock Young (eds), *The Manufacture of News* (revised edition), London: Constable, pp. 226–43.

—— (2006) [1980] 'Encoding/Decoding' in Douglas Kellner and Meenakshi Gigi Durham (eds) *Media and Cultural Studies: KeyWorks* (revised edition), Malden, MA: Blackwell, pp. 163–73.

Hallin, Daniel C. (1986) *The 'Uncensored War': The Media and Vietnam*, Berkeley: University of California Press.

Harcup, Tony and O'Neill, Deirdre (2001) 'What Is News? Galtung and Ruge Revisited', *Journalism Studies*, vol. 2, no. 2, pp. 261–80.

Hargittai, Eszter (2001) 'Radio's Lessons for the Internet', *Communications of the ACM*, vol. 43, no. 1, January, pp. 51–7.

—— (2007) 'The Social, Political, Economic, and Cultural Dimensions of Search Engines: An Introduction', *Journal of Computer-Mediated Communication*, vol. 12, no. 3, <http://jcmc.indiana.edu/vol12/issue3/hargittai.html>, accessed 4 May 2011.

Hargreaves, Ian and Thomas, James (2002) *New News, Old News*, Independent Television Commission and Broadcasting Standards Commission, <http:// www.cardiff.ac.uk/jomec/research/researchgroups/journalismstudies/funded projects/newnews.html>, accessed 23 December 2010.

Harriet J (2010) 'Fuck You, Google', *Fugitivus*, 11 February, <http://fugitivus.wordpress.com/2010/02/11/fuck-you-google>, accessed 19 August 2010.

Hartley, John (2000) 'Communicative Democracy in a Redactional Society: The Future of Journalism Studies', *Journalism: Theory, Practice and Criticism*, vol. 1, no. 1, pp. 39–48.

—— (2001) 'The Infotainment Debate' in Glen Creeber (ed.) *The Television Genre Book*, London: British Film Institute, pp. 118–20.

—— (2003) *A Short History of Cultural Studies*, London: Sage.

—— (2008) *Television Truths*, Malden, MA: Blackwell.

—— (2009a) *Uses of Digital Literacy*, St. Lucia: University of Queensland Press.

—— (2009b) 'Less Popular But More Democratic? *Corrie*, Clarkson and the Dancing *Cru*' in Graeme Turner and Jinna Tay (eds) *Television Studies After TV: Understanding Television in the Post-Broadcast Era*, London: Routledge, pp. 20–30.

—— (2009c) 'From the Consciousness Industry to the Creative Industries: Consumer-Created Content, Social Network Markets, and the Growth of Knowledge' in Jennifer Holt and Alisa Perren (eds) (2009) *Media Industries: History, Theory, and Method*, Chichester: Wiley-Blackwell, pp. 231–44.

—— (ed.) (2005) *Creative Industries*, Malden, MA: Blackwell.

—— and McWilliam, Kelly (eds) (2009) *Story Circle*, Malden, MA: Blackwell.

Harvey, Eric (2011) 'Same as the Old Boss? Changes, Continuities, and Careers in the Digital Music Era' in Mark Deuze (ed.) *Managing Media Work*, London: Sage, pp. 237–48.

Harvey, David (1989) *The Condition of Postmodernity*, Oxford: Blackwell.

Hawke, Jo (1995) 'Privatising the Public Interest' in Jennifer Craik, Julie James Bailey and Albert Moran (eds), *Public Voices, Private Interests*, St Leonards: Allen and Unwin, pp. 33–50.

Hepworth, David (2008) 'The Man Who Changed TV Forever: An Interview with *The Wire*'s David Simon', *The Word*, 11 September, <http://www.wordmagazine.co.uk/content/the-man-who-changed-tv-forever-an-interview-with-the-wires-david-simon-part-iii>, accessed 21 January 2011.

Herman, Bill (2009) 'Opening Bottlenecks: On Behalf of Mandated Network Neutrality', *Federal Communications Law Journal*, vol. 59, no. 1, pp. 107–59.

Herman, Edward S. and Chomsky, Noam (1988) *Manufacturing Consent*, New York: Pantheon.

Herman, Edward S. and McChesney, Robert (1997) *The Global Media: the New Missionaries of Corporate Capitalism*, London: Cassell.

Hesmondhalgh, David (2005) 'Media and Cultural Policy as Public Policy', *International Journal of Cultural Policy*, vol. 11, no. 1, pp. 95–109.

—— (2007) *The Cultural Industries* (second edition), London: Sage.

Hewitt, Duncan (2009) 'Net Effects', *Index on Censorship*, vol. 38, no. 4, pp. 60–9.

Higgins, Michael (2008) *Media and Their Publics*, Maidenhead: Open University Press.

Hills, Matt (2002) *Fan Cultures*, London: Routledge.

—— (2007) '"TVIII" and the Cultural/Textual Valorisations of DVD', *New Review of Film and Television Studies*, vol. 5, no. 1, pp. 41–60.

Himanen, Pekka (2001) *The Hacker Ethic*, New York: Random House.

Hindman, Matthew (2009) *The Myth of Digital Democracy*, Princeton, NJ: Princeton University Press.

Hjorth, Larissa (2011) *Games and Gaming*, Oxford: Berg.

Horrocks, Peter (2009) 'The End of Fortress Journalism' in Charles Miller (ed.) *The Future of Journalism: Papers from a Conference Organised by the BBC College of Journalism*, <http://www.bbc.co.uk/blogs/theeditors/future_of_journalism.pdf>, pp. 6–17, accessed 6 August 2009.

Howkins, John (2005) 'The Mayor's Commission on the Creative Industries' in John Hartley (ed.) *Creative Industries*, Malden, MA: Blackwell, pp. 117–25.

Huang, Edgar (2007) 'A DVD Dilemma: Ripping for Teaching', *Convergence*, vol. 13, no. 2, pp. 129–41.

Innis, Harold (1999) [1951] *The Bias of Communication*, Toronto: University of Toronto Press.

—— (2007) [1950] *Empire and Communications*, Toronto: Dundurn Press.

Ito, Mimi (2005) 'Intertextual Enterprises: Writing Alternate Places and Meanings in the Media Mixed Networks of Yugioh' in Debbora Battaglia (ed.) *E.T. Culture: Anthropology in Outerspaces*, Durham, NC: Duke University Press, pp. 180–99.

Ito, Mizuko, Baumer, Sonia, Bittanti, Matteo, boyd, danah, Cody, Rachel, Herr-Stephenson, Becky, Horst, Heather A., Lange, Patricia G., Mahendran, Dilan, Martinez Katynka Z., Pascoe, C. J., Perkel, Dan, Robinson, Laura, Sims, Christo and Tripp, Lisa (2010) *Hanging Out, Messing Around and Geeking Out*, Cambridge, MA: MIT Press.

Jacka, Elizabeth (2003) '"Democracy as Defeat": The Impotence of Arguments for Public Service Broadcasting', *Television & New Media*, vol. 4, no. 2, pp. 177–91.

Jacobs, Andrew (2010) 'Heartthrob's Blog Challenges Chinese Leaders', *New York Times*, 12 March, <http://www.nytimes.com/2010/03/13/world/asia/13hanhan.html>, accessed 15 March 2010.

Jardin, Xeni (2010) 'The Elements for iPad: Hands-on Review' *Boing Boing*, 1 April, <http://boingboing.net/2010/04/01/the-elements-for-ipa.html>, accessed 16 February 2011.

Jarrett, Kylie (2008) 'Beyond Broadcast Yourself™: The Future of YouTube', *Media International Australia*, no. 126, pp. 132–44.

Jenkins, Henry (1992) *Textual Poachers*, London: Routledge.

—— (2001) 'Convergence? I Diverge', *Technology Review*, June, p. 93.

—— (2003) 'Quentin Tarantino's Star Wars? Digital Cinema, Media Convergence, and Participatory Culture' in David Thorburn and Henry Jenkins (eds) *Rethinking Media Change*, Cambridge, MA: MIT Press, pp. 281–312.

—— (2004) 'The Cultural Logic of Media Convergence', *International Journal of Cultural Studies*, vol. 7, no. 1, pp. 33–43.

—— (2006b) *Fans, Bloggers and Gamers: Exploring Participatory Culture*, New York: New York University Press.

—— (2008) [2006a] *Convergence Culture* (updated edition), New York: New York University Press.

—— and Deuze, Mark (2008) 'Editorial: Convergence Culture', *Convergence*, vol. 14, no. 1, pp. 5–12.

Jensen, Klaus Bruhn (2010) *Media Convergence*, London: Routledge.

Jordan, Ken (2008) 'Stop. Hey. What's That Sound?' in Paul D. Miller (ed.) *Sound Unbound: Sampling Digital Music and Culture*, Cambridge, MA: MIT Press, pp. 245–64.

Jordan, Tim (2007) 'Online Direct Action: Hacktivism and Radical Democracy' in Lincoln Dahlberg and Eugenia Siapera (eds) *Radical Democracy and the Internet*, Basingstoke: Palgrave Macmillan, pp. 73–88.

—— and Taylor, Paul (2004) *Hacktivism and Cyberwars: Rebels With a Cause*, London: Routledge.

Joyce, Don (2005) 'An Unsuspected Future in Broadcasting: Negativland' in Annemarie Chandler and Norie Neumark (eds) *At A Distance: Precursors to Art and Activism on the Internet*, Cambridge, MA: MIT Press, pp. 176–89.

Juul, Jesper (2001) 'Games Telling Stories? A Brief Note on Games and Narratives, *Game Studies*, vol. 1, no. 1, <http://www.gamestudies.org/0101/juul-gts>, accessed 10 May 2011.

Kaplan, Benjamin (1967) *An Unhurried View of Copyright*, New York: Columbia University Press.

Katz, Elihu (1992) 'The End of Journalism? Notes on Watching the War', *Journal of Communication*, vol. 42, no, 3, pp. 5–13.

Kavka, Misha (2011) 'Industry Convergence Shows' in Michael Kackman, Marnie Binfield, Matthew Thomas Payne, Allison Perlman and Bryan Sebok (eds) *Flow TV*, New York: Routledge, pp. 75–92.

Kay, Alan and Goldberg, Adele (1999) [1977] 'Personal Dynamic Media' in Paul A. Mayer (ed.) *Computer Media and Communication: A Reader*, Oxford: Oxford University Press, pp. 111–19.

Keane, John (1991) *The Media and Democracy*, Cambridge: Polity.

Keen, Andrew (2007) *The Cult of the Amateur: How Today's Internet is Killing Our Culture*, New York: Doubleday.

—— (2011) 'Your Life Torn Open, essay 1: Sharing is a trap', *Wired UK*, 3 February, <http://www.wired.co.uk/magazine/archive/2011/03/features/sharing-is-a-trap>, accessed 11 March 2011.

Kelly, Kevin (2005) 'We Are the Web', *Wired*, 13.08, <http://www.wired.com/wired/archive/13.08/tech.html>, accessed 4 February 2011.

—— (2008) 'Better Than Free', *The Technium*, <http://www.kk.org/thetechnium/archives/2008/01/better_than_fre.php>, accessed 22 December 2010.

Kern, Stephen (1983) *The Culture of Time and Space 1880–1918*, Cambridge, MA: Harvard University Press.

Khatchadourian, Raffi (2010) 'No Secrets: Julian Assange's Mission for Total Transparency', *New Yorker*, 7 June, <http://www.newyorker.com/reporting/2010/06/07/100607fa_fact_khatchadourian>, accessed 5 November 2010.

Kilker, Julian Albert (2003) 'Shaping Convergence Media: "Meta-Control" and the Domestication of DVD and Web Technologies', *Convergence*, vol. 9, no. 3, pp. 20–39.

Klein, Naomi (2000) *No Logo*, London: Flamingo.

Knabb, Ken (ed.) (1981) *Situationist International Anthology*, Berkeley: Bureau of Public Secrets.

Knobel, Michele and Lankshear, Colin (eds) (2010) *DIY Media: Creating, Sharing and Learning with New Technologies*, New York: Peter Lang.

Kompare, Derek (2006) 'Publishing Flow: DVD Box Sets and the Reconception of Television', *Television & New Media*, vol. 7, no. 4, 335–60.

—— (2011) 'More "Moments of Television": Online Cult Television Authorship' in Michael Kackman, Marnie Binfield, Matthew Thomas Payne, Allison Perlman and Bryan Sebok (eds) *Flow TV*, New York: Routledge, pp. 95–113.

Krotoski, Aleks (2010) 'Meet the Cyber Radicals Using the Net to Change the World', *Observer*, 28 November, 'New Review' section, pp. 8–11.

Küng, Lucy, Picard, Robert G. & Towse, Ruth (eds) (2008) *The Internet and the Mass Media*, London: Sage.

Küng-Shankleman, Lucy (2000) *Inside the BBC and CNN: Managing Media Organisations*, London: Routledge.

Kunzru, Hari (1997) 'You Are Cyborg' *Wired*, 5.02, February, <http://www.wired.com/wired/archive/5.02/ffharaway.html>, accessed 19 November 2010.

Lasica, J. D. (2003) 'Random Acts of Journalism', *J. D. Lasica*, 12 March, <http://www.jdlasica.com/blog/archives/2003_03_12.html>, accessed 6 August 2009.

Lanier, Jaron (2006) 'Digital Maoism: The Hazards of the New Online Collectivism', *Edge*, 30 May, <http://www.edge.org/3rd_culture/lanier06/lanier06_index.html>, accessed 10 November 2010.

—— (2010) *You Are Not a Gadget*, New York: Vintage.

Lasn, Kalle (1999) *Culture Jam: The Uncooling of America™*, New York: Eagle Brook.

Lasswell, Harold D. (1995) [1948] 'The Structure and Function of Communication in Society' in Oliver Boyd-Barrett and Chris Newbold (eds) *Approaches to Media*, London: Arnold, pp. 93–4.

Latour, Bruno (1991) 'Technology is Society Made Durable' in John Law (ed.) *A Sociology of Monsters: Essays on Power, Technology and Domination*, London: Routledge, pp. 103–31.

—— (2005) *Reassembling the Social: An Introduction to Actor-Network-Theory*, Oxford: Oxford University Press.

Leadbeater, Charles (1999) *Living on Thin Air*, London: Vintage.

—— (2008) *We-Think*, London: Profile.

—— and Miller, Paul (2004) *The Pro-Am Revolution: How Enthusiasts are Changing Our Economy and Society*, London: Demos.

Leaver, Tama (2008) 'Watching *Battlestar Galactica* in Australia and the Tyranny of Digital Distance', *Media International Australia*, no. 126, pp. 145–54.

Leavitt, Neal (2005) 'Audi's Art of the Heist Captured Leads', *iMedia Connection*, 26 July, <http://www.imediaconnection.com/content/6386.imc>, accessed 4 November 2010.

Leiner, Barry M., Cerf, Vinton G., Clark, David D., Kahn, Robert E., Kleinrock, Leonard, Lynch, Daniel C., Postel, Jon, Roberts, Larry G. and Wolff, Stephen (2000) 'A Brief History of the Internet', *Internet Society*, <http://www.isoc. org/internet/history/brief.shtml>, accessed 4 October 2010.

Lemley, Mark A. and Lessig, Lawrence (2004) 'The End of End-to-End', in Mark N. Cooper (ed.) *Open Architecture as Communications Policy*, Stanford: Centre for Internet and Society, pp. 41–91.

Lessig, Lawrence (2000) *Code and Other Laws of Cyberspace*, New York: Basic Books.

—— (2001) *The Future of Ideas*, New York: Vintage.

—— (2004) *Free Culture*, New York: Penguin.

—— (2006) *Code 2.0*, New York: Basic Books.

—— (2008) *Remix*, London: Bloomsbury Academic.

Letts, Don (director) (1996) 'Planet Rock', *Dancing In The Streets*, episode 10, London: BBC Television.

Levinson, Paul (1997) *The Soft Edge: A Natural History and Future of the Information Revolution*, London: Routledge.

—— (2004) *Cellphone*, New York: Routledge.

Lévy, Pierre (1997) *Collective Intelligence*, Cambridge, MA: Perseus Books.

Levy, Steven (1984) *Hackers: Heroes of the Computer Revolution*, New York: Anchor Press/Doubleday.

—— (2011) *In the Plex: How Google Works, Thinks and Shapes Our Lives*, New York: Simon & Schuster.

Lewis, Justin, Williams, Andrew and Franklin, Bob (2008a) 'A Compromised Fourth Estate?' *Journalism Studies*, vol. 9, no. 1, pp. 1–20.

—— (2008b) 'Four Rumours and an Explanation' *Journalism Practice*, vol. 2, no. 1, pp. 27–45.

Liang, Lawrence (2011) 'A Brief History of the Internet from the 15th to the 18th Century' in Geert Lovink and Nathaniel Tkacz (eds) *Critical Point of View: A Wikipedia Reader*, Amsterdam: Institute of Network Cultures, pp. 50–62.

Lichtenberg, Judith (2000) 'In Defence of Objectivity Revisited', in James Curran and Michael Gurevitch (eds), *Mass Media and Society* (third edition), London: Arnold, pp. 238–54.

Liebes, Tamar and Katz, Elihu (1990) *The Export of Meaning: Cross-Cultural Readings of Dallas*, Oxford: Oxford University Press.

Lievrouw, Leah A. (2011) *Alternative and Activist New Media*, Cambridge: Polity.

—— and Livingstone, Sonia (eds) (2006) *The Handbook of New Media* (updated student edition), London: Sage.

Ling, Rich and Donner, Jonathan (2009) *Mobile Communication*, Cambridge: Polity.

Lipsitz, George (1994) *Dangerous Crossroads: Popular Music, Postmodernism, and the Poetics of Place*, London: Verso.

Lister, Martin, Dovey, Jon, Giddings, Seth, Grant, Iain and Kelly, Kieran (2009) *New Media: A Critical Introduction* (second edition), London: Routledge.

Livingstone, Sonia (2005) 'Media Audiences, Interpreters and Users' in Marie Gillespie (ed.) *Media Audiences*, Maidenhead: Open University Press, pp. 9–50.

—— (2008) 'Taking Risky Opportunities in Youthful Content Creation: Teenagers' Use of Social Networking Sites for Intimacy, Privacy and Self-expression', *New Media & Society*, vol. 10, no. 3, pp. 393–411.

Long, Geoffrey (2007) *Transmedia Storytelling: Business, Aesthetics and Production at the Jim Henson Company*, PhD thesis, Massachusetts Institute of Technology.

Lotz, Amanda D. (2007) *The Television Will Be Revolutionized*, New York: New York University Press.

Lovink, Geert (2002) *Uncanny Networks*, Cambridge, MA: MIT Press.

—— (2007) *Zero Comments*, London: Routledge.

—— (2008) 'The Art of Watching Databases', in Geert Lovink and Sabine Niederer (eds) *Video Vortex Reader*, Amsterdam: Institute of Network Cultures, pp. 9–12.

—— and Rossiter, Ned (2007) 'Proposals for Creative Research', in Geert Lovink and Ned Rossiter (eds) *MyCreativity Reader: A Critique of Creative Industries*, Amsterdam: Institute of Network Cultures, pp. 11–17.

—— and Rossiter, Ned (2011) 'Urgent Aphorisms: Notes on Organized Networks for the Connected Multitudes' in Mark Deuze (ed.) *Managing Media Work*, London: Sage, pp. 279–90.

Lundby, Knut (ed.) (2008) *Digital Storytelling, Mediatized Stories*, New York: Peter Lang.

Lyon, David (2007) *Surveillance Studies: An Overview*, Polity: Cambridge.

MacKenzie, Donald and Wajcman, Judy (eds) (1999) *The Social Shaping of Technology* (second edition), Buckingham: Open University Press.

MacKinnon Rebecca (2010) 'Google Rules', *Index on Censorship*, vol. 39, no. 1, pp. 32–45.

Madden, Mary (2010) 'Older Adults and Social Media', *Pew Internet & American Life Project*, 27 August, <http://pewinternet.org/Reports/2010/Older-Adults-and-Social-Media.aspx>, accessed 5 February 2011.

—— and Smith, Aaron (2010) 'Reputation Management and Social Media', *Pew Internet & American Life Project*, 26 May, <http://pewinternet.org/Reports/2010/Reputation-Management.aspx>, accessed 5 February 2011.

Manovich, Lev (2001) *The Language of New Media*, Cambridge, MA: MIT Press.

—— (2003) 'New Media from Borges to HTML' in Noah Wardrip-Fruin and Nick Montfort (eds) *The New Media Reader*, Cambridge, MA: MIT Press, pp. 13–25.

—— (2008) 'The Practice of Everyday (Media) Life: From Mass Consumption to Mass Cultural Production?' *Critical Inquiry*, no. 35, pp. 319–31.

Marcus, Greil (1989) *Lipstick Traces: a Secret History of the Twentieth Century*, London: Picador.

Marinetti, F. T., Corra, Bruno, Settimelli, Emilio, Ginna, Arnaldo, Balla, Giacomo and Chiti, Remo (2001) [1916] 'The Futurist Cinema' in Randall Packer and

Ken Jordan (eds) *Multimedia: From Wagner to Virtual Reality*, New York: W. W. Norton, pp. 10–15.

Marinucci, Mimi (2010) 'You Can't Front on Facebook' in D. E. Wittkower (ed.) *Facebook and Philosophy*, Chicago: Open Court, pp. 65–74.

Marriott, Stephanie (2007) *Live Television: Time, Space and the Broadcast Event*, London: Sage.

Marshall, P. David (1997) *Celebrity and Power*, Minneapolis: University of Minnesota Press.

—— (2009) 'Screens: Television's Dispersed "Broadcast"' in Graeme Turner and Jinna Tay (eds) *Television Studies After TV: Understanding Television in the Post-Broadcast Era*, London: Routledge, pp. 41–50.

Marvin, Carolyn (1988) *When Old Technologies Were New: Thinking About Communications in the Late Nineteenth Century*, Oxford: Oxford University Press.

Mathiesen, Thomas (1997) 'The Viewer Society: Michel Foucault's "Panopticon" Revisited', *Theoretical Criminology*, vol. 1, no. 2, pp. 215–34.

McCaughey, Martha and Ayers, Michael (eds) (2003) *Cyberactivism: Online Activism in Theory and Practice*, New York: Routledge.

McChesney, Robert W. (1996) 'The Internet and U.S. Communication Policy-Making in Historical and Critical Perspective', *Journal of Communication*, vol. 46, no. 1, pp. 98–125.

—— (1999) *Rich Media, Poor Democracy: Communication Politics in Dubious Times*, Urbana: University of Illinois Press.

—— (2007) *Communication Revolution*, New York: The New Press.

—— (2011) 'The Crisis of Journalism and the Internet' in Graham Meikle and Guy Redden (eds) *News Online*, Basingstoke: Palgrave Macmillan, pp. 53–68.

McCombs, Maxwell (2004) *Setting The Agenda: The Mass Media and Public Opinion*, Cambridge: Polity.

McDonough, Tom (ed.) (2002) *Guy Debord and the Situationist International: Texts and Documents*, Cambridge, MA: MIT Press.

McKay, George (ed.) (1998) *DiY Culture: Party & Protest in Nineties Britain*, London: Verso.

McLeod, Kembrew (2005) *Freedom of Expression: Overzealous Copyright Bozos and Other Enemies of Creativity*, New York: Doubleday Books.

McLuhan, Marshall (1964) *Understanding Media*, London: Routledge.

—— and Fiore, Quentin (1967) *The Medium is the Massage*, San Francisco: Hardwired.

McNair, Brian (2006) *Cultural Chaos: Journalism, News and Power in a Globalised World*, London: Routledge.

McPherson, Tara (2006) 'Reload: Liveness, Mobility, and the Web' in Wendy Hui Kyong Chun and Thomas Keenan (eds) *New Media, Old Media*, New York: Routledge, pp. 199–208.

McQuail, Denis (1997) *Audience Analysis*, Thousand Oaks, CA: Sage.

—— (2010) *Mass Communication Theory* (sixth edition), London: Sage.

Meadows, Daniel (2003) 'Digital Storytelling: Research-Based Practice in New Media', *Visual Communication*, vol. 2, no. 2, pp. 189–93.

Meikle, Graham (2002) *Future Active: Media Activism and the Internet*, New York: Routledge.

—— (2007) 'Stop Signs: An Introduction to Culture Jamming' in Kate Coyer, Tony Dowmunt and Alan Fountain (eds) *The Alternative Media Handbook*, London: Routledge, pp. 166–79.

—— (2008a) 'Whacking Bush: Tactical Media As Play' in Megan Boler (ed.) *Digital Media and Democracy: Tactics In Hard Times*, Cambridge, MA: MIT Press, pp. 367–82.

—— (2008b) 'Electronic Civil Disobedience and Symbolic Power' in Athina Karatzogianni (ed.) *Cyber-conflict and Global Politics*, London: Routledge, pp. 177–87.

—— (2009) *Interpreting News*, Basingstoke: Palgrave Macmillan.

—— (2010) 'Intercreativity: Mapping Online Activism' in Jeremy Hunsinger, Lisbeth Klastrup and Matthew Allen (eds) *International Handbook of Internet Research*, Dordrecht: Springer, pp. 363–77.

Merrin, William (2008) 'Media Studies 2.0 – My Thoughts...' *Media Studies 2.0 Forum*, 4 January, <http://twopointzeroforum.blogspot.com/2008/01/media-studies-20-my-thoughts.html >, accessed 28 January 2008.

—— (2009) 'Media Studies 2.0: Upgrading and Open-Sourcing the Discipline', *Interactions*, vol. 1, no. 1, pp. 17–34.

Meyrowitz, Joshua (1985) *No Sense of Place*, New York: Oxford University Press.

—— (1995) 'Mediating Communication: What Happens?' in John Downing, Ali Mohammadi and Annabelle Sreberny-Mohammadi (eds) *Questioning the Media*, Thousand Oaks: Sage, pp. 39–53.

Miller, Daniel (2011) *Tales From Facebook*, Cambridge: Polity.

Miller, Paul D. (2004) *Rhythm Science*, Cambridge, MA: MIT Press.

—— (2008) (ed.) *Sound Unbound: Sampling Digital Music and Culture*, Cambridge, MA: MIT Press.

Miller, Toby (2009) 'Media Studies 3.0', *Television & New Media*, vol. 10, no. 1, pp. 5–6.

Miller, Vincent (2008) 'New Media, Networking and Phatic Culture', *Convergence*, vol. 14, no. 4, pp. 387–400.

Mills, Jane (2001) *The Money Shot: Cinema, Sin and Censorship*, Sydney: Pluto Press

Milne, Esther (2010) *Letters, Postcards, Email: Technologies of Presence*, London: Routledge.

Mirzoeff, Nicholas (2009) *An Introduction To Visual Culture* (second edition), London: Routledge.

Mitchell, Tony (ed.) (2001) *Global Noise: Rap and Hip-Hop Outside the USA*, Middletown, CT: Wesleyan University Press.

Moe, Hallvard (2008) 'Discussion Forums, Games and *Second Life*: Exploring the Value of Public Broadcasters' Marginal Online Activities', *Convergence*, vol. 14, no. 3, pp. 261–76.

Morley, David (1980) *The Nationwide Audience*, London: British Film Institute.

—— (1992) *Television, Audiences and Cultural Studies*, London: Routledge.

Morozov, Evgeny (2011) *The Net Delusion: How Not to Liberate the World*, London: Allen Lane.

Mosco, Vincent (2009) 'The Future of Journalism', *Journalism: Theory, Practice and Criticism*, vol. 10, no. 3, pp. 350–2.

MSNBC (2010) 'Facebook inches past Google for Web users' minutes', *MSNBC*, 9 September, <http://www.msnbc.msn.com/id/39087743/ns/technology_and_science-tech_and_gadgets>, accessed 23 December 2010.

Munster, George (1985) *A Paper Prince*, Harmondsworth: Penguin.

Murdoch, James (2009) 'The Absence of Trust', Edinburgh International Television Festival MacTaggart Lecture, 28 August.

Murdock, Graham (2000) 'Digital Futures: European Television in the Age of Convergence' in Jan Wieten, Graham Murdock and Peter Dahlgren (eds) *Television Across Europe*, London: Sage, pp. 35–57.

Murphie, Andrew and Potts, John (2003) *Culture and Technology*, Basingstoke: Palgrave Macmillan.

Murray, Janet H. (1997) *Hamlet on the Holodeck: The Future of Narrative in Cyberspace*, New York: Simon & Schuster.

—— (2003) 'Inventing the Medium' in Noah Wardrip-Fruin and Nick Montfort (eds) *The New Media Reader*, Cambridge, MA: MIT Press, pp. 3–11.

—— (2004) 'From Game-Story to Cyberdrama' in Noah Wardrip-Fruin and Pat Harrigan (eds) *First Person: New Media as Story, Performance, and Game*, Cambridge, MA: MIT Press, pp. 2–11.

Naughton, John (1999) *A Brief History of the Future*, London: Weidenfeld & Nicolson.

—— (2009) 'Everyone's Invited to the Birthday Bash for Blogger', *Observer*, 13 September, <http://www.guardian.co.uk/technology/2009/sep/13/blogging-john-naughton-comment>, accessed 15 February 2011.

Negativland (1995) *Fair Use: The Story of the Letter U and the Numeral 2*, Concord, California: Seeland.

Negroponte, Nicholas (1995) *Being Digital*, London: Hodder and Stoughton.

Neil, Andrew (1996) *Full Disclosure*, London: Macmillan.

Neilson, Brett and Rossiter, Ned (2005) 'From Precarity to Precariousness and Back Again: Labour, Life and Unstable Networks', *Fibreculture Journal*, no. 5, <http://five.fibreculturejournal.org/fcj-022-from-precarity-to-precariousness-and-back-again-labour-life-and-unstable-networks>, accessed 20 January 2011.

Nelson, Ted (2001) [1974] 'Computer Lib/Dream Machines' in Randall Packer and Ken Jordan (eds) *Multimedia: From Wagner to Virtual Reality*, New York: W. W. Norton, pp. 160–72.

Newman, James (2004) *Videogames*, London: Routledge.

—— (2008) *Playing With Videogames*, London: Routledge.

Newman, Nic (2009) 'The Rise of Social Media and its Impact on Mainstream Journalism', *Reuters Institute for the Study of Journalism* (working paper), <http://reutersinstitute.politics.ox.ac.uk/fileadmin/documents/Publications/The_rise_of_social_media_and_its_impact_on_mainstream_journalism.pdf>, accessed 8 February 2011.

News Corporation (2010) *Annual Report 2010*, <http://www.newscorp.com/Report2010/index.html>, accessed 17 February 2011.

Nightingale, Virginia (2007) 'Emergence, Search and Social Networking', in Virginia Nightingale and Tim Dwyer (eds), *New Media Worlds: Challenges for Convergence*, London: Oxford University Press, pp. 291–307.

—— (2011) 'Search and Social Media' in Virginia Nightingale (ed.) *The Handbook of Media Audiences*, Malden, MA: Blackwell, pp. 86–108.

OECD [Organization for Economic Co-operation and Development] (2007) 'Participative Web and User-Created Content: Web 2.0, Wikis and Social Networking', <http://www.oecd.org/document/40/0,3343,en_2649_34223_39428648_1_1_1_1,00.html>, accessed 17 October 2008.

OECD Working Party on the Information Economy (2010) 'The Evolution of News and the Internet', *Organisation for Economic Co-operation and Development*, <http://www.oecd.org/dataoecd/30/24/45559596.pdf>, accessed 8 February 2011.

Ofcom [Office of Communications, UK] (2008) *Social Networking: A Quantitative and Qualitative Research Report into Attitudes, Behaviours and Use*, 2 April, <http://www.ofcom.org.uk/advice/media_literacy/medlitpub/medlitpubrss/socialnetworking/report.pdf>, accessed 17 October 2008.

—— (2010a) *The Consumer's Digital Day*, 14 December, <http://stakeholders.ofcom.org.uk/market-data-research/market-data/digital-day>, accessed 1 September 2011.

—— (2010b) *Communications Market Report*, 19 August, <http://stakeholders.ofcom.org.uk/market-data-research/market-data/communications-market-reports/cmr10/uk>, accessed 14 September 2010.

—— (2011) *Communications Market Report*, 4 August, <http://stakeholders.ofcom.org.uk/market-data-research/market-data/communications-market-reports/cmr11>, accessed 1 September 2011.

O'Reilly, Tim (2005) 'What Is Web 2.0? Design Patterns and Business Models for the Next Generation of Software', *O'Reilly Media*, 30 September, <http://oreilly.com/web2/archive/what-is-web-20.html>, accessed 16 September 2010.

—— (2006) 'Web 2.0 Compact Definition: Trying Again' *O'Reilly Media*, 10 December <http://radar.oreilly.com/2006/12/web-20-compact-definition-tryi.html>, accessed 16 September 2010.

Örnebring, Henrik (2007) 'Alternate Reality Gaming and Convergence Culture: The Case of *Alias*', *International Journal of Cultural Studies*, vol. 10, no. 4, pp. 445–62.

Orwell, George (1949) *Nineteen Eighty-Four*, London: Secker & Warburg.

Oudshoorn, Nelly and Pinch, Trevor (eds) (2003) *How Users Matter: The Co-Construction of Users and Technologies*, Cambridge, MA: MIT Press.

Packer, Randall and Jordan, Ken (2002) *Multimedia: From Wagner to Virtual Reality*, New York: W.W. Norton.

Page, Bruce with Potter, Elaine (2003) *The Murdoch Archipelago*, London: Simon & Schuster.

Papacharissi, Zizi (ed.) (2011) *A Networked Self: Identity, Community, and Culture on Social Network Sites*, London: Routledge.

Park, Robert E. (1967) [1940] 'News as a Form of Knowledge' in his *On Social Control and Collective Behavior* (ed. Ralph H. Turner), Chicago: University of Chicago Press, pp. 33–52.

Pearce, Matthew (2000) 'Structured Action in Australian Broadcasting Policy: Pay TV', *Media, Culture and Society*, vol. 22, no. 3, pp. 347–54.

Penley, Constance (1990) 'Time Travel, Primal Scene and the Critical Dystopia' in Annette Kuhn (ed.) *Alien Zone: Cultural Theory and Contemporary Science Fiction Cinema*, London: Verso, pp. 116–27.

—— (1991) 'Brownian Motion: Women, Tactics, and Technology' in Constance Penley and Andrew Ross (eds) *Technoculture*, Minneapolis: University of Minnesota Press, pp. 135–61.

Peretti, Jonah (2001) 'My Nike Media Adventure', *The Nation*, 9 April, <http://www.thenation.com/article/my-nike-media-adventure>, accessed 26 August 2010.

Perryman, Neil (2008) '*Doctor Who* and the Convergence of Media: A Case Study in "Transmedia Storytelling"', *Convergence*, vol. 14, no. 1, pp. 21–39.

Peters, John Durham (1999) *Speaking Into The Air: A History of the Idea of Communication*, Chicago: University of Chicago Press.

Plant, Sadie (1992) *The Most Radical Gesture: The Situationist International in a Post-modern Age*, London: Routledge.

Pool, Ithiel de Sola (1983) *Technologies of Freedom*, Cambridge, MA: Belknap Press of Harvard University Press.

Poole, Christopher 'moot' (2010) 'The Case for Anonymity Online', *TED*, June, <http://www.ted.com/talks/lang/eng/christopher_m00t_poole_the_case_for_anonymity_online.html>, accessed 11 February 2011.

Postman, Neil (1985) *Amusing Ourselves to Death*, London: Methuen.

—— (1992) *Technopoly*, New York: Vintage.

—— and Paglia, Camille (2007) [1991] 'Two Cultures — Television Versus Print' in David Crowley and Paul Heyer (eds) *Communication in History* (fifth edition) Boston: Allyn & Bacon, pp. 283–95.

Pöttker, Horst (2003) 'News and its Communicative Quality: The Inverted Pyramid — When and Why did it Appear?' *Journalism Studies*, vol. 4, no. 4, pp. 501–11.

Pras, Aiko, Sperotto, anna, Moura, Giovane C. M., Drago, Idilio, Barbosa, Rafael, Sadre, Ramin, Schmidt, Ricardo and Hofstede, Rick (2010) 'Attacks by "Anonymous" WikiLeaks Proponents Not Anonymous', *Simple Web*, 10 December, <http://www.simpleweb.org/reports/loic-report.pdf>, accessed 12 February 2011.

Project for Excellence in Journalism (2010) 'Understanding the Participatory News Consumer', 1 March, <http://www.journalism.org/analysis_report/news_and_internet>, accessed 16 February 2011.

Purcell, Kristen, Rainie, Lee, Mitchell, Amy, Rosenstiel, Tom and Olmstead, Kenny (2010) 'Understanding the Participatory News Consumer: How Internet and Cell Phone Users Have Turned News Into a Social Experience', *Pew Internet &*

American Life Project, 1 March, <http://www.pewinternet.org/Reports/2010/Online-News.aspx>, accessed 8 February 2011.

Raboy, Marc (2002) 'Introduction — Media Policy in the New Communications Environment', in Marc Raboy (ed.) *Global Media Policy in the New Millennium,* Luton: University of Luton Press, pp. 3–16.

Radway, Janice (1987) *Reading the Romance,* London: Verso.

Raymond, Eric S. (2001) *The Cathedral and the Bazaar,* Sebastopol, CA: O'Reilly.

Reith, J. C. W. (1924) *Broadcast Over Britain,* London: Hodder and Stoughton.

Resnick, David (1998) 'Politics on the Internet: The Normalization of Cyberspace' in Chris Toulouse and Timothy W. Luke (eds) *The Politics of Cyberspace: A New Political Science Reader,* New York: Routledge, pp. 48–68.

Rettberg, Jill Walker (2008) *Blogging,* Cambridge: Polity.

Rheingold, Howard (1993) *The Virtual Community: Homesteading on the Electronic Frontier,* Reading, MA: Addison-Wesley.

—— (2000) 'Community Development in the Cybersociety of the Future', in David Gauntlett (ed.) *Web.Studies: Rewiring Media Studies for the Digital Age,* London: Arnold, pp. 170–8.

—— (2002) *Smart Mobs: The Next Social Revolution,* Cambridge, MA: Perseus.

Rice, Ronald E. (1999) 'Artifacts and Paradoxes in New Media', *New Media & Society,* vol. 1, no. 1, pp. 24–32.

Richter, Hans (1965) *Dada: Art and Anti-Art,* London: Thames & Hudson.

Rizzo, Teresa (2007) 'Programming Your Own Channel: An Archaeology of the Playlist' in Andrew T. Kenyon (ed.) *TV Futures: Digital Television Policy in Australia,* Carlton: Melbourne University Press, pp. 108–31.

Robertson, Roland (1992) *Globalization,* London: Sage.

Robinson, Andrew (2003) [1995] 'The Origins of Writing' in David Crowley and Paul Heyer (eds) *Communication in History: Technology, Culture, Society* (fourth edition), Boston: Allyn and Bacon, pp. 34–40.

Rodriguez, Clemencia (2001) *Fissures in the Mediascape: An International Study of Citizens' Media,* Cresskill, NJ: Hampton Press.

Roper, Jonathan (1995) 'The Heart of Multimedia: Interactivity or Experience?' *Convergence,* vol. 1, no. 2, pp. 23–5.

Rose, Tricia (1994) *Black Noise: Rap Music and Black Culture in Contemporary America,* Hanover, NH: Wesleyan University Press.

Rosen, Jay (2006) 'The People Formerly Known as the Audience', *PressThink,* 27 June, <http://journalism.nyu.edu/pubzone/weblogs/pressthink/2006/06/27/ppl_frmr_p.html>, accessed 6 January 2010.

—— (2010) 'The Afghanistan War Logs Released by Wikileaks, the World's First Stateless News Organization', *Pressthink,* 26 July, <http://archive.pressthink.org/2010/07/26/wikileaks_afghan.html>, accessed 5 November 2010.

Ross, Andrew (2007) 'Nice Work If You Can Get It: The Mercurial Career of Creative Industries Policy', in Geert Lovink and Ned Rossiter (eds) *MyCreativity Reader: A Critique of Creative Industries,* Amsterdam: Institute of Network Cultures, pp. 17–41.

Ross, Karen and Nightingale, Virginia (2003) *Media and Audiences: New Perspectives*, Maidenhead: Open University Press.

Ross, Sharon Marie (2008) *Beyond the Box: Television and the Internet*, Oxford: Blackwell.

Ruddock, Andy (2001) *Understanding Audiences: Theory and Method*, London: Sage.

Rushkoff, Douglas (2009) 'The Web's Dirtiest Site', *Daily Beast*, 11 August, <http://www.thedailybeast.com/blogs-and-stories/2009-08-11/the-webs-dirtiest-site>, accessed 11 February 2011.

Samuels, Edward (2000) *The Illustrated Story of Copyright*, New York: Thomas Dunne Books.

Scannell, Paddy (1989) 'Public Service Broadcasting and Modern Public Life', *Media, Culture & Society*, vol. 11, no. 2, pp. 135–66.

—— (2000) 'For-Anyone-As-Someone Structures', *Media, Culture & Society*, vol. 22, no. 1, pp. 5–24.

—— and Cardiff, David (1991) *A Social History of British Broadcasting: Volume 1 1922–1939 Serving The Nation*, Oxford: Basil Blackwell.

Schiller, Herbert I. (1989) *Culture Inc.*, New York: Oxford University Press.

Schlesinger, Philip (2008) 'Communications Policy' in Neil Blain and David Hutchison (eds) *The Media in Scotland*, Edinburgh: Edinburgh University Press, pp. 35–51.

Schmidt, Eric (2006) 'A Note to Google Users on Net Neutrality' *Google Help Center*, <http://www.google.com/help/netneutrality_letter.html>, accessed 16 February 2011.

Schudson, Michael (1978) *Discovering the News: A Social History of American Newspapers*, New York: Basic Books.

—— (1995) *The Power of News*, Cambridge, MA: Harvard University Press.

Schultz, Julianne (1998) *Reviving the Fourth Estate*, Cambridge: Cambridge University Press.

Sconce, Jeffrey (2004) 'What If?: Charting Television's New Textual Boundaries' in Lynn Spigel and Jan Olsson (eds) *Television After TV: Essays on a Medium in Transition*, Durham: Duke University Press, pp. 93–112.

Sexton, Jamie (2009) 'Digital Music: Production, Distribution and Consumption' in Glen Creeber and Royston Martin (eds) *Digital Cultures*, Maidenhead: Open University Press, pp. 92–101.

Shapiro, Peter (1992) 'Deck Wreckers: The Turntable as Instrument' in Rob Young (ed.) *Undercurrents: The Hidden Wiring of Modern Music*, London: Continuum, pp. 163–76.

Shawcross, William (1992) *Rupert Murdoch: Ringmaster of the Information Circus*, Sydney: Random House.

Shirky, Clay (2003) 'Social Software and the Politics of Groups', *Clay Shirky's Writings About the Internet*, 9 March, <http://www.shirky.com/writings/group_politics.html>, accessed 1 September 2010.

—— (2008) *Here Comes Everybody*, London: Allen Lane.

—— (2009) 'How Social Media Can Make History', *TED*, <http://www.ted.com/talks/clay_shirky_how_cellphones_twitter_facebook_can_make_history.html>, accessed 6 January 2010.

—— (2010) *Cognitive Surplus*, London: Allen Lane.

Shoemaker, Pamela J. (1991) *Gatekeeping*, Newbury Park: Sage.

Silver, David (2009) 'The Difference Between Thin and Thick Tweets', *Silver in SF*, 25 February, <http://silverinsf.blogspot.com/2009/02/difference-between-thin-and-thick.html>, accessed 27 July 2010.

Silverstone, Roger (1995) 'Convergence Is a Dangerous Word', *Convergence*, vol. 1, no. 1, pp. 11–13.

Singer, Jane B. (2010) 'Journalism in the Network' in Stuart Allan (ed.) *The Routledge Companion to News and Journalism*, London: Routledge, pp. 277–86.

—— and Ashman, Ian (2009) 'User-Generated Content and Journalistic Values' in Stuart Allan and Einar Thorsen (eds) *Citizen Journalism: Global Perspectives*, New York: Peter Lang, pp. 233–42.

Smaill, Belinda (2004) 'Online Personals and Narratives of the Self: Australia's RSVP', *Convergence*, vol. 10, no. 1, pp. 93–107.

Smith, Marc A. and Kollock, Peter (eds) (1999) *Communities in Cyberspace*, London: Routledge.

Smith, Merrit Roe and Marx, Leo (eds) (1994) *Does Technology Drive History?*, Cambridge, MA: MIT Press.

Smith, Owen F. (2005) 'Fluxus Praxis: An Exploration of Connections, Creativity, and Community' in Annmarie Chandler and Norie Neumark (eds) *At A Distance: Precursors to Art and Activism on the Internet*, Cambridge, MA: MIT Press, pp. 116–38.

Smith, Paul (2006) 'The Politics of UK Television Policy: The Making of Ofcom', *Media, Culture & Society*, vol. 28, no. 6, 929–40.

Snyder, Donald (2000) 'Webcam Women: Life on Your Screen' in David Gauntlett (ed.) *Web.Studies: Rewiring Media Studies for the Digital Age*, London: Arnold, pp. 68–73.

Snyder, Ilana (1996) *Hypertext: The Electronic Labyrinth*, Melbourne: Melbourne University Press.

Sobel, Jon (2010) 'State of the Blogosphere 2010', *Technorati*, 3 November, <http://technorati.com/blogging/article/state-of-the-blogosphere-2010-introduction>, accessed 15 February 2011.

Solove, Daniel J. (2007) *The Future of Reputation: Gossip, Rumor, and Privacy on the Internet*, New Haven: Yale University Press.

Spigel, Lynn and Olsson, Jan (eds) (2004) *Television After TV*, Durham: Duke University Press.

Stallman, Richard (2003) [1985] 'The GNU Manifesto' in Noah Wardrip-Fruin and Nick Montfort (eds) *The New Media Reader*, Cambridge, MA: MIT Press, pp. 545–50.

Stam, Robert (2000) *Film Theory: An Introduction*, Oxford: Blackwell.

Standage, Tom (1998) *The Victorian Internet*, London: Weidenfeld & Nicolson.

—— (2006) 'The Culture War', *Wired*, 14.04, April, <http://www.wired.com/wired/archive/14.04/war.html>, accessed 22 December 2010.

Stephens, Mitchell (2007) *A History of News* (third edition), New York: Oxford University Press.

Sumiala, Johanna (2008) 'Circulation' in David Morgan (ed.) *Keywords in Religion, Media, and Culture*, London: Routledge, pp. 44–55.

Sussman, Elisabeth (ed.) (1989) *On the Passage of a Few People Through a Rather Brief Moment in Time: The Situationist International, 1957–1972*, Cambridge, MA: MIT Press.

Sutherland, Ivan (2003) [1963] 'Sketchpad: A Man-Machine Graphical Communication System' in Noah Wardrip-Fruin and Nick Montfort (eds) *The New Media Reader*, Cambridge, MA: MIT Press, pp. 109–26.

Taylor, Paul A. (2005) 'From Hackers to Hacktivists: Speed Bumps on the Global Superhighway?' *New Media & Society*, vol. 7, no. 5, pp. 625–46.

Taylor, T. L. (2006) *Play Between Worlds: Exploring Online Game Culture*, Cambridge, MA: MIT Press.

Terranova, Tiziana (2004) *Network Culture*, London: Pluto.

Tessler, Joelle (2010) 'FCC poised to adopt network neutrality rules', *Bloomberg Businessweek*, <http://www.businessweek.com/ap/financialnews/D9K7U87G0.htm>, accessed 21 December 2010.

Thompson, John B. (1995) *The Media and Modernity*, Cambridge: Polity.

—— (2000) *Political Scandal*, Cambridge: Polity.

—— (2005) 'The New Visibility', *Theory, Culture & Society*, vol. 22, no. 6, pp. 31–51.

Thurman, Neil (2008) 'Forums for Citizen Journalists? Adoption of User Generated Content Initiatives by Online News Media', *New Media & Society*, vol. 10, no. 1, pp. 139–57.

—— (2011) 'Making "The Daily Me": Technology, Economics and Habit in the Mainstream Assimilation of Personalized News', *Journalism: Theory, Practice & Criticism*, vol. 12, no. 4, pp. 395–415.

Tofts, Darren and McKeich, Murray (1998) *Memory Trade: a Prehistory of Cyberculture*, Sydney: Interface.

Tofts, Darren, Jonson, Annemarie and Cavallaro, Alessio (eds) (2002) *Prefiguring Cyberculture: An Intellectual History*, Sydney: Power Publications and Cambridge, MA: MIT Press.

Tomlinson, John (2007) *The Culture of Speed*, London: Sage.

Tönnies, Frederic (1963) *Community and Society*, New York: Harper & Row.

Toop, David (1984) *The Rap Attack: African Jive to New York Hip Hop*, London: Pluto Press.

Tracey, Michael (1998) *The Decline and Fall of Public Service Broadcasting*, Oxford: Oxford University Press.

Trippenbach, Philip (2009) 'Video Games: A New Medium for Journalism' in Charles Miller (ed.) *The Future of Journalism: Papers from a Conference Organised by the BBC College of Journalism*, <http://www.bbc.co.uk/blogs/theeditors/future_of_journalism.pdf>, pp. 39–49, accessed 6 August 2009.

Tuchman, Gaye (1972) 'Objectivity as Strategic Ritual: An Examination of Newsmen's Notions of Objectivity', *American Journal of Sociology*, vol. 77, no. 4, pp. 660–79.

Turkle, Sherry (1984) *The Second Self*, Cambridge, MA: MIT Press.

—— (1995) *Life on the Screen*, London: Phoenix.

Turner, Graeme (2004) *Understanding Celebrity*, London: Sage.

—— (2010) *Ordinary People and the Media*, London: Sage.

—— and Tay, Jinna (2009) 'Introduction' in Graeme Turner and Jinna Tay (eds) *Television Studies After TV: Understanding Television in the Post-Broadcast Era*, London: Routledge, pp. 1–6.

Uricchio, William (2004) 'Television's Next Interface: Technology/Interface Culture/Flow' in Lynn Spigel and Jan Olsson (eds) *Television After TV: Essays on a Medium in Transition*, Durham: Duke University Press, pp. 163–82.

Urry, John (2007) *Mobilities*, Cambridge: Polity.

Van De Donk, Wim, Loader, Brian D., Nixon, Paul G., and Rucht, Dieter (eds) (2004) *Cyberprotest: New Media, Citizens and Social Movements*, London: Routledge.

Virilio, Paul (1997) *Open Sky*, London: Verso.

—— (2002) 'The Visual Crash' in Thomas Y. Levin, Ursula Frohne, and Peter Weibel (eds) (2002) *CTRL [Space]*, Cambridge, MA: MIT Press, pp. 108–13.

—— (2007) [1995] 'Red Alert in Cyberspace' in David Bell and Barbara M. Kennedy (eds) *The Cybercultures Reader* (second edition), London: Routledge, pp. 106–7.

—— and Lotringer, Sylvere (1983) *Pure War*, New York: Semiotext(e).

Vnuk, Helen (2003) *Snatched: Sex and Censorship in Australia*, Sydney: Vintage.

Wagner, Richard (2001) [1849] 'Outlines of the Artwork of the Future' in Randall Packer and Ken Jordan (eds) *Multimedia: From Wagner to Virtual Reality*, New York: W. W. Norton, pp. 3–9.

Wajcman, Judy (1994) 'Technological A/genders: Technology, Culture and Class,' in Lelia Green and Roger Guinery (eds) *Framing Technology*, Sydney: Allen & Unwin, pp. 3–14.

Wang, Stephanie and Faris, Robert (2008) 'Welcome to the Machine', *Index on Censorship*, vol. 37, no. 2, pp. 106-113.

Wardle, Claire and Williams, Andrew (2008) *ugc@thebbc: Understanding its Impact Upon Contributors, Non-Contributors and BBC News*, Cardiff School of Journalism, Media and Cultural Studies, available from <http://www.bbc.co.uk/blogs/knowledgeexchange/cardiffone.pdf>, accessed 5 January 2011.

—— (2010) 'Beyond User-Generated Content: A Production Study Examining the Ways in which UGC is Used at the BBC', *Media, Culture & Society*, vol. 32, no. 5, pp. 781–99.

Wark, McKenzie (1992) 'The Information War,' *21C*, no. 7, pp. 60–5.

—— (1994) *Virtual Geography*, Bloomington: Indiana University Press.

—— (1997) 'Technofear' in Ashley Crawford and Ray Edgar (eds) *Transit Lounge*, Sydney: Craftsman House, pp. 170–2.

—— (1999) *Celebrities, Culture and Cyberspace*, Sydney: Pluto Press.

—— (2000) 'Cellphones and the Cancer of Cellspace', posted to the *Nettime* list at <http://www.nettime.org/Lists-Archives/nettime-l-0011/msg00078.html>, 10 November, accessed 27 July 2007.

—— (2004) *A Hacker Manifesto*, Cambridge, MA: Harvard University Press.

—— (2011) *The Beach Beneath the Street: The Everyday Life and Glorious Times of the Situationist International*, London: Verso.

Warren, Samuel D. and Brandeis, Louis, D. (1890) 'The Right to Privacy', *Harvard Law Review*, vol. IV, no. 5, <http://www.jjllplaw.com/The-Right-to-Privacy-Warren-Brandeis-Harvard-Law-Review-1890.html>, accessed 9 May 2011.

Werner, Craig (1998) *A Change Is Gonna Come: Music, Race and the Soul of America*, Edinburgh: Payback Press.

Westbury, Marcus (2010) 'How Social Media Saved Renew Newcastle', *Marcus Westbury. My Life. On the Internets*, 23 October, <http://www.marcuswestbury.net/2010/10/23/how-social-media-saved-renew-newcastle-vapac-talk>, accessed 11 February 2011.

White, David Manning (1950) '"The 'Gatekeeper": A Case Study in the Selection of News' *Journalism Quarterly*, vol. 27, pp. 383–90.

White, Michele (2003) 'Too Close to See: Men, Women and Webcams', *New Media & Society*, vol. 5, no. 1, pp. 7–28.

Wikström, Patrik (2009) *The Music Industry: Music in the Cloud*, Cambridge: Polity.

Williams, Raymond (1961) *Culture and Society 1780–1950*, London: Chatto & Windus.

—— (1965) *The Long Revolution*, London: Pelican.

—— (1974) *Television: Technology and Cultural Form*, London: Fontana.

Willson, Michele (2007) [1997] 'Community in the Abstract: A Political and Ethical Dilemma?' in David Bell and Barbara M. Kennedy (eds) *The Cybercultures Reader* (second edition), London: Routledge, pp. 213–26.

Winner, Langdon (1977) *Autonomous Technology: Technics-out-of-Control as a Theme in Political Thought*, Cambridge, MA: MIT Press.

—— (1986) *The Whale and the Reactor: A Search for Limits in an Age of High Technology*, Chicago: University of Chicago Press.

Winston, Brian (2005) *Messages: Free Expression, Media and the West from Gutenberg to Google*, London: Routledge.

Wise, David A. (2005) *The Google Story*, New York: Bantam Dell.

Wolfe, Tom (1968) *The Electric Kool-Aid Acid Test*, New York: Farrar, Straus and Giroux.

Wolff, Michael (2010) *The Man Who Owns The News*, New York: Vintage.

Wray, Stefan (1998) 'On Electronic Civil Disobedience', <http://www.thing.net/~rdom/ecd/oecd.html>, accessed 12 February 2011.

Wu, Tim (2010) *The Master Switch: The Rise and Fall of Information Empires*, New York: Alfred A. Knopf.

Xia, Bill (2008) 'Cat and Mouse', *Index on Censorship*, vol. 37, no. 2, pp. 114–19.

Yoo, Christopher (2006) 'Network Neutrality and the Economics of Congestion', *Georgetown Law Journal*, vol. 94, no. 6, pp. 1847–908.

Young, Sherman (2007) *The Book is Dead, Long Live the Book*, Sydney: UNSW Press.

Zelizer, Barbie (ed.) (2009) *The Changing Faces of Journalism: Tabloidization, Technology and Truthiness*, New York: Routledge.

Zhou, Shuguang (2008) 'Notes on the Net', *Index on Censorship*, vol. 37, no. 2, pp. 90–6.

Zickuhr, Kathryn and Rainie, Lee (2011) 'Wikipedia, Past and Present', *Pew Internet & American Life Project*, 13 January, <http://pewinternet.org/Reports/2011/Wikipedia.aspx>, accessed 14 February 2011.

Zittrain, Jonathan (2008) *The Future of the Internet: And How to Stop It*, London: Allen Lane.

Zuckerman, Ethan (2008) 'The Cute Cat Theory Talk at ETech', *My Heart's in Accra*, 8 March, <http://www.ethanzuckerman.com/blog/2008/03/08/the-cute-cat-theory-talk-at-etech>, accessed 10 May 2011.

—— (2011) 'The First Twitter Revolution?' *Foreign Policy*, 14 January, <http://www.foreignpolicy.com/articles/2011/01/14/the_first_twitter_revolution>, accessed 16 February 2011.

Index